YOUNG CHILDREN'S NAIVE THINKING ABOUT THE BIOLOGICAL WORLD

ESSAYS IN DEVELOPMENTAL PSYCHOLOGY

North American Editors:
Henry Wellman, University of Michigan at Ann Arbor and
Janet Werker, University of British Columbia

United Kingdom Editor:
Peter Bryant, University of Oxford

Essays in Developmental Psychology is designed to meet the need for rapid publication of brief volumes in developmental psychology. The series defines developmental psychology in its broadest terms and covers such topics as social development, cognitive development, developmental neuropsychology and neuroscience, language development, learning difficulties, developmental psychopathology and applied issues. Each volume in the series makes a conceptual contribution to the topic by reviewing and synthesizing the existing research literature, by advancing theory in the area, or by some combination of these missions. Authors in this series provide an overview of their own highly successful research program, but they must also include an assessment of current knowledge and identification of possible future trends in research. Each book is a self-contained unit supplying the advanced reader with a coherent review of important research as well as its context, theoretical grounding, and implications

IN PREPARATION
Goldin-Meadow: *The Resilience of Language*
Tager-Flusberg: *Autism and William's Syndrome*
Trehub: *Infants and Music*

PUBLISHED TITLES
Bryne: *The Foundation of Literacy*
Cox: *Children's Drawings of the Human Figure*
Forrester: *The Development of Young Children's Social-Cognitive Skills*
Garton: *Social Interaction and the Development of Language*
Goodnow/Collins: *Development According to Parents*
Goswami: *Analogical Reasoning in Children*
Goswami/Bryant: *Phonological Skills and Learning to Read*
Harris: *Language Experience and Early Language Development*
Hobson: *Autism and the Development of Mind*
Howe: *Language Learning*
Inagaki & Hatano: *Young Children's Naive Thinking About the Biological World*
Langford: *The Development of Moral Reasoning*
Meadows: *Parenting Behavior and Children's Cognitive Development*
Meins: *Security of Attachment and Cognitive Development*
Perez-Pereira & Conti-Ramsden: *Language Development and Social Interactions in Blind Children*
Siegal: *Knowing Children (2nd Edn)*
Smith: *Necessary Knowledge and Constructivism*

YOUNG CHILDREN'S NAIVE THINKING ABOUT THE BIOLOGICAL WORLD

Kayoko Inagaki

Chiba University

Giyoo Hatano

Keio University

Essays in Developmental Psychology

Psychology Press
New York • Brighton

Published in 2002 by
Psychology Press
29 West 35th Street
New York, NY 10001

Published in Great Britain by
Psychology Press Ltd
27 Church Road
Hove, East Sussex
BN3 2FA

10 9 8 7 6 5 4 3 2 1

Library of Congress Cataloging-in-Publication Data
Inagaki, Kayoko, 1944–
    Young children's naive thinking about the biological world / Kayoko Inagaki and Giyoo Hatano.
        p. cm. — (Essays in developmental psychology)
    Includes bibliographical references (p.).
    ISBN 1-84169-041-4
    1. Biology—Study and teaching (Elementary)—Psychological aspects. 2. Cognition in children.   I. Hatano, Giyoo, 1935– II. Title. III. Series.

QH315 .I55 2002
372.3'57—dc21
                                                                        2002017789

CONTENTS

v

ACKNOWLEDGMENTS

Are there any special cultural or historical reasons why Japanese cognitive developmentalists investigate young children's thinking about the biological world? The answer is probably "No." The two of us began in the early 1980s to do the research that eventually provided us with the foundational data for this book, but initially we did not see our subject matter as about naive biology. Both of us, though deeply impressed by Piaget's vivid descriptions of young children's active and constructive mind, felt some dissatisfaction with his conceptualization of children's (lack of) competence, as many developmentalists did at that time. We thus wanted to reveal young children's competence by studying their reasoning, including analogical reasoning in knowledge-rich domains.

Soon after we began our research, we were struck by young children's personification, their attempts to predict and explain behaviors and properties of animals and plants by using their relatively rich knowledge about humans. However, this was a few years before the publication of the monumental book by Susan Carey, and at that time we did not know that personification was so specifically relevant to young children's naive biology. Fortunately, a number of our American colleagues pointed out that our idea of personification as analogy is closely related to Susan's and recommended us to contact her. A few years later we found ourselves in a circle of active researchers on naive biology. We were pleased that our ideas as well as findings were openly welcomed by our colleagues in North America, Europe, and Australasia. As we became involved deeply in this domain, we realized that naive biology is a domain to which we Japanese may be able to make unique contributions, because such aspects of young children's naive biology as vitalistic causality, the mind-body interdependence, the status of plants as human-like living things, and so forth, which tended to be neglected in Western culture, are recognizable in Japanese society.

However, writing a book had been beyond our imagination until Henry Wellman invited us to consider it as one for this series for which he is an editor. We are grateful to Henry for his invitation in the first place, and his warm, continued encouragement and help, without of which we could have never completed this book.

We also thank our colleagues who invited us to give addresses and colloquia and who shared ideas and interests with us in informal conversations as well as formal sessions like symposia and workshops. Among others, we owe a great deal to Susan Carey—even when we disagreed with her (as we often did), she trusted our data, considered our arguments seriously, and tried to incorporate them in her framework.

We have found that writing a book is one of the best ways to learn. Our outline of the book was reviewed by Carey, Terry Au, John Coley, Susan Gelman, and Frank Keil, from whom we had learned a lot. Their reviews were so positive that we were greatly encouraged. The initial draft of the book was reviewed by Henry, and as expected, he gave us many good suggestions. A second draft was reviewed by Frank and Ken Springer. Although their reviews were very favorable, they also pointed out arguments and issues in need of further development.

Much of the research described in this book was supported by Grants-in-Aid for Scientific Research from the (Japanese) Ministry of Education to the first author (No. 02610036, 05610095, 07610114) and the second author (No. 02255223, 06301015, 09207105). Tables 2.1, 2.2, and 4.2 originally appeared in our articles (Inagaki & Hatano, 1993; 1996) in *Child Development* and are reproduced by permission of the Society for Research in Child Development. Figure 2.1, which originally appeared in our chapter (Hatano & Inagaki, 1999) of D. Medin and S. Atran's edited book *Folkbiology*, are reproduced by permission of MIT Press. Table 3.1 and Figures 7.1, 7.2, and 7.3 originally appeared in our articles (Inagaki & Hatano, 1991; Inagaki & Sugiyama, 1988) in *Cognitive Development* and are reproduced by permission of Elsevier Science.

We really hope that this small book will increase professional and lay people's interest in studies on, as well as understanding of, naive biology. In addition, we hope our colleagues worldwide will increasingly recognize that some interesting cognitive studies are done outside of North American and Europe.

1

Naive Biology as a Core Domain of Thought

Girl (6 years, 0 month): [Interviewer: Hanako's family has had a baby. Hanako wants to keep him the same size forever because he is small and cute. Can she do that?] "No, she can't. If he eats, he will become bigger and bigger and be an adult." [Suppose someone is given the bud of tulip that's just coming out and wants to keep it in the same size forever. Can he do that?] "No, he can't. Because if he doesn't water it, it will wither, but if he waters it, it will become bigger and bigger."

Boy (6 years, 10 months): [Interviewer: Who is more likely to catch a cold, a girl eating a lot or another girl eating little every day?] "The girl eating little, because she has little nutriment. You know there are germs in the air. They enter easily through the film at her throat (pointing to his own throat) if she has little nutriment."

Girl (6 years, 4 months): [Interviewer: What will happen to us when we eat nothing every day?] "We'll die." [Why?] "'Cause we'll have no nutriment." [What does the nutriment do inside our body?] "It gives us power, though I don't know much about that."

These are excerpts obtained from our interview studies with young children before they had any formal schooling. How shall we interpret their remarks? Apparently we may claim the following: Either young children lack understanding of the world, or their reasoning skills are immature, because mapping the relationship between a human and food to that between a plant and water is not scientifically acceptable, and attributing the contagion process not to germs' multiplication but to their physical invasion is clearly false. Even when they know difficult words such as *germs* and *nutriment*, their thought processes have severe limitations.

However, it is also possible to emphasize positive aspects of the thinking reflected in these remarks. Young children are intellectually active and inventive enough not only to make novel predictions but also to seek causal explanations for the predictions, at least for such topics as bodily phenomena. Their reasoning is plausible and firmly based on their acquired knowledge. They seem to understand, for instance, that eating is the key to growing as well as to being active and vigorous, assuming that humans take some "power" from food. They exploit their relatively rich knowledge about humans to make educated guesses about other entities, such as a tulip in the above example.

This issue of how much young children know about important aspects of the world is central to the contemporary research on conceptual development. Unlike Piagetians who focused on the structural aspect of thought and indicated that developing individuals' competence depended on their stages, contemporary researchers pay attention to children's representations or understandings of the world, that is, the content of thought. They also emphasize domain specificity instead of domain-general stages; now, it is almost taken for granted that children's as well as adults' knowledge is divided into domains, and that the acquisition and elaboration of the knowledge in each domain is supported by a variety of domain-specific constraints (factors and conditions that narrow down what are to be observed and considered). While preserving the Piagetian constructivist view, current views are at best skeptical about the Piagetian assumption that children's thought is uniform across domains.

A growing number of conceptual development investigators have also come to agree that even young children possess "naive theories" or theory-like knowledge systems about selected aspects of the world (Wellman & Gelman, 1992, 1998). Because the term "naive theories" means coherent bodies of knowledge that involve causal explanatory devices, this conceptualization is also a distinct departure from the Piagetian position, which assumed young children to be preoperational and thus incapable of offering more or less plausible explanations in any domain. The emphasis on early competence (e.g., R. Gelman, 1979) is almost the slogan of contemporary researchers, but an important qualification here is "selected aspects of." In other words, young children are assumed to possess naive theories only in a few selected domains, presumably those domains that have been critical for the survival of the human species.

Since the publication of the highly influential article by Wellman and Gelman (1992), consensus has built that (a) naive physics, (b) theory of mind or naive psychology, and (c) naive biology are core domains. These domains concern major kinds of understandings of the external world with which we interact and are typically represented by a grasp of, respectively, (a) the movement of solid objects, (b) goal-directed behaviors of humans, and (c) life-sustaining activities of the body of humans and other living entities. It is contemporary researchers' hope that we can eventually build an integrated theory of conceptual development that replaces the Piagetian theory by closely studying each of these and several other core domains of thought and finding commonalities and differences among them.

In this monograph on young children's naive biology, we examine such theoretical issues as the processes, conditions, and mechanisms for conceptual development using the development of biological understanding as the target case. Why do we choose naive biology instead of other domains, say, naive physics or psychology? Historically, children's biological understanding has been central to major theories of children's thinking. For example, Piaget (1929) asserted that young children were animistic and took this animistic tendency as a sign of immaturity, reflecting the fact that young children had not yet differentiated between animate and inanimate objects. However, this is not a major reason for our choice.

☐ Why Do We Need to Study Children's Biological Thought?

We give below several theoretical and practical reasons why the study of children's biological thought will provide us with the perspective necessary to comprehend the growth of the mind and people's attempt to understand the world. First, the targets of naive biology, that is, human bodily processes and nonhuman animals and plants, are topics of apparent concern and importance to young children themselves. The children's remarks presented at the beginning of this chapter reveal that young children are fairly knowledgeable about these targets and willing to talk about them.

When toddlers begin to speak, they do so to request food and drink to satisfy physiological needs. Young children may talk with their parents about cuts and illnesses, especially when they have them. They may also be curious why a balanced diet is important or, more concretely for instance, why they have to eat some foods they do not like. In addition, even infants show an interest in the pets around them. Young children love to "read" picture books on nonhuman animals, watch TV programs about nature, and visit zoos. In short, naive biology is a cognitive product of young children's interaction with a part of the world to which they spontaneously pay attention.

Second, naive biology reveals both natural schemes of the human mind and cross-cultural universalities on the one hand, and cultural influences and specificities on the other. Because humans are supposed to have domain-specific schemes of mind through which they "conceptually perceive" different aspects of the world differently (Atran, 1998), how people divide the world must be highly similar across cultures. People everywhere in the world classify entities into humans, other animals, plants, and nonliving things. At the same time, however, there are some significant and interpretable cross-cultural differences in how these categories are represented and explained. Thus, "folkbiology" (see, e.g., Medin & Atran, 1999) is central in studies on culture and cognition. Naive biology is acquired and revised in different ecological niches of faunas and floras and also in varied cultural niches (Super & Harkness, 1986). Compared with naive physics and cognitive aspects of naive psychology called a theory of mind, naive biological understanding can be expected to reveal larger cultural variations, though its core is universal.

Third, naive biology is probably the most revealing domain for the personification-based understanding of the world, an attempt to comprehend a novel entity by assuming it to be human-like. This may take the form of the person analogy or the projection of self into the target, which probably constitutes one of our most basic and useful fallback strategies for knowing.

As we will see a number of times in the following chapters, young children's biological understanding is personifying (Carey, 1985; Inagaki & Hatano, 1987); they try to understand behaviors of other animals and plants by inductively projecting human properties and/or analogically attributing human processes based on structure mapping. Although professional biologists may claim that humans are an atypical animal, humans serve for both children and lay adults as the most familiar exemplar of biological entities against which other animals, and sometimes even plants, are compared. In contrast, naive physics is seldom human-centered; usually its prototypical entities are nonliving, solid objects. Naive psychology is seldom extended to nonhuman entities except for dogs, cats, and other pets.

Fourth, naive biology, especially naive systematics, provides us with an excellent domain to study human categorization and its resultant categories, as well as how such categories may be used in inferences. Human categorization is not solely dependent on perceptual similarities, nor on shared pragmatic values. People may be able to develop highly similar hierarchically organized structures even when they are exposed to different taxons, interact with these taxons in diverse ways, and are taught about them differently (López, Atran, Coley, Medin, & Smith, 1997). At the same time, however, they may arrange species in terms of similarity to a few important exemplars (Carey, 1985). Moreover, people may make both category-based and similarity-based inferences, probably depending on the amount and organization of their relevant pieces of knowledge (Inagaki & Sugiyama, 1988). Similarly, sophisticated categories may be used differently in inferences. We can thus profitably study the developmental trajectories of categorical knowledge and inference in naive biology.

Fifth, the study of naive biology is expected to show interactions between the theoretical mode of understanding entities and the engineering mode of cultivating their usefulness for us. It seems reasonable to assume that the evolutionary bases of our biological interest and comprehension are to obtain food (Wellman & Gelman, 1992) and to take care of one's own and family members' health (Inagaki & Hatano, 1993). Likewise, naive biology is not just a rudimentary natural science; it includes knowledge about how to grow plants, raise animals, and avoid being taken ill due to contagion and contamination.

Such close interactions between basic theories and engineering have been lost in naive physics, at least in technologically advanced societies. Nowadays artifacts are too sophisticated to be reconstructed from the knowledge in naive physics. Naive psychology may include elements of practical skills, but they often remain at the level of how-to, without being tied specifically to naive psychological principles even among lay adults.

Finally, the study of naive biology reveals how children and lay adults explain biological phenomena, which are about neither nonliving, solid objects nor human social-psychological behaviors. They may adopt either mechanical causality from naive physics or intentional causality from naive psychology, with or without recognizing that biological phenomena do not resonate with either. Alternatively, they may use, from the beginning, an intermediate form of causality that lies between mechanical and intentional forms (a teleological or vitalistic causality, for instance). In other words, by studying young children's biological understanding, we can examine whether there are only two primitive types of causality or there is something in-between in human cognition. This information is critical for our understanding of how our knowledge about the world is divided, considering that theories are characterized primarily in terms of causal devices.

We do not claim that naive biology constitutes a more important domain of thought than any other domain. However, we believe that its study has unique advantages. When we study naive biology, we exploit these advantages in order to add to our understanding of how the mind works and develops.

☐ Theoretical and Empirical Issues Within the Study of Naive Biology

As indicated at the beginning of this chapter, one of the goals of this book is to offer a description of young children's naive biology. The ongoing research programs by contemporary investigators of conceptual development have yet to produce complete description of children's thought even in the core domains (except possibly for theory of mind in young children), by answering such questions as, what the initial theory is like, when it is constructed, how it emerges, what experiential factors facilitate or inhibit its acquisition, how it is revised, and so on. As Carey (1985) aptly pointed out, we need accurate and rich descriptions of conceptual development before we can refine theoretical explanations. Moreover, there have been several topics in naive biology that have been the target of heated debates in recent decades. This monograph reviews experimental findings to derive reasonable, though tentative, conclusions on these debatable issues.

Early Piaget's Contributions

Like many other aspects of children's naive thinking, the study of children's biological understanding was initiated by Piaget's (1929) book, *The Child's Conception of the World*, which was one of his earliest publications. As the title of this book indicates, early Piaget, unlike middle Piaget and most of the Piagetians, was seriously interested in young children's understandings of the world. Through a series of ingenious questions, he demonstrated how qualitatively different young children's thought is from adults'. For instance, he asserted that young children were animistic in thinking: They tended to label nonliving entities as alive, to attribute characteristics of animals (typically, humans) to these entities, and to make predictions or explanations about the entities based on knowledge about animals (again, usually represented by humans). As we will see later in this book, his characterization of young children's biological reasoning as personifying hit the mark. Assigning mental states (desire, beliefs, and consciousness) to nonliving things, including extraterrestrial entities (e.g., the sun) and geographical features (e.g., a mountain), provided the most impressive example of animistic (and personifying) responses. For example, "The sun is hot because it wants to keep people warm." This animistic (or personifying) tendency was taken by Piaget as a sign of immaturity, reflecting the fact that young children had not yet differentiated between animate and inanimate objects.

Piaget (1929), using a clinical interview method, indicated that children's understanding of living entities progresses through four stages; from the first stage, where children regard entities that perform a function or are active as alive and/or conscious, to the second and third stages, where only entities that move or move autonomously are considered as alive and/or conscious, to the fourth stage, where either animals or both animals and plants are regarded as alive. Piaget asserted that it takes 11 or 12 years to reach the fourth stage. Unlike the middle Piaget or Piagetian logico-mathematical stages, these stages regarding the understanding of an aspect of the world provided a sequence of vivid descriptions of children's beliefs and reasoning about the target content. Let us give an example of a Stage 1 child's animistic responses shown in the Piaget's (1929) clinical interview.

VEL *(8 years, 6 months):* [Interviewer: Does a bicycle know it goes?] "Yes." [Why?] "Because it goes." [Does it know when it is made to stop?] "Yes." [What does it know?] "The pedals." [Why?] "Because they stop going." [You think so really?] "Yes." (We laugh.) (p. 175). . . . [Is the sun alive?] "Yes." [Why?] "It gives light." [Is a candle alive?] "No." [Why not?] "(Yes) because it gives light. It is alive when it is giving light, but it isn't alive when it is not giving light" (p. 196).

Piaget's work on child animism motivated a large amount of subsequent research, especially in the 1950s and 1960s (see Looft & Bartz, 1969). Among others, Laurendau and Pinard (1962) interviewed a large number of children between the ages of 4 and 12 years in the same fashion as Piaget did. On the whole, they confirmed Piaget's basic findings. Young children's animistic responses were often cited in child psychology textbooks as evidence for their intellectual immaturity.

Carey and Beyond

Studies in conceptual development since the late 1970s, which have emphasized early competence (R. Gelman, 1979), especially in a few selected core or privileged domains of thought (Keil, 1981), have led developmentalists to doubt Piaget's view on animism as a sign of immaturity and of young children's general lack of understanding of the world. Carey (1985), among others, provided a pivotal reinterpretation of Piaget's insightful observations. Interestingly, she, too, characterized young children's reasoning about biological phenomena as animistic and personifying. She attributed this not to domain-general intellectual immaturity, however, but to the lack of domain-specific knowledge in biology. Since young children are familiar with humans while necessarily ignorant of most other entities, she assumed, they have to use their knowledge about humans as a reference point in inferring about other biological phenomena.

In spite of this innovative reconceptualization of the childhood animism, Carey (1985) agreed with Piaget that children's biological understanding emerged rather late in development. Based on her own experimental findings as well as reviews of earlier studies, she concluded that children's characteristically biological thinking emerged fairly late, at least much later than their physical and psychological understandings. She claimed that young children's human-centered inference or personification would lead to a distorted, psychological interpretation of biological phenomena, because it meant to her that young children tended to make predictions and explanations based on their intuitive psychology, that is, on intentional causality. Applying mechanical causality to the workings of the bodily machine would become possible only around age 10. Younger children would not accept that our bodily functions are independent of our intention to operate the bodily machine. They would not admit the inevitability of growth or death for any living thing, because they lacked the knowledge that the biological processes that produce these phenomena are autonomous.

Carey (1985) also claimed that children younger than 10 years of age could not possess biology because they are "totally ignorant of the physiological mechanisms involved" (p. 45); they know that input (e.g., eating too much) is related to output (becoming fat or upsetting the stomach), but nothing about what mediates them. She proposed the idea that naive biology emerges from intuitive psychology (p. 200). All of these claims came from the fact that she regarded the domain of biology not as a privileged domain (Siegler & Crowley, 1994) or an innate domain (Carey, 1995), but as a derivative.

Thus, in addition to reviving the issue of animism, Carey (1985) raised three more, mutually related and theoretically intriguing issues in the study of young children's biological understanding: (a) whether children younger than 10 years of age lack a domain of biology that is separated from other systems of knowledge, (b) whether a domain of naive biology emerges from that of naive psychology, and (c) whether the development of naive biology involves a theory change, or what Carey termed, a radical form of conceptual change. (Although Carey sometimes discussed (b) and (c) as if they denoted almost the same, we separate them because they are conceptually distinguishable.)

In the years since Carey's book was published, there has been vigorous debates over these three issues, as well as the issue of animism. Arguments against Carey have been both empirical and conceptual. Some investigators have tried to show that children much younger than 10 years of age do possess some intuitive grasp of biological structures and functions as well as considerable knowledge about biological phenomena. Others have pointed out that, though young children lack an understanding of mechanical causality, they may rely on nonintentional causality for predicting and explaining biological phenomena, and that young children's ignorance of physiological mechanisms does not mean that they do not have any form of biology, because they may have something that is similar to endogenous biology, which was shared by both non-Westerners and Westerners before the establishment of modern biology (Hatano & Inagaki, 1994b, 1996).

Among these challengers to Carey, Keil (1989, 1992) has been highly influential, partly because his position is in sharp contrast with Carey's. Keil asserts that (a) even preschoolers possess fairly advanced biological understanding, (b) reasoning about biological phenomena is never psychological, and (c) the development of naive biological thought involves no discontinuities. His ideas are closer to scholars such as Atran (1990, 1998), who emphasize the modular nature of folkbiology. These ideas have stimulated as well as been supported by a lot of experiments in both Keil's and S. Gelman's laboratories. Through the debates, we have learned a lot, such as young children's animistic and personifying tendencies, their differentiation between biological and psychological processes, the distinctions they make between natural kinds and artifacts, their intuitive grasp of the essence of living things, their nonpsychological, functional causal understanding of biological processes, and so forth. We will review these studies in chapters that follow.

Preview of the Present Argument

Unlike Piaget, we argue that preschool children think consistently and causally about biological phenomena. Unlike Carey, we think that young children have a distinctive biological, not merely psychological, knowledge system. Like both Piaget and Carey, we too believe that young children's understanding of biological phenomena is "qualitatively" different from that of older children and lay adults. We, however, attribute the differences primarily to the paucity of young children's biology-relevant experience and specific knowledge, and emphasize the insightful and adaptive nature of their biological understanding. Although we characterize young children's naive biology in detail in Chapters 2–5, let us present a quick preview here.

First, biological phenomena that are targets of young children's spontaneous attention and interest are quite limited, more limited than older children's and lay adults' that have been influenced in various ways by the modern science of biology through schooling and other channels. According to our informal survey and conversational analysis, young children are concerned mainly with human bodily processes such as eating, growing, and being taken ill, with everyday observations about characteristic shapes, body parts, and behaviors of pets and other animals, and maybe with a few other issues. In other words, the initial form of naive biology is built upon a data set primarily regarding these phenomena, and thus can offer plausible predictions and explanations only within this range.

Second, young children's *salient* modes of biological inferences are also distinctly different. Young children's biology, unlike older children's and lay adults', is personifying: They tend to predict nonhuman animals' and sometimes even plants' behaviors and properties based on these organisms' similarity to humans. Often they have to rely on personification because of their limited knowledge about biological categories and their paucity of representative exemplars. Although their use of personification is skillful and does not produce overly personifying errors as often as Piaget claimed, it cannot be error free.

Young children's preferred biological causality is vitalistic. More specifically, instead of seeking some exact mechanisms, they assume that life-sustaining processes in living organisms are governed by laws of vitalism, that is, that organisms can be active and lively by ingesting vital power from food and/or water and circulating it within them. They also assume a surplus of vital power produces growth, and its loss causes illness. However, they may leave other phenomena unexplained.

☐ Developmental Issues That Can Be Examined in the Study of Naive Biology

As mentioned at the beginning, the other of the two goals of this book is to clarify processes, conditions, and mechanisms of conceptual development through a case study of naive biology. Such an attempt is promising, we believe, because the current formulation of conceptual development needs further refinement, and this can be achieved only with a more advanced understanding of a particular domain of thought. For background, we summarize current views on conceptual development in contrast with the Piagetian theory that dominated the research area in the 1960s and early 1970s and raise a few unsolved issues in the current views.

Summary of Current Views of Conceptual Development

How does conceptual development take place? Many proponents of the current views of conceptual development probably agree that it can be characterized in succinct and coherent ways as the domain-specific construction and revision of theory-like knowledge systems under both cognitive and sociocultural constraints. The idea that knowledge is constructed is inspired by Piaget, among others, and it constitutes the *Zeitgeist* shared by contemporary researchers. Humans interact with the environment, find regularities, and construct condition-action rules and more elaborate forms of knowledge. In the course of development, knowledge must be modified, as every developmental researcher knows.

As indicated in the above characterization, there are three notable differences between the Piagetian theory and current views. The Piagetian theory assumed that developing individuals' competence depended on their stages, in other words, logico-mathematical structures applicable across domains. This assumption implied that young children who had not yet acquired "concrete operations" would not possess a coherent system of knowledge in any domain. Those children would proceed from the preoperational to the concrete-operational stage by elaborating logico-mathematical structures. In contrast, the current views assume that (a) processes as well as products of construction are domain-specific, (b) products can be theory-like knowledge systems even in early childhood, and (c) processes of knowledge construction are constrained cognitively and socioculturally. These new features of the current views have been introduced by several different groups of scholars who found some aspect of the Piagetian theory particularly unsatisfactory (Hatano & Inagaki, 2000), including those who wanted to stress the competence of young (preoperational) children in a few selected domains of thought (e.g., R. Gelman, 1979), those who paid special attention to within-individual variations in problem-solving competence due to accumulated experience in the relevant domain (e.g., Chi, Glaser, & Rees, 1982), and those who emphasized roles of the sociocultural context that serves as cognitive scaffolding (e.g., Rogoff, 1990). Each of these groups were active reformers and have reinforced, successfully to some extent, a soft point of the Piagetian theory.

However, these views still face some serious conceptual confusion and conflict, partly because they have been formed through the collective enterprise of groups with diverse interests and perspectives, not by a leading authority or a small group whose members share most of opinions. In particular, the notions of domains and constraints, which play key roles in the current views of conceptual development, are not yet well articulated. Many contemporary scholars tend to interpret these notions in biased ways, stressing their favorite aspects and deemphasizing, if not ignoring, competing or opposing aspects. This is probably because of such traditional dichotomies as nativism versus emergentism, cognitivism versus cultural determinism, and so on.

In addition, we have not yet succeeded in properly characterizing theory-like knowledge systems or "naive theories." The "theory theory" (Gopnik & Wellman, 1994), a view that children's conceptual structures are theories, has many opponents as well as proponents (Gopnik & Meltzoff, 1997; Russell, 1992). As a result, we are far from building a powerful and integrated theory of conceptual development that can replace the Piagetian theory. We will discuss these problems as an initial step toward proposing an integrative and moderate model in later chapters in this book.

Domains and Domain Specificity

The current views indicate that both processes and products of knowledge construction and revision are domain-specific. Higher order cognitive activities, such as problem solving and comprehension, usually take place within a domain, using only the knowledge of a domain most relevant to the target problem or set of phenomena for cognitive economy. When new pieces of knowledge are produced by these activities, they are also incorporated into the relevant domain for future use. In this sense, many current investigators assume, knowledge is acquired domain by domain. This represents the most remarkable difference between Piagetian and current views. Intraindividual variations in the ability for problem solving, comprehension, and memory are now explained in terms of domain-specific prior knowledge. Children as well as adults reveal high levels of competence in those domains in which they possess rich and well-structured bodies of knowledge (e.g., Chi, Hutchinson, & Robin, 1989; Chi et al., 1982). Horizontal decalage, which was regarded as exceptional and puzzling for Piagetians, is taken for granted now.

Our knowledge constructed in the course of development is divided into domains and, because theory-like knowledge systems include characteristic causal devices, modes of causal understanding vary between domains accordingly. These ideas are intuitively appealing. Carey (1985) suggested that there are a dozen or so such domains. It is generally agreed that at least naive physics, naive psychology, and naive biology are included among them (Wellman & Gelman, 1992, 1998). However, it is very hard to indicate how knowledge is divided. How domains are divided is, in a sense, a cultural product (Laboratory of Comparative Human Cognition, 1983), as clearly indicated in the case of the grouping of academic disciplines at universities. At the same time, how knowledge is divided into domains is also determined on cognitive bases (Lutz & Keil, in press) that are at least partially innate. As a result, defining the term "domain" in a way acceptable to everyone is almost impossible. Hirschfeld and Gelman (1994) characterize domains as "a body of knowledge that identifies and interprets a class of phenomena assumed to share certain properties and to be of a distinct and general type" (p. 21). This carefully phrased definition based on an extensive review of the literature seems reasonable, but leaves the issue of "by whom it is assumed" open.

A related difficult question to answer that is directly relevant to the present monograph is whether human beings are genetically endowed to acquire core domains of thought. Each core domain probably emerges as a framework for predicting and interpreting typical "behaviors" of representative objects that are covered by the domain; in the case of naive physics, such "behaviors" are motion of nonliving, solid objects, and in the case of naive psychology, social activity of humans. This far almost everyone would agree. But why do these domains emerge? In the chapters that follow, we will seek better characterization of domains, and examine how young children build the core domains, by using naive biology as a test case.

Constraints

Virtually all contemporary researchers assume that the process of knowledge acquisition proceeds under a variety of constraints. Here the term *constraints* refers to conditions or factors that eliminate part of the set of physically or logically possible alternatives (moves, hypotheses, or interpretations) in advance. In the case of learning or development, constraints thus facilitate the process of acquisition as well as restrict its possible range. As Keil (1990) pointed out, some sorts of constraints on learning are needed because, without constraints, we cannot succeed in choosing a most promising hypothesis or interpretation for the given set of observations from among a very large number of possible alternatives. Some constraints are domain-general (e.g., architectural constraints as well as logico-mathematical knowledge a la Piaget), and others are domain-specific (Keil, 1990). Whereas Piaget considered only domain-general constraints, proponents of the current views of conceptual development have concerned themselves mostly with domain-specific constraints, in correspondence with their emphasis on domain-specificity. The acquisition of some forms of knowledge is easy, but others are difficult to learn due to the difference in domain-specific constraints. The construction and successive revision of knowledge in a domain takes place under the same set of constraints so that the acquired knowledge in the domain is often similar, if not identical, between different individuals.

The necessity of assuming constraints is even more obvious in conceptual development in which such basic knowledge systems as naive physics, psychology, and biology are acquired early and uniformly. A number of studies (e.g., Wellman & Inagaki, 1997) have shown that naive physics and psychology have been acquired even among 3-year-olds, and naive biology, a little later but surely before formal schooling. Thus, we have to explain, by assuming a variety of constraints, (a) how a child determines which aspects of the world he or she should pay attention to and how he or she should segment and encode them, and (b) how a child can pick out a good candidate when an almost infinite number of hypotheses and interpretations are consistent with the sample observations.

Many investigators agree that there are three types of domain-specific constraints: acquired prior knowledge of the domain, innate tendencies and biases relevant to the domain, and sociocultural constraints. The first two are called cognitive constraints and are supposed to operate within individual minds; sociocultural constraints interactively control a child's attention and search for an interpretation or hypothesis. These three constraints have been advocated by those who belong to the three successor positions to Piaget, those who emphasize expert knowledge, early competence, and sociocultural scaffolding, respectively. Depending upon their theoretical orientation, a majority of the investigators emphasize one type while belittling others.

Nobody doubts that rich and well-organized knowledge in the domain enables children to acquire new pieces of knowledge or elaborate prior pieces of knowledge readily and easily (Chi, 1978), as it enhances all forms of higher order cognition in the domain (e.g., Bransford & McCarrell, 1975). Even young children learn efficiently and reveal advanced modes of reasoning in a domain in which they have accumulated and elaborated knowledge. However, this constraint may not be as effective in conceptual development, especially at its early phase, as in expertise (Wellman, in press).

The other two types of constraints, innate and sociocultural, should play a more critical role in the initial construction of naive theories. We will try to specify their nature in Chapter 6, again taking naive biology as the target example. In Chapter 8, we will also analyze extensively how these three types of constraints help young children, in a coordinated and compensatory way, to build knowledge systems in the core domains.

Naive Theories

Conceptual development consists of the construction and revision of a set of knowledge systems that concern important aspects of the world. These knowledge systems are often called naive theories, primarily because they are somewhat similar to scientific theories rather than to schemas or scripts, which do not involve any deep causal explanatory principles (e.g., Carey, 1985). Naive theories include coherent pieces of knowledge involving characteristic causal principles or devices. In other words, children can predict, construe, or even explain in coherent and principled ways a set of phenomena that are targets of each theory, relying on the causal devices. However, investigators vary widely in attributing which other aspects of scientific theories belong to naive theories.

It is obvious that naive theories are dissimilar in some respects from scientific theories. Again, investigators vary in their opinions on which aspects of scientific theories and naive theories differ from each other. However, even strong proponents of the "naive theories" view would agree that young children are very poor at designing experiments to falsify their theories and revising the theories based on results of the experiments (see Kuhn, 1989). Some researchers may emphasize that children's "theories" are not for making novel predictions but for providing the children with interpretations for observed events, and thus might better be called interpretive schemas or *modes of construal* (Keil, 1992). There are a number of scholars who do not want to use the term naive theories, because children's or even lay adults' theories are not highly coherent and therefore deserve only such labels as *a set of mental models* (diSessa, 1983; Yates et al., 1988). Naive theories do not cover all the phenomena they could, and their implications are not fully extended or exploited.

However, we use the term *naive theories* interchangeably with *theory-like knowledge systems* in this book not just for brevity but for the following reasons: (a) they enable children or lay adults to offer some principled and coherent predictions and explanations; (b) the construction of more concrete and specific mental models, which seem to vary from situation to situation, is constrained to some extent by the relevant naive theory, as a framework scientific theory constrains specific scientific theories; and (c) they are also used to guide the learning of new pieces of information and the invention of additional pieces.

As the starting point for this book, we adopt the following tentative criteria for recognizing that children have a naive theory in the target domain:

1. We judge children to possess a naive theory when they can make co-
    herent, reasonable, and differentiated predictions (probably based on
    a proper causal device in the domain), even though they cannot offer
    explanations themselves. This is because such a coherent, reasonable,
    and differentiated use of the causal device probably reveals a basic
    explanatory schema, which is the essential constituent of a naive theory,
    possessed by young children or even preverbal infants (Keil & Wilson,
    2000). In order to differentiate the responding based on an explana-
    tory schema from that relying on specific pieces of knowledge, this
    criterion requests coherent responses within a subdomain of a naive
    theory, though young children cannot be expected to apply the ex-
    planatory schema to all subdomains.
2. A stricter criterion is that children be able to offer a causal explanation
    that is relevant and appropriate to some important phenomenon of
    the domain or, at the least, that they can choose such an explanation
    from among a few alternatives. However, considering that "the ability
    to express explanations explicitly is likely to be an excessively strin-
    gent criterion" (Keil & Wilson, 2000, p. 3) and also that this criterion
    excludes the possibility of attributing a theory to preverbal infants and
    nonhuman animals, we prefer the above lenient one, though we ad-
    mit that meeting this strict criterion gives stronger evidence for the
    possession of a theory.
3. We credit a precursor of a naive theory when children can differenti-
    ate from among other entities, target entities, the behaviors of which
    constitute important phenomena of the domain.

We reflect on these criteria in the final chapter after reviewing studies on
naive biology.

How to characterize the knowledge system children possess is a very
important job for conceptual development researchers in general, and for
this book in particular, but it is also very difficult due to problems related
to assessment. We are now well aware that the target piece of knowledge,
that can serve as the basis for answering the experimenter's varied questions in coherent ways, may not be used, especially when the knowledge
is not salient or fragile. Thus, subtle differences in questioning may activate different pieces of knowledge and induce different answers from the
same child. Our general strategy is to ask participant-friendly questions
that require inferences, by (a) avoiding ambiguities about the target entity, property, or process, and (b) clarifying the context of questions as
much as possible. At the same time, we carefully arrange questions lest
children answer them all based on their specific memories.

To summarize, we are convinced that it is time to review what we have
learned in recent decades about young children's biological understand-

ing. More specifically, our review has two goals. At a specific level, we claim that children as young as 5 years of age, that is, before formal schooling, possess a naive theory of biology that is personifying and vitalistic but that is differentiated from naive theories of psychology and physics. At a more general level, we try to offer an integrative and moderate model of conceptual development as a domain-specific construction of theory-like knowledge systems under cognitive and sociocultural constraints, taking naive biology as a good example.

The Living/Nonliving Distinction

Boy (3 years), while seeing young sweet potato plants droop: "Poor thing! Are you thirsty? I give lots of water (to you). So, cheer up." (Group El Sol, 1987)

Girl (5 years, 5 months), when asked what would happen to a tulip if it was not watered for a whole day: "The tulip will wither. 'Cause, if the tulip doesn't drink water, it won't become lively."

Some readers may think that the above utterances by 3- and 5-year-olds show immature children's "animistic" responses to plants—treating the plants as if they had consciousness. Other readers may think that these utterances indicate the children's recognition of commonalities between animals and plants, because taking something from outside is essential for living things, including plants, to live or to be lively. Although whether young children recognize plants as well as animals as living has drawn researchers' attention only very recently, the distinction between living entities, including animals and plants, and nonliving things is essential not only in biology but also for our understanding of the world. If we know that an entity is alive, we can reasonably infer that entity's other important properties and behaviors, such as that it grows, needs nutriment, reproduces, and so on (see Keil, 1992). If children use different criteria for the living/nonliving distinction than adults do, they must think very differently about a number of entities in the world. This is one of the major reasons why children's or indigenous people's animism has received so much attention for such a long time.

Thus, although studies on childhood animism have primarily concerned the distinction between animals (humans) and nonliving things, it is more important to examine whether young children distinguish both animals and plants from nonliving things. The acquisition of the concept of living things including animals and plants is essential for the establishment of naive biology (Carey, 1985). However, most of the previous studies have neglected, or at least dealt with only incidentally, plants in the living/nonliving distinction; in other words, they focused on the animate/inanimate distinction, omitting plants. The studies on childhood animism represented by Piaget did not pay due attention to "animistic responses" to plants.

Can young children recognize commonalities between animals and plants to construct a concept of living things? Animals and plants are perceptually very different; for instance, plants have no self-initiated movement, no face, and so on. Linguistic factors also seem to be an obstacle to recognizing commonalities between animals and plants. For example, the English word *animate* easily reminds us of an animal. The Hebrew word for animal is very close to that for living and alive, but the word for plant has no obvious relation to these terms (Stavy & Wax, 1989). The Japanese be-verb has two forms, *iru* and *aru*; *iru* is applied to humans and other animals, whereas *aru* is applied to plants and nonliving things.

For these reasons and others, it has been believed that young children have great difficulty acquiring the concept of living things including animals and plants; Piaget (1929) claimed that the concept of life is not acquired before late childhood, and Carey (1985) reported that the acquisition of the concept of living things is not achieved until middle childhood. Similar findings were reported by Richards and Siegler (1986) and Stavy and Wax (1989) by asking children whether certain sets of entities are alive. However, recent studies using more sophisticated methodologies than the previous ones indicate that much younger children can recognize commonalities between animals and plants.

We claim that children as young as 5 years of age make the living/nonliving distinction including animals and plants, at least for taking food/water, growth, and some related properties. We assume that ingesting something (i.e., taking food or water) and its related properties, including growth, may constitute the core of young children's concept of living things. In this chapter, we first discuss why the previous studies represented by Piaget and Carey failed to find that young children distinguish both animals and plants from nonliving things, and then present some data from recent studies suggesting that young children can treat both animals and plants as different from nonliving things. We also present some data to indicate that young children grasp commonalities between animals and plants and thus form a superordinate category of living things. Next, we briefly review studies on the animate/inanimate distinction as a

foundation, or a precursor, of the living/nonliving distinction. That review will reveal that the animate/inanimate distinction (i.e., the distinction between animals and nonliving things) is acquired earlier. Finally,
we discuss theoretical implications of what has been revealed in this
chapter.

Although our aim in this book is to integrate an increasingly large literature from an increasingly large number of researchers and countries,
we do this in part by organizing the larger sets of studies around some
exemplary ones of our own. In doing so, we provide details about some
of our studies. In addition, we focus primarily on preschool children before their formal schooling has started, and more specifically on children
aged 3–6 years (preschoolers through kindergartners). We place our main
focus on this age for several reasons. First, this age is theoretically important because Carey (1985) claimed that preschool children (4- to 6-year-
olds) have no naive biology differentiated from psychology and Piaget
(1929) also asserted that preschool children, who are supposed to be "preoperational," are so immature that they cannot help being animistic in
thinking. Second, most research on children's biological understanding
has focused on the preschool age. Third, children of this age have had no
formal schooling and no systematic instruction on biology, and thus we
can examine their "naive" thinking. (We note that, unlike American kindergartens, Japanese kindergartens usually include children aged 3–6 years
and do not belong to the formal schooling system.)

☐ The Living/Nonliving Distinction

Studies Denying That Children Make
the Living/Nonliving Distinction

The questionable conclusion that young children do not make the living/
nonliving distinction comes from two sources. One source is the studies
represented by Piaget (1929). In these studies children were directly asked
whether animals, plants, and inanimate objects are alive (e.g., Piaget,
1929; Richards & Siegler, 1984) or what characteristics living things have
(Richards & Siegler, 1986). However, the children's failures to make the
living/nonliving distinction in these cases might be due to the ambiguity
of the questions posed to them. The terms *alive* or *living* are especially
complex and contain multiple definitions that young children may find
confusing.

The other source of the alleged evidence against young children's understanding of the living/nonliving distinction is Carey's (1985) study,
which examined whether children's induction of a given property would

be constrained by biological categories. In her study, after 6-year-old children were taught about a novel property (e.g., that X has *golgi*, a technical word which was beyond their understanding) of dogs and bees, of dogs and flowers, or only of flowers. They were then asked whether other living and nonliving entities (including astronomical ones) would also have it. The results provided no evidence that the concept of living things constrained their induction. Children who were taught about dogs and flowers tended to attribute *golgi* more widely than those who were taught about dogs and bees or just flowers, but often overattributed the novel property even to inanimate objects. However, the failure here may be attributed to low retrievability of the concept of living things. The children did not rely on biological boundaries in inductive projection because they may have failed to activate the concept of living things in attributing the novel and incomprehensible property of having *golgi*, not because they did not possess the concept.

To induce the ability to make the living/nonliving distinction, which is not yet firmly established in young children, we need to use more sophisticated methods than before—methods that are "child-friendly." In what follows, we provide data from studies using such methods.

Recognition of Both Animals and Plants as "Growers"

Recent studies on the living/nonliving distinction have examined whether children would make predictions for representative animals and plants differently than for typical nonliving things in specified situations. These studies often avoid exclusive reliance on verbal responses. As one such study, we describe Experiment 1 of Inagaki and Hatano (1996), who examined whether young children can distinguish animals and plants from nonliving things in terms of growth. We focus on growth here because it constitutes one of the few significant biological phenomena that young children pay attention to and that are familiar to them. It is also considered an advantage that the word *grow* seems to have no "language barrier" in application to animals and plants. Keil (1983) reported that kindergartners correctly applied the predicate *grow* to both animals and plants, though they applied other animal-plus-plant predicates, such as alive, sick, and starve, to animals only. Thus, young children are assumed to characterize plants as "growers," as expressed in Hebrew (Stavy & Wax, 1989).

We (Inagaki & Hatano, 1996) extended Rosengren, Gelman, Kalish, and McCormick's (1991) method, which successfully established young children's animal/artifact distinction in terms of growth, to include plants, so that the results could reveal children's ability to make the living/nonliving distinction. However, unlike Rosengren et al. (1991), we avoided the use of words implying differences in size, such as "a baby" and "an adult," and constructed nearly identical questions for animals, plants, and artifacts. The stimulus materials consisted of four sets of three animal pictures each, four sets of three plant pictures each, and four sets of three artifact pictures each. Two of the three pictures in each set were identical, and the third item was either larger (i.e., size change) or both larger and different in shape (i.e., size and shape change). The four sets of animals, those of plants, and those of artifacts each consisted of two size-change sets and two size-and-shape-change sets. Examples of size-and-shape-change sets are shown in Figure 2.1. Forty-eight 4-year-olds and forty-

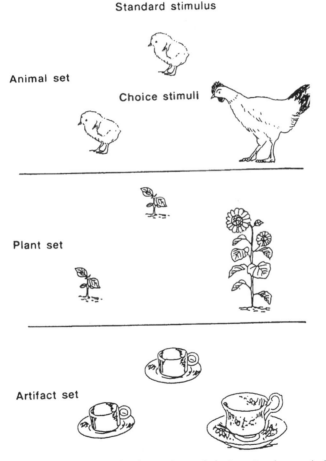

FIGURE 2.1. An example of standard stimulus and choice stimulus cards for animals, plants, and artifacts. From Hatano and Inagaki (1999).

eight 5-year-olds were recruited from a kindergarten and participated in this study.

The child was presented with a standard stimulus, for example, a picture of a flower bud / a small tree/a young animal/a new artifact, and was then asked to choose which of two other pictures would show the plant/ animal/artifact a few hours later and several months or years later. One of the pictured stimuli to be chosen was identical to the standard, and the other pictured item was either larger or larger and different in shape. Instructions for the tree stimuli in the plant condition are as follows: "This is a picture of a pine tree. Taro saw this tree when he arrived at the kindergarten in the morning. If he sees it again when he leaves the kindergarten for home, which of these trees will he be able to see?"; "Then, if he sees it once again after a very, very long time, many years later, which of these trees will he be able to see?" For the flower sets, "after a very long time, in summer" was used instead of "after a very, very long time, many years later." Instructions for all sets in the other two conditions were almost the same as those for the tree sets described above except that the situations in which Taro saw the target stimuli were different, and thus the wordings were changed accordingly. For example, a zoo, not a kindergarten, was the setting for the animal sets. For the artifact sets, for example, the experimenter said, "Taro put a cup in the box and left home to play outside," and actually put the picture of the cup in a small cardboard box.

The children's choice responses were classified into *same size, same size* (SS) for the two questions of "a few hours later" and "several months/ years later," *same size, larger size* (SL), *larger size, larger size* (LL), or *larger size, same size* (LS). Table 2.1 shows the frequencies of these four types of responses for animals, plants, and artifacts in each age group.

TABLE 2.1. Frequencies of four types of responses for animals, plants, and artifacts in each age group

Types of responses	4 Years			5 Years		
	Animal	Plant	Artifact	Animal	Plant	Artifact
SS response	9	7	37	6	0	52
SL response	36	37	12	44	50	7
LL response	6	11	5	2	9	0
LS response	13	9	10	12	5	5

Note. The total number of responses for each condition was 64 (16 participants with 4 responses). S=same size; L=larger size. First letter of each two-letter pair indicates the child's response to an-a-few-hours-later question; second, response to a several-months/years-later question. From Inagaki & Hatano (1996).

Both 4- and 5-year-olds made SL responses most often for both animals and plants, whereas they made SS responses most often for artifacts. That is, for animals and plants the children predicted changes in size (and also in shape) after a long time (though not after a few hours), whereas for artifacts they expected no changes in size over time. This tendency was found clearly among the 5-year-olds. They made SL responses 69% of the time for animals and 78% of the time for plants. In contrast, they seldom made SS responses for animals or plants, but did 81% of the time for artifacts. Thus the average percent correct across these three types of entities was 76% among the 5-year-olds. Although the average among the 4-year-olds was only 57% and they made a considerable number of responses other than SS for artifacts, they too made few SS responses for animals and plants.

The children made some LL responses, especially for plants. This result was probably due to the overestimation of the growing speed, derived from their characterization of plants (and sometimes animals, too) as rapid growers. Another reason for LL responses may be that these children had difficulty conceptualizing time; they may have regarded "a few hours" to be as long as "a few months/years." Alternatively, considering that LL responses occurred even for artifacts, some children may have preferred a larger alternative and/or referred to magical change.

The above findings clearly indicated that the 4- and 5-year-olds treated animals and plants (but not artifacts) as entities growing in size (and also changing in shape) over time. Hickling and Gelman (1995) further found that older 4-year-olds but not younger 4-year-olds recognized plant growth as cyclical; the older children could order pictures depicting the seed, plant, and fruit or flower in the correct sequence (e.g., seed → plant → fruit/flower, plant → fruit/flower → seed) above chance, irrespective of the differences in the starting point (item types) from which the children were asked to reason.

Backscheider, Shatz, and Gelman (1993) reported that preschool children recognize that when damaged, both animals and plants can recover through regrowth, while artifacts must be fixed by a person. Inagaki and Hatano (1987) revealed that when 5- and 6-year-olds were asked to predict behaviors of an animal or a plant in situations involving four biological phenomena (e.g., growth, spontaneous recovery, etc.), the children relied on personification (the person analogy) to make predictions for an animal and a plant, but not for a stone (a representative nonliving thing). Their predictions concerning growth and related phenomena were generally reasonable.

A number of studies dealing with other phenomena than growth or regrowth also corroborate the above findings. For example, Springer and Keil (1991) found that 4- and 5-year-old children differentiated animals and plants from artifacts in terms of mechanisms of color acquisition. That is, when asked to choose one from among five alternative mechanisms, these children chose natural mechanisms of inheritance for animals and plants most often, whereas for artifacts the children considered human intervention to be necessary. S. Gelman and Kremer (1991), who examined the natural kind/artifact distinction in children's causal explanations through such questions as "Why does a rabbit hop?", "Why does a flower open up?", "Why does a guitar play music?" reported that preschool children referred to human intervention for artifacts but not for natural kinds, and that the children appropriately attributed natural causes (e.g., "It grew that way") to natural kinds more often than to artifacts.

☐ Recognition of Commonalities Between Animals and Plants

Some readers may wonder whether the findings so far are conclusive for the acquisition of the category of living things, because most of the above studies only showed that children attribute to both animals and plants an isolated property or that they predict that animals and plants respond similarly to a single situation. However, we emphasize that these findings are promising for the claim that much younger children than Piaget or Carey claimed recognize commonalities between animals and plants for some phenomena or processes.

As indicated in the previous section, growth is one property that even young children recognize as being shared by animals and plants. This is supported by daily observation, too. Children seem to have learned that animals are born as babies and become bigger in size (e.g., Rosengren et al., 1991). Plants, especially flowers, are likely to grow markedly (i.e., change from sprouts to blooms) in a short period. Though trees grow in size much more slowly, they often undergo changes corresponding to the seasons, having tiny fresh green leaves in spring, growing thick in summer, and so on. These apparently incremental changes suggest that trees are alive, though they are not active in the literal sense.

It has also been suggested that children associate growth with feeding or watering. Remember the two children's statements about plants quoted at the beginning of this chapter. We thus assume that growth and growth-related properties as well as taking food or water may constitute the core of young children's concept of living things. These properties may include those that make living entities lively and cause growth, such as taking in energy from food/water or even from air, as well as those involving changes in the life course other than growth in size, such as being taken ill, being restored to health, or becoming old and dying. These properties may serve as the basis for children to recognize commonalities between animals and plants to the extent that they are applied to both animals and plants in children's linguistic-cultural environments. For example, we expect that the properties of growing and dying or withering, which are seemingly used often for plants as well as animals, will help children grasp the commonalities. Based on these considerations, we ran a series of experiments (Inagaki & Hatano, 1996). Let us describe these experiments in detail below.

Experiments Using Inductive Projection

The inductive projection paradigm enabled us to ask children about various properties within a short period of time. Inductive patterns can illuminate concepts children possess, because the processes of projection are generally constrained by one of the concepts. However, it should be noted that both "false negative" and "false positive" conclusions about the possession of a given concept (e.g., "living things") may be derived by analyzing the patterns of induction. On the one hand, a concept children possess may not be activated and thus may fail to affect their patterns of induction. For example, it is likely that the acquired concept of living things fails to affect induction when a given property is phrased using a predicate readily applicable to humans or animals only, because that concept is difficult to activate in such a condition. On the other hand, attributional patterns identical to those generated by constrained induction may be obtained when children know specifically which objects possess the target characteristic. Carey (1985) used totally novel properties (e.g., having a *golgi*) in order to eliminate this "false positive" possibility. However, as discussed earlier, it is possible that the children in her study failed to activate their concept (e.g., "living things") because they could not understand the functions of novel properties that were taught to them on the spot.

We employed somewhat familiar properties in the sense that most children might know that humans have them. We assumed that although children might know that humans (including themselves) possess these properties, they would be uncertain as to which other entities do, because the properties are not directly observable and because they do not encounter such entities often. In attributing such properties, they would thus have to make inferences based on an intuitive grasp of the functions of these properties. In order to reduce further the possibility of obtaining a "false negative" result, we, following Gutheil, Vera, and Keil (1998), provided half the children with a biological context that was expected to trigger their biological knowledge system. Although the effect of giving a biological context was limited to animals in the Gutheil et al. (1998) study, we expected that the effect would extend to plants when properly phrased all-living-thing properties were used. Thus children's knowledge of a living/nonliving distinction could be examined.

We conducted two experiments (see Inagaki & Hatano, 1996, Experiments 2 and 2a). In what follows we discuss both experiments in combination, because they were highly similar. In both experiments two conditions were set up: the context condition and the no-context condition. In the context condition we gave short, vitalistic descriptions about the function of the target property for a person, that is, the descriptions referring to taking in or exchanging vital power or energy. In the no-context condition we did not give such descriptions. If giving vitalistic accounts of properties for a person enhances children's use of the concept of living things in their inductive projection, it implies that children consider both animals and plants to be biological entities with the same underlying mechanisms.

Fifty-two 5-year-old kindergarten children participated in Experiment 1 and forty 5-year-olds did so in Experiment 2. They were randomly assigned to either the context condition or the no-context condition. As the target properties, we used growth and being taken ill in Experiment 1, and taking food and water, and being taken ill (in another phrasing) in Experiment 2. These are properties that animals and plants share and are also major properties in young children's vitalistic biology. We also asked about filler (animal) properties, that is breathing, eating, and defecating. These were included to check whether children attributed the target property just mechanically. For breathing and eating, some analogous properties could be found among plants, but in the phrasing we used, they were applicable to animals alone. For example, the action verbs "eats" and "breathes" are applicable to animals alone.

What follows are example descriptions of properties given to the children. The underlined words were given only to the children in the context condition.

> *Grows:* A person becomes bigger and bigger <u>by taking in energy from food and water</u>. Well, does X become bigger and bigger? (Exp. 1)
>
> *Needs food/water:* A person needs water and/or food. <u>If he does not take in energy or vital power from water and/or food, he will die.</u> Well, does X need water and/or food? (Exp. 2)
>
> *Is taken ill:* A person is sometimes taken ill <u>because his energy or vital power is gradually weakened by germs going into his body</u>. Well, is X sometimes taken ill? (Exp. 1)
>
> *Is taken ill:* A person is sometimes taken ill <u>because his energy or vital power is gradually weakened when he feels too cold or too hot</u>. Well, is X sometimes taken ill? (Exp. 2)

(We felt that a mixture of the vitalistic explanation and the germ explanation in Exp. 1 did not represent children's biological beliefs accurately enough. Thus, we modified the description into diminution of vital power due to a loss of balance in Exp. 2.)

Properties described using action verbs were used as fillers. Examples are as follows:

> *Breathes:* A person breathes <u>in order to take in vital power from fresh air</u>. Well, does X breathe? (Exp. 1)
>
> *Eats:* A person eats food every day. <u>If he doesn't eat food and cannot take in energy or vital power from it, he will die</u>. Well, does X eat something? (Exp. 1)

There were nine target objects, three each from the animal, plant, and nonliving thing categories: squirrel, alligator, grasshopper, tulip, dandelion, pine tree, stone, pencil, and chair. Each property question was asked about all the objects before the inquiry proceeded to another property. The target objects were given in random order for each child.

We counted individual children's numbers of "yes" responses to three instances each of animals, plants, and nonliving things. Then we classified their patterns of induction into three patterns: an animal-and-plant pattern ("Yes" responses to all three instances of animals and plants but not to any of the nonliving things); an animal pattern ("Yes" responses only to animals); or a human pattern ("Yes" responses to none). We allowed one unexpected response; thus, for example, 3/2/0 (three "yes" responses to three animal questions; two to three plant questions; none to three nonliving questions) or 3/3/1 were classified as an animal-and-plant pattern. Patterns not satisfying any of the above criteria were classified as "others."

We anticipated finding one of the following three possible results.

1. Children possess object-specific knowledge. In this case, children in both the context condition and the no-context condition would often show the animal-and-plant pattern, and thus there would be no difference between the context and no-context conditions.
2. Children possess a concept of living things but the concept is not salient and is fragile. From this we predict that children in the context condition would show the animal-and-plant pattern more often than those in the no-context condition.
3. Children do not possess a concept of living things. In this case children both with and without context would seldom show the animal-and-plant pattern, and thus there would be no difference between the context and no-context conditions.

Figure 2.2a shows occurrence rates of the animal-and-plant pattern for each property in the context and no-context conditions. The inductive

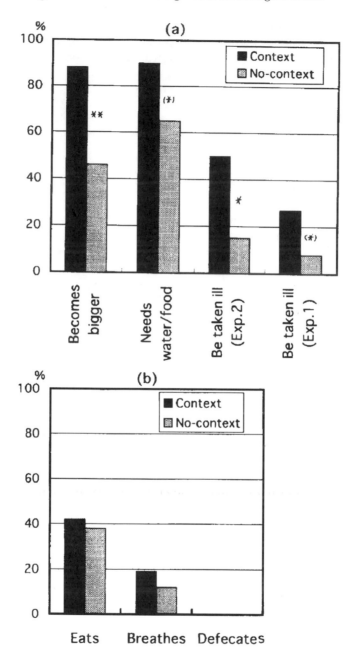

FIGURE 2.2. Occurence rates of animal and plant patterns for (a) all-living-thing properties and (b) animal properties. **shows a significant difference between the two conditions at $p < .01$; * $p < .05$; (*) $p < .10$.

projections from humans were extended up to plants by a majority of the children in the context condition for growth, needing food/water, and being taken ill when they were phrased properly. Children in the context condition made animal-and-plant patterns for the four target properties 63% of the time on average, whereas children in the no-context condition did so 33% of the time. For the three target properties excluding being taken ill (which was poorly phrased), corresponding percentages were 77 versus 42. The second possibility was thus supported; that is, the present findings strongly suggest that the children already possessed the concept of living things, because the given description was too brief for them to acquire the concept. This consideration excluded the third possibility. The first possibility was also rejected. If the children responded based on their object-specific knowledge, there would not have been any difference in the frequency of the animal-and-plant patterns between the two conditions.

For the filler properties, percentages of animal-and-plant patterns were low (Figure 2.2b). There was no effect of context. It is clear that the children made "Yes" responses not just mechanically. For the property of eating, quite a number of the children hesitated to answer "Yes" or "No" in attributing eating to plants. Nine children said, "It drinks water" without answering "Yes" or "No." These responses (19 in all) were counted as "Yes." In spite of this, animal patterns were most dominant for the property of eating. As described earlier, this was supposed to be an animal property in the present phrasing. It contrasted with the attribution of needing food/water, which used the verb involving functional or emerging processes. The latter property produced the animal-and-plant pattern most often.

How connected are these properties with one another? In the context condition, more than half (13) of the 23 children who showed the animal-and-plant pattern for growth made the same pattern at least once for other properties (7 for being taken ill and 10 for eating) in Experiment 1, and about half of the children in Experiment 2 showed this pattern for both needing food/water and being taken ill. This strongly suggests that these children possessed not a collection of simple associations but a more or less coherent belief that a set of properties is shared by animals and plants.

In sum, children as young as 5 years of age consider humans, nonhuman animals, and plants to be similar entities in terms of biological ways of life, suppressing a similarity metric based on behaviors. To put it differently, 5-year-old children recognize commonalities between animals and plants. However, this result is not enough for us to assert that young children have consciously grasped commonalities between animals and plants. We dealt with this issue in the next experiment.

Experiment Using Forced Analogy

We explored a few alternative methods of directly asking children about commonalities between animals and plants. The use of generic terms like animals and plants is desirable (e.g., "What do animals and plants have in common?"), but was not possible with our participating children, mainly because the term *plants* (*shokubutsu* in Japanese) is incomprehensible for most of them.[1] Asking children about the commonalities between an example of animals and one of plants often induced local comparisons that were not applicable to these categories in general. The only method that proved to work was asking children whether a few examples of plants show phenomena similar to those observed for a few examples of animals. In other words, we required children to generate analogies from animals to plants.

Here, too, we asked children about varied "biological" properties or behaviors, including growth and taking food/water, that they might believe animals and plants share (Inagaki & Hatano, 1996, Experiment 3). We expected that this "forced analogy" experiment would not only reveal whether children could recognize commonalities between animals and plants more readily than those between animals and nonliving things, but also suggest which properties children use as cues to recognize animal/plant commonalities.

Participants were forty 5-year-old children. After being asked to identify each drawing of six exemplars of animals, plants, and inanimate things to be described below, each child was told that animals (a squirrel and an alligator) reveal such-and-such a phenomenon and was then asked whether plants (a tulip and a pine tree) or artifacts (a chair and a public telephone) would reveal any similar one. When the child replied, "Yes," he or she was further asked what it was.

The target phenomena covered major biological functions that young children understand, that is, nutrition, growth and death, excretion, respiration, and reproduction. Specifically, they were (a) feeding needed to maintain life, (b) growing in size as time passes, (c) becoming older and ultimately dying, (d) discarding waste matter as feces or urine, (e) taking in fresh air, (f) growing in number by having babies or laying eggs, (g) overfeeding causing ill health, and (h) being ill-fed producing little growth. All are phenomena common to advanced animals, but, in Japanese language, only growth can be applied to plants without changing phrasings. In other words, participants were in fact required to find functionally equivalent phenomena for plants, by mapping between animals and plants. Example questions for feeding and growing in size were as follows: "A squirrel or an alligator will die if we do not feed it. Do you think anything similar to this occurs with a tulip or a pine tree/with a chair or a pay phone?" (feeding); "A squirrel or an alligator becomes bigger, though it was small when it was a baby. Do you think anything similar to this occurs with a tulip or a pine tree/with a chair or a pay phone?" (growth in size).

Half the children were given the feeding question first, and the other half, the growth in number question first. All of them were asked the first item initially for plants, then for artifacts. Here, when children did not give any answer or answered "No" for this first question for plants, they were given a simple hint to help them understand what they were asked. Irrespective of whether the child recognized the common phenomenon for plants after this simple hint, the experimenter moved on to the same question for artifacts, then all other questions.

The order of the questions about the eight phenomena was randomized for each child, except for the first item (i.e., feeding or growth in number) and the last item (being ill-fed). The questions for plants and for artifacts were asked about a phenomenon before the inquiry proceeded to another phenomenon. Half the children in each series were asked about plants first, and the other half, artifacts first, except for the first item.

Table 2.2 shows the percentages of "Yes" responses, that is, the children's recognition that plants or artifacts revealed a phenomenon similar to that for animals. Here the responses to the first items (for both plants and artifacts), irrespective of whether the hint was given, are excluded. As is evident, the children very often recognized similar phenomena for plants, but almost never for artifacts. We compared the frequency of Yes/No patterns (recognizing a similar phenomenon for plants but not for artifacts) with that of No/Yes patterns (recognizing a similar phenomenon for artifacts but not for plants), and found statistically significant differences between them for all the phenomena except for excretion. The differential responding for plants and artifacts was especially clear for feeding and growth in size; for the former, 85% (17/20) of the children showed Yes/No patterns, and for the latter, 90% (36/40) of them did so. About 70%

Table 2.2. Percentages of children's recognition that plants or artifacts reveal a similar phenomenon

	Feed-ing	Growing in number	Growing in size	Becoming older and dying	Over feed-ing	Excret-ing	Breath-ing	Being ill-fed
Plants	90	50	93	80	33	3	45	50
Artifacts	5	5	3	13	3	0	0	0

Note. N = 20 each for feeding, growing in number, and being ill-fed, and 40 each for the other items. From Inagaki and Hatano (1996).

of the children indicated Yes/No patterns for becoming older and dying, about 50% of them did so for being ill-fed, growth in number, and breathing, and 30% of them showed this pattern for overfeeding. Children did not appear to respond mechanically by saying "Yes" to plants and "No" to artifacts, because a majority of them responded "No" to plants for excretion.

What phenomena in plants did the children give as similar to the target phenomenon for animals? For feeding, almost all children (94%) who gave "Yes" responses for plants answered, "A tulip or a pine tree withers if we do not water it." For growing in size, 12 of the 37 children who gave "Yes" responses for plants offered the phenomenon of a plant's getting bigger from a seed or a bud. Another 14 children referred to watering as corresponding to feeding as a condition for growth, saying, "If we give it water, it will become bigger and bigger." One of these children explicitly asserted, "(A tulip or a pine tree) becomes bigger, because water is food for it."

For becoming older and dying, a great majority (88%) of the 32 children who gave "Yes" responses for plants offered, without considering their becoming old, the phenomenon that plants wither or die, saying, "If we do not give water, a tulip or a pine tree will wither," or "A tulip or a pine tree withers. That point is similar." Only a small number referred to becoming older; one child said, "Even if we give water to (a tulip or pine tree), it will wither after living long."

For growth in number by reproduction, 6 of the 10 children who recognized the similarity between animals and plants referred to seeds. They stated that buds come out from seeds buried in the ground and grow in number (or produce many flowers) as a phenomenon similar to animals' increasing by having babies or laying eggs. Other children seemed to regard plants' having flowers again and again or becoming thickly covered by leaves as a similar phenomenon.

For being ill-fed, almost all the children referred to the relation between watering and growth, for example, "If we give it (a tulip or pine tree) only a little water, it will not become bigger," or "A small amount of water will keep it (a tulip or a pine tree) small." For overfeeding, 10 of the 13 who recognized similar phenomena for plants pointed out the fact that too much watering causes plants to wither or die. One of them said, "If we give too much water, a tulip and a pine tree will have a tummyache."

As partly inferable from the above description, almost all who answered that there was a similar phenomenon for plants to any of the eight questions were able to give a concrete example. In other words, "No" answers and "Don't know" answers were negligible in number. However, for breathing, half of the 18 who gave "Yes" responses could not specify the similar phenomena and another three gave incomprehensible answers.

Almost all of the affirmative answers for artifacts were metaphorical;

for example, for feeding, "A pay phone cannot be used if we don't put a coin in it" or "If a person doesn't sit on the chair, there is no need to have it"; for growing in number, "If a chair is broken, a person can make another one"; for becoming old and dying, "If a pay phone is old and broken, a person discards it."

In sum, the data suggests that children as young as 5 years of age grasp explicitly the commonalities between animals and plants, and can thus differentiate both animals and plants from nonliving things. This conscious grasp of the commonalities is at a functional level and may often be achieved first with feeding/watering and growth in size, and then generalized to other biological phenomena.

Conclusion About the Living/Nonliving Distinction

Our experiments using inductive projection and forced analogy offer three pieces of strong evidence for young children's recognition of commonalities between animals and plants. First, for 5-year-old children, inductive projection that was extended to plants was enhanced by vitalistic explanations of the target properties for humans. We interpret this result to imply that "biological" functions that had been assigned to humans were applied to plants as well as to other animals. In other words, humans, other animals, and plants were regarded as entities that were covered by a single theory of biology. Second, a considerable number of the children showed an inductive projection pattern constrained by the category of living things for plural properties. It is unlikely that they attributed a given property to both animals and plants independently but correctly. Third, a majority of the 5-year-olds could offer for plants specific phenomena analogous to those observed for animals. They consciously recognized that animals and plants are so similar that most (biological) phenomena can be mapped from the former to the latter.

We would like to emphasize that growth and taking in food/water and a few other related characteristics are not mutually independent but form a coherent configuration. For example, children often connect growth to taking food/water, as illustrated by the results for the "ill-fed" question of our forced analogy experiment ("A small amount of watering makes plants grow only a little"). It should be pointed out that the children in our induction experiment generalized growth to plants much more readily when they were given the context referring to food and water as the source for vital power that induces growth. Being taken ill may also be connected to the loss of vital power, and thus, like becoming older and dying, may be linked to food and water; energy taken in from food or water may prevent or inhibit animals' or plants' death or ill-health.

Thus, we conclude that, at the least, 5-year-old children have an integrated concept of living things including animals and plants. Although the acquisition of this concept of living things may be delayed when a meta-level understanding is required as Jaakkola (under review) insists, it is certain that by 5 years of age children can recognize commonalities for a few biological properties and behaviors between animals and plants.

☐ The Animate/Inanimate Distinction

Here we briefly review studies on the animate/inanimate distinction. We believed that distinction serves as a foundation, or a precursor, for the living/nonliving distinction. Moreover, compared with studies on the living/nonliving distinction including plants, there are many more studies on the animate/inanimate distinction.

Evidence Against Piaget's Claim on Animism

In the current trend to reconsider preschoolers' competence, a considerable number of researchers have examined whether young children really lack such basic distinctions as the animate/inanimate distinction, as Piaget (1929) claimed. R. Gelman, Spelke, and Meck (1983) questioned whether young children are truly animistic all the time. They pointed out the possibility that the anomalous questions Piaget used, such as, "Does the sun know where it is going?", lead children into a "play mode" and thus prevent them from thinking biologically (or seriously). In other words, animistic responses may reflect children's capacity for fantasy, not their insufficient knowledge about entities. Moreover, they asserted, extraterrestrial entities (e.g., sun or cloud) as target objects and psychological states like volition, thinking, and feeling as target properties are problematic, because these are not well known to children, and, in addition, extraterrestrial objects are misleading in terms of moving without an apparent external cause. Thus, children may have made incorrect, "animistic" responses out of ignorance or confusion.

From these considerations, R. Gelman et al. (1983) interviewed 3- to 5-year-old children using familiar objects as targets; specifically, a person, a cat, and a rock were used as typical examples of animate and inanimate objects, and a doll or a puppet as a typical example of somewhat ambiguous entities. Using more direct (i.e., nonambiguous) questions about properties of four categories, such as "Can an X walk?" or "Does an X have a mouth?", they found that not only the 4- and 5-year-olds but also the 3-

year-olds made correct responses 90% of the time on average for each of the target objects, and for a person, all the children answered 100% correct for all target properties. This indicates that children aged 3–5 years know well a lot about humans and also that they have the knowledge needed to distinguish typical animate objects from inanimate ones. Moreover, these children did not show any animistic responses for puppets or dolls.

It is interesting that, when asked the Piaget-type questions consisting of predicate-complement sentences (e.g., "Do the clouds know that they are moving?" or "Does the rain like to water the flowers?"), the same children who had correctly answered the previous direct questions readily gave typical animistic responses. In other words, children switched from a reality to a nonreality mode, depending on the types of questions asked.

Richards and Siegler (1984) also indicated that types of questions influenced the occurrence of animistic responses. When asked either to name living things or to judge whether the object was alive, 4- and 5-year-old children almost never gave animistic responses (i.e., they seldom judged inanimate objects as alive). However, when asked to justify their judgments, they often referred to the object's capacity for movement. In addition, when questions were worded so as to emphasize an object's motion state, a majority of the children gave animistic responses in that they judged whether objects were alive on the basis of whether the objects were moving. S. Gelman and Kremer (1991) also reported that young children are sensitive to modes induced by question types with regard to the child's artificialism (i.e., the belief that natural kinds are created by people). Whereas children aged 4–7 years often provided artificialistic explanations when asked about the origins of things using open-ended questions like those used by Piaget (1929), they distinguished between human and natural causes when simply asked whether or not an object was made by people; for instance, they knew that people made dolls and TVs but not clouds and flowers.

These findings strongly suggest that, contrary to Piaget's claim, young children are not always animistic but are able to engage in biologically reasonable thinking in response to appropriate questions. It is true that young children may not be able to activate the biological knowledge needed to make inferences about life-sustaining processes or properties of entities when questions are ambiguous, concern objects about which the children know very little (e.g., extraterrestrial entities), or require metacognitive understanding of the processes/properties. In this sense, Piaget was not entirely wrong. However, the fact that young children can make coherent and reasonable responses to child-friendly questions indicates, we believe, that they possess the knowledge needed to differentiate living things from nonliving things.

Attention to an Object's Capacity for Self-Initiated Movements

The R. Gelman et al. (1983) study described above revealed that pre-school children distinguished familiar animate objects from familiar in-animate ones. Similar results were reported by Bullock (1985), who used a person, a rabbit, a toy worm, and a block as targets.

Massey and Gelman (1988), using unfamiliar animate and inanimate entities as target objects, found that preschool children can correctly judge whether animals and inanimate objects have a capacity for self-initiated movement or not. The 3- and 4-year-olds were shown photographs of unfamiliar objects, including mammals (e.g., echidna), nonmammalian animals (e.g., shiny-shelled insect), statues with familiar animal-like forms and parts, wheeled vehicles, and multipart rigid objects, and asked whether each of these objects could go up and down a hill by itself.

These children were correct on about 85% of their first yes/no answers, meaning that they answered that animals could go up and down a hill by themselves, while inanimate objects, even if they looked like animals, couldn't. Analyses of explanations that the children gave spontaneously or in response to a request for justification of their yes/no responses suggested that these children tended to change kinds of explanations de-pending on the types of the objects. When talking about an animal, children often focused on body parts that enable the target to move (e.g., "It can move because it has feet") or referred to some general feature of the target's appearance (e.g., "It's an animal because it has a face") and the fact that the target object was alive or active. For the animal-looking statues, they also talked about whether the target was alive, real, or just pretend (e.g., "It's not a real piggy"). For the wheeled vehicles or rigid objects, they also referred to parts enabling movement (e.g, "It can roll down on its wheels") or to an agent needed to move the object (e.g., "It needs a push and then it goes," or "You have to carry it down").

Based on these results, R. Gelman (1990) proposed a hypothesis that children at early ages possess skeletal principles focusing on particular features of entities. More specifically, they have the innards principle, "the principle of causal mechanism that governs attention to those natu-ral objects that move on their own" (p. 91), and "the external-agent prin-ciple that draws attention to objects that do not move on their own" (p. 91), and these principles lead one to rapidly acquire knowledge about the animate/inanimate distinction.

Consistent with R. Gelman's (1990) idea, a number of recent studies have revealed that even infants distinguish humans from nonliving things in terms of self-initiated movement versus movement caused by external agents. For example, Golinkoff and Harding (1980; cited in Golinkoff, Harding, Carlson, & Sexton, 1984) found that 24-month-old toddlers showed surprise when a real chair appeared to move by itself (a hidden person was pulling on plastic wires connected to the chair's legs). Similar results are reported for young infants by more recent studies using habituation methods (e.g., Poulin-Dubois & Shultz, 1990; Spelke, Phillips, & Woodward, 1995). Mandler and McDonough (1993) examined 7- to 11-month-old infants' conceptual categorization, using an object examination task, and reported that the process of global differentiation of animals from nonanimals (including artifacts) had begun by the end of the first year.

The Animate/Inanimate Distinction in Terms of Essence _

Young children seem to distinguish animals from artifacts by taking into account the nonobvious, such as the inside of the body. Simons and Keil (1995) claimed that before acquiring detailed factual knowledge, children possess "abstract" knowledge. They, as an example of such knowledge, examined whether young children could properly expect different insides for animals and artifacts. Children of 3, 4, and 8 years of age were presented with three photographs of an animal inside (e.g., a set of bones), a machine inside (e.g., a set of gears), and an aggregate substance (e.g., a pile of rocks or blocks), and asked to choose one as a picture representing the inside of either an animal or a machine. They found that by 8 years almost all children responded accurately; that is, they consistently picked out the corresponding insides for animals and artifacts. Fewer than half of the preschoolers were consistently correct. However, most of the remaining children responded systematically, like all correct responses to the machine inside but not the animal. Moreover, when these preschoolers erred, they tended to assign natural kind inside (e.g., rocks) to the animals and artifact insides (e.g., blocks) to the artifacts. This indicates, according to the authors, that preschool children expect the insides of animals and artifacts to differ, though they lack concrete knowledge of insides.

Keil's (1989) transformation study demonstrates that in some contexts, preschool children can recognize that inside and essence are more important than external appearances among animate objects. Here children were asked to consider animals and artifacts that had undergone transformations leading them to appear to be something else; for example, they were shown a picture of a horse that was transformed so that it looked like a zebra, and asked to judge its identity. When told that such a transformation was made by a physician, 5-year-olds answered that it was a zebra, whereas 7-year-olds judged that animal identity was unchanged and answered that it was still a horse. The younger children judged the animal based on overt appearance, but the older children relied on judgments about the animal's "inside." However, when told that an animal (e.g., a horse) was dressed in a costume that resembled another animal (e.g., a zebra), even 5-year-olds judge on the basis of the inside and answered that it was still a horse. For transformed artifacts (e.g., a coffeepot transformed by a doctor so that it looked like a birdfeeder), both the 7- and 5-year-olds judged that the transformation could change the thing's "identity" and pronounced that the object was now a birdfeeder. These findings suggest that 5-year-old children can distinguish animals from artifacts, taking the inside as the nonobvious into account, though their understanding is still fragile.

Rosengren et al. (1991) examined children's beliefs about naturally occurring transformations. They found that preschool children recognized that animals get larger with age, while artifacts remain the same size over time, though younger preschoolers (3-year-olds) were less systematic in their responses about artifacts than about animals.

The studies so far reviewed clearly indicate that young preschool children can distinguish animals from nonliving things. In addition, they strongly suggest that the acquisition of the animate/inanimate distinction begins very early in life. The acquisition seems be helped by an intuition that animals have something inside their bodies that enables them to move on their own, along with the intuition that animals have an essence as nonobvious. We will discuss this issue in detail in Chapter 6.

☐ Young Children's Grasp of Ontological Categories

Let us summarize here what the preceding sections have revealed and discuss some theoretical implications. Contrary to Piaget's claim, recent developmental studies indicated that young children can distinguish not only between animate and inanimate entities but also between living and nonliving entities. The animate/inanimate distinction seems to be established early in childhood, say by 3 years of age, probably helped by children's tendency to direct attention to the self-initiated movements that animals engage in. Although the acquisition of the living/nonliving distinction is delayed, relative to the animate/inanimate one, it too occurs much earlier than Piaget (1929) and Carey (1985) claimed and does not wait until children become 11- or 12-years-old (Piaget, 1929) or even 10-years-old (Carey, 1985). The current studies indicated that children as young as 5 years of age can grasp commonalities between animals and plants, which are perceptually different, and thus distinguish living entities together from nonliving entities, although their first grasp of commonalities between plants and animals seems to be limited to taking food/

water and its related biological phenomena and needs some context that directs their attention to biological aspects.

To put the above summary differently, young children do not commit animistic errors as often as Piaget claimed. Even when they do, the errors do not reflect their general intellectual immaturity but a lack of domain-specific (often object-specific or property-specific) knowledge; for example, it is likely for them to err when they are asked questions about extraterrestrial entities (e.g., sun or cloud) or mental properties such as consciousness, which they are usually ignorant of. Also, some questions may induce play mode or nonbiological mode response in children. Recent studies have also showed that, contrary to Carey's (1985) claim, as long as typical examples are concerned, children have enough biological knowledge to differentiate living things from nonliving things. Thus we conclude that by about the age of 5, children have acquired the living/nonliving distinction as one of the important elements constituting a naive theory of biology.

Let us consider how young children might begin the difficult job of recognizing commonalities between the two very different ontological classes of animals and plants, given that they do not have histological and physiological knowledge. The findings reviewed so far suggest that taking food/water and growth serve as the basis for this recognition and constitute the core of young children's concept of living things. However, we do not believe that young children build a (superordinate) category of living things by paying attention to these shared properties simply based on perceptual salience. Growth, especially unidirectional and/or long-term cyclic (seasonal) changes in plants, may be obvious, but cannot be grasped readily because it takes time to occur. Thus, recognizing growth requires the ability to remember the past state of the target object. Taking food/ water is even less conspicuous for plants unless they are potted.

Instead of noticing perceptually salient properties, we assume that recognizing commonalities between animals and plants involves two component processes. First, young children causally connect "feeding or watering" and "an animal or a plant being lively and healthy." In this process, innate and interactive sociocultural constraints direct children's attention to these activities and resultant states and help them interpret the observed connections in terms of what might be called vital power. Second, the combined category of animals and plants can be constructed by personification, as will be reviewed in the next chapter. More specifically, animals and plants are considered alike because both of them are functionally similar to humans. A more detailed scenario of both these processes will be presented at the end of Chapter 6.

Through these processes, young children come to differentiate living

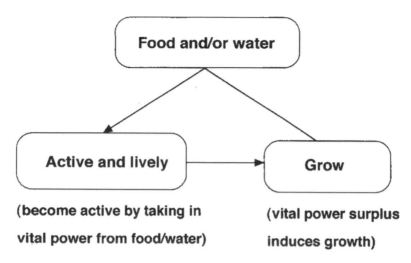

FIGURE 2.3. Triangular relationships among taking food and/or water, being active and lively, and growth.

things from nonliving entities and to recognize that living things are similar to humans in that they take vital force from food and/or water to maintain vigor, with the surplus inducing growth. This triangular structural relationship among (a) taking food and/or water, (b) the characteristics of being active and lively ("becomes active by taking in vital power from food"), and (c) growth ("vital power surplus induces growth") (see Figure 2.3) can be applied readily to a variety of animals. It may also be applied to plants, partly because children lack the understanding of photosynthesis. We assume that this triangular relationship constitutes "the core" of young children's understanding of biological entities and also of their naive biology.

Note

1. The Japanese word corresponding to "plant" is not an everyday household item. It is not used nearly as much frequently as the English word. Japanese people usually refer to less inclusive categories like flowers, trees, or grasses. "Plant" is a word for scientific discourse. In our pilot testing thus nine out of 12 first-graders answered that they had never heard of the word.

3
CHAPTER

Personification as Analogy in Biological Understanding

Girl (5 years), after having the experience of growing flowers: "Flowers are like people. If flowers eat nothing (are not watered), they will fall down of hunger. If they eat too much (are watered too often), they will be taken ill." (Motoyoshi, 1979)

Boy (5 years), who himself is shy, while looking at a bulb of hyacinth under the water: "These roots must be shy, 'cause they get longer when nobody looks at them. Roots become longer in the dark." (Shimizu, 1964)

In Chapter 2 we saw that young children possess the knowledge needed to distinguish between living and nonliving things and that preschool children seldom commit animistic errors unless they are induced to answer in the play mode. However, this play-mode explanation seems to be only a partial answer, because anecdotal instances reported by observant preschool educators have indicated that young children sometimes spontaneously make personifying or animistic remarks in everyday situations when they are intellectually serious. The two children's utterances given at the beginning of this chapter are good examples of this.

Why do young children make spontaneous personifying or animistic remarks? What roles does personification play in young children's understanding of the world, particularly biological phenomena? Is young children's understanding of animals' behavior through personification always an attempt to interpret biological phenomena psychologically, or can it be an attempt to grasp them biologically? In this chapter we deal with these issues and propose a positive view of personification for the understanding of biological phenomena and entities.

We begin with our definition of personification and animism. *Personification* means the extension and application of human properties and behaviors to any nonhumans. It can often be regarded as a person analogy in that it relies on a mapping between a person as the source and the entity as the target, that is, it involves applying what one knows about the relation among a set of elements in humans to the relation among a different set in another entity. In the case of the girl's remark about watering flowers given at the beginning of the chapter, the known relationship between eating too much and ill-health in people is mapped to that between being watered too often and wilting for the flowers; in the case of the boy's remark, a shy person's reluctance to display himself is mapped to plant roots' growing in the dark.

Animism means attributing characteristics and activities of animate objects (typically humans) to inanimate objects. Thus animistic reasoning can usually be thought of as personification of inanimate objects. We assume that personifying and animistic reasoning involve many cognitive components in common, most notably "structure mapping" (Gentner, 1983) between a human as the source and a less familiar entity as the target. However, we prefer the term "personification" to "animism" to indicate this general mode of reasoning for several reasons: (a) "personification" implies the mind's active attempt to understand less familiar entities by analogy, whereas animism has been regarded as indicating confusion, if not intellectual immaturity; (b) whereas "animism" may well characterize indigenous adults' thinking, "personification" can neatly indicate a general tendency to rely on the most familiar source analog of humans (see, e.g., Lakoff & Johnson, 1980); and (c) in the discussion of naive biology, the structural alignment of human bodily processes and properties to those of animals, which is naturally termed personification, seems critical.

The idea that personification is a person analogy is supported by mainstream researchers in studies on analogy (e.g., Gentner & Markman, 1997; Holyoak & Thagard, 1995). Current studies on analogy have indicated that even preschool children can aptly use analogy when they have relevant knowledge about the source analog (e.g., Goswami, 1996). The major barrier to young children relying on analogies is that they do not possess rich knowledge about a variety of entities, which would allow them to choose a proper source analog. Young children's person analogy, however, often produces impressive outcomes, such as those presented above, because they possess fairly rich knowledge about humans, compared with their knowledge about other animals and plants. They themselves are humans and are captured in their own bodies. They interact with other humans very often and thus get information about them based on observation and conversation. Therefore, their active mind tends to map any target onto the most familiar source, the analog of humans. Moreover, as will be seen later in this chapter, they can use this source analog flexibly and differentially depending on the target and the context of reasoning.

It is expected, therefore, that personification is not only ubiquitous but also a powerful device in young children's understanding of the world, including biological phenomena and entities. It enables them not only to predict behaviors of less familiar animals but also to make sense of and offer a good justification for what they have experienced with animals and plants. Considering that the body metaphor in adults' everyday language is ubiquitous and worldwide (e.g., Lakoff & Johnson, 1980), knowledge about human bodily structures and functions constitutes an important part of the source analog of humans in personification.

In what follows, we first describe our idea about constrained personification, more specifically how personification can be used productively without producing too many errors. In contrast to Piaget (1929), who regarded personifying or animistic responses as a sign of immaturity, we consider personification to be a form of plausible reasoning that generates "educated guesses"; we see it as adaptive in nature, especially when a cognizer does not possess rich knowledge about the target entity or its close neighbors. Moreover, personification can often be used as a sort of inference in the biological mode for understanding biological phenomena. Next, we present experimental evidence from our studies to support our idea of constrained personification. In the third and fourth sections, we discuss the essential roles personification plays in the construction of naive biology, specifically in the acquisition of the concept of living things and the expansion of biological knowledge, respectively.

☐ Young Children's Constrained Personification

Why Do Young Children Use Personification?

As revealed in Chapter 2, young children have the factual knowledge needed to distinguish between humans, nonhuman animals, plants, and typical nonliving things. However, compared with adults, children's experience is generally so limited that their specific knowledge about animals and plants is still scarce and not always hierarchically structured; they do not have enough knowledge to make correct or reliable predictions about specific objects' attributes and behaviors. In contrast, even young children have fairly rich knowledge about humans, because they themselves are humans, and it is humans as conspecifics that they most often interact with in their life. In the R. Gelman et al. (1983) study described earlier, almost all the 3-year-olds correctly attributed to a person those properties that humans possess, such as body parts (e.g., ears, stomach), overt actions (e.g., walk, eat), or mental states and acts (e.g., feel sad, think). Other studies dealing with anatomical/physiological properties, such as eats, has a heart, has bones, etc., also have demonstrated that most preschool children know that people have such properties (e.g., Carey, 1985; Inagaki & Sugiyama, 1988), although there is debate concerning whether children consider these properties to be biological.

Consistent with Carey's (1985) claim that humans function as a prototype of animals for preschool children, Quinn and Eimas (1998), using the familiarization-novelty preference procedure, provided evidence suggesting that humans (in their terminology, "a broadly inclusive categorical representation of humans") may work as a cognitive reference point even for young infants. First, 3- to 4-month-old infants were familiarized with either 12 pictorial examples of humans or 12 examples of horses (as a nonhuman animal species), and then were given three sets of novelty preference tests, where a different novel member of the familiarized category (humans or horses) was paired with a member of the nonfamiliarized category (horses or humans), a novel fish, or a novel car.

It was found that there was an asymmetry concerning categorical exclusivity in the results after familiarization with examples of humans and horses. That is, the novelty preference for humans after familiarization with horses was significantly greater than the chance estimate of 50%, whereas the novelty preference for horses after familiarization with humans was not significantly different from chance. In other words, the infants familiarized with horses discriminated horses from humans, whereas those familiarized with humans did not distinguish humans from horses. In addition, the novelty preference for humans after familiarization with the horses was larger than that for horses after familiarization with humans. Both the infants who were familiarized with humans and those familiarized with horses almost equally strongly showed the novelty preference for cars, indicating that those infants discriminate humans or horses from cars. In other words, these findings suggest that infants who had been familiarized with humans formed a categorical representation that contained novel humans, horses, and fish, but not cars; infants familiarized with horses formed a categorical representation including novel horses, but excluding humans, fish, and cars.

Quinn and Eimas speculated that "even over the course of a time span as short as the first 3 to 4 months of life, the differential experience that infants have with humans versus non-human animal species drives infants to become 'experts' at categorizing humans" (p.169). This speculation is tenable, but a rival interpretation is also possible: Human infants have an innate tendency to use humans as the basic schema to observe other animals. In either case, it is interesting that a categorical representation of humans may function as a reference point even for young infants, although their categorical representation of humans is perceptually based and may not yet be conceptual.

Constraints Operating in Personification

The findings so far strongly suggest that knowledge about humans constitutes a privileged knowledge base for young children. Therefore we claim that when children do not have enough knowledge about a target (animate) object, they tend to use their knowledge about humans as the source for analogically attributing properties to the less familiar animate object or predicting reactions of the object to novel situations. However, it should be emphasized that they do not use knowledge about humans blindly and indiscriminately. If they always applied personification and accepted its inferred outcome, they would commit many errors. In actuality, they recognize where to apply personification and when to accept its inference. In other words, they opt for using personification or the person analogy selectively, and accept the conclusion derived from it also in a selective way. As a result, they can generate reasonable predictions without committing many overpersonifying errors. How is it possible for young children who have not acquired an articulated taxonomy of properties (e.g., all-living-thing properties, animal properties, etc.) to do so? They seem to be helped by two constraints on reasoning when they transfer knowledge about humans to other animals, and sometimes even to plants.

One is the similarity constraint, which requires the target object to be more or less similar to a human in order for personification or person analogy to be applied to it. As Vosniadou (1989) asserts, children tend to apply an analogy on the basis of salient similarity between the target and the source, though the "depth" of this perceived similarity varies with the richness and structuredness of the knowledge base children have. Judged similarity also varies with contexts given (Gentner & Markman, 1997). For instance, when behavioral contexts are given plants are almost never perceived as similar to people, whereas in biological contexts, they can be regarded as close to people in terms of their way of life. Thus giving a particular context may change the pattern of inductive projection (e.g., Gutheil et al., 1998). Generally, however, the closer the target object is phylogenetically to a human being, the more often children recognize its similarity and thus apply personification or the person analogy.

In fact, a number of studies have found that young children attribute human characteristics to targets in proportion to the extent that they are perceived as being similar to people (Carey, 1985; Inagaki & Sugiyama, 1988). Note that the perceived similarity is not simple physical similarity, because although a mechanical monkey or doll looks more like a person than a fish does, children seldom attribute to the mechanical monkey or doll animal properties, such as eating, which they do to the fish (Carey, 1985; Inagaki, 1989). This differential application of personification or person analogy tends to reduce both erroneous over- and under-attributions, to the extent that children's criteria for judging similarity correspond to those of adults or biologists. Thanks to this constraint, it is rare that children personify nonliving objects, unless the target object apparently reveals some human properties (e.g., the sun seems to move spontaneously).

The other constraint in young children's personification or person analogy is a factual check or feasibility constraint. This requires that the predicted behavior or property of the target object derived through the personification be feasible and that, if not, the prediction be rejected. This constraint works after the personification is attempted, that is, one examines whether the inference through personification is plausible on the basis of factual knowledge about the target object. Even young children know basic specific facts about a living thing (e.g., R. Gelman, et al., 1983) and thus may use this knowledge to check the plausibility of predictions reached by the personification, even though the knowledge is not powerful enough to generate predictions in itself. For example, if personification leads children to predict that a tree runs to avoid fire, they should reject this prediction on the basis of their knowledge that trees cannot run. Because it is governed by such constraints, personification as analogy can avoid producing many animistic errors.

To put it reversely, if reasoners do not have enough specific knowledge to constrain the prediction reached by personification, they may commit personifying or animistic errors. Because many young children do not know that a developed brain is necessary to have such sophisticated mental states as feeling sad (C. Johnson & Wellman, 1982), they cannot reject their personification-based attribution that grasshoppers would mourn over the death of their caretaker, as we will see later. Moreover, the feasibility constraint does not work in the play or fantasy mode, so, as R. Gelman et al. (1983) asserted, young children generate many animistic errors when such a mode is induced. Hence, animistic or personifying errors are considered to be accidental by-products of this reasoning process.

Our notion of constrained personification is similar to Carey's (1985) "comparison-to-people" model, but differs from it in that we consider the second constraint as well. Taking the feasibility constraint into account helps us notice positive aspects that young children's personification has in the sense that children are likely to generate reasonable predictions through personification. We may also estimate to a greater extent than Carey the flexibility of young children's similarity metric and the operation of the similarity constraint.

Personification Can Be Used in Biological Inference

Personification, or person analogy, is a general mode of inference and thus can be used in biological as well as psychological reasoning. Recognizing structural or functional similarity between humans and the target nonliving, solid object by mapping between them is usually difficult, and there are only a few attempts to use person analogy for understanding physical (or mechanical) phenomena (e.g., Murayama, 1994). In contrast, a mapping between humans as the source and animate objects as the target is fairly easy for biological phenomena as well as psychological phenomena. However, previous studies have not paid due attention to personification or person analogy as a biological inference device. For example, Carey (1985) considered personification, which she thought was realized as inductive projection based on a comparison-to-people model, to be *psychological* inference in an attempt to understand biological phenomena. She claimed that young children attribute animal properties to a variety of animals based on comparison with people, and thus they do not attribute them to animals that behave so differently from people, such as worms. To her, this indicated that young children see animals as behaving beings or psychological beings, not as biological beings.

Unlike Carey, we claim that young children can use personification or person analogy also in biological inference. First, there is evidence showing that preschool children can appropriately apply different explanatory reasoning systems to a variety of human behaviors, namely those with psychological, biological, or physical impetus (Wellman, Hickling, & Schult, 1997). In the Wellman et al. (1997) study, 4-year-olds, and sometimes 3-year-olds, generated biological explanations for biological human behaviors, referring to such biological processes as growth or fatigue, while they gave psychological explanations for psychological human behaviors, referring to the actor's desires, preferences, beliefs, and so on. For physical human behaviors, they gave explanations that appealed to physical factors, such as gravity or the wind. These data strongly suggest that young children can use personification in different ways, for example, as a biological inference device.

Second, we would like to emphasize the fact that young children use personification for plants, notwithstanding that plants are not included in the domain of psychology (Carey, 1985). This indicates that personification applied to biological phenomena may not be used as a psychological inference device. Indeed, the anecdotal examples of the 5-year-old girl quoted at the beginning of this chapter and other children's utterances for animals and plants, which we will present later, illustrate that such personification is children's attempts to understand plants as well as animals biologically.

Since humans are a species of living things, though an atypical one, inferences based on knowledge about humans are very useful in everyday biological problem solving and understanding. Young children's reliance on person analogies may reflect their active and adaptive mind. In the next section, we present experimental data to support this idea.

☐ Experimental Evidence for Constrained Personification

Frequent but Differential Use of Personification

First, we show how often young children rely on personification for biological phenomena and how differentially they apply it, depending upon situations. In Study 1 (Inagaki & Hatano, 1987) kindergarten children aged 5–6 years were asked to predict a rabbit's, a tulip's, or a stone's reactions to unfamiliar situations concerning four biological phenomena— inevitable growth, too much water, spontaneous recovery, and no water intake—and then to justify their responses. As a control, the children were also posed comparable questions about a person. For example, the children were asked, "Suppose someone is given a baby rabbit/a tulip bud/a small stone and wants to keep it forever the same size because it's so small and cute. Can he or she do that? Why do you think so?" (inevitable growth); "Suppose a rabbit/a tulip is dead tired and not lively/a stone is broken in two. Will it become fine again/become a whole as it was before if we leave it as it is? Why do you think so?" (spontaneous recovery). We call these situations the *similar situation*, because a person and a living target object will make functionally similar reactions.

Children's responses for a rabbit or a tulip were scored in terms of whether they were personifying responses. Two types of such responses were identified. One was explicit personification, which was operationally defined as a child's describing the reaction in person-relevant terms that are almost never used by adults for the target object (e.g., "thirsty" for the tulip, "birthday" for the rabbit or tulip) or justifying his or her prediction by referring to a person ("just as a human does"). The other was implicit personification, which was scored when the child's prediction *and* explanation for the target were essentially the same as those for a person. For example, to the inevitable growth question, for a person: "No, we cannot keep the baby the same size forever, because he takes food. If he eats, he will become bigger and bigger and be an adult; for a tulip: "No, we can't. Because if we don't water it, it will wither, but if we water it, it will become bigger and bigger." Implicit personification was never scored when the child's explanation was tautological, incomprehensible, or missing. Explicit personification was given priority when a response could also be scored as implicit personification. Both explicit and implicit personifying responses were supposed to reflect the use of the person analogy.

Results indicated that for a rabbit, 75% (30 out of the 40) of the children made at least one personifying response (explicit or implicit personification) for the four prediction questions, and for a tulip, 63% (25/40) did so. However, they gave virtually no personifications for a stone as a typical nonliving object. It should be noted that these children answered seriously—not in the play mode—because they answered 100% correctly for simple questions concerning observable properties, such as, "Does X have a mouth?" or "Does X walk?"

Let us give two examples of explicit personification for a rabbit and tulip as targets.

> *Boy (5 years, 11 months)*, for the inevitable growth question: "We can't keep it (rabbit) forever the same size. Because, like me, if I were a rabbit, I would be 5 years old and become bigger and bigger."
>
> *Girl (5 years, 6 months)*, for the spontaneous recovery question: "A tulip is the same as a person only on this point. [Interviewer: What point is the same?] If we leave it as it is . . . if we water it a little bit and let it take a rest, it will become fine again."

Another group of forty 6-year-olds from the same kindergarten were asked to predict a rabbit's or tulip's reaction to another type of situation in which a person and the target would behave differently, and thus the use of personification would lead to implausible predictions. We call this type the *contradictory situation* hereafter. One such contradictory situation was as follows: "Suppose a woman buys a rabbit/a potted tulip. On her way home she drops in at a store with this caged rabbit (her tulip). After shopping, she is about to leave the store without the rabbit/the tulip. What will the rabbit/tulip do?" The children were given questions about either a rabbit or a tulip and questions about a person.

None of the 20 children who were given the question about the tulip and only 7 out of the 20 children who were asked about the rabbit gave personifying responses in this type of situation. The seven personifying responses observed for the questions about the rabbit were almost within the rabbit's behavioral repertoire, such as its struggling in the cage to signal that it is being left behind. Almost all the reasons why the tulip could do nothing to get out of the "trouble" concerned the difference between the tulip and a person. For example, "Because it (the tulip) doesn't move/walk," "It doesn't have feet/arms, eyes," and so on. Two of the children explicitly compared the tulip to a person as "unlike a person." Although children did not show implausible personifying responses, they still seemed to use a person as the point of reference. For the caged rabbit, on the contrary, children tended to refer to the cage in explaining why it could not get out of the trouble even though it would try something in the cage (e.g., jumping, just waiting, etc.).

In Study 2 (Inagaki & Hatano, 1991), a grasshopper, along with a tulip, was used as an animal that was more dissimilar to people than a rabbit as the target object. This study aimed at examining whether the same children would use personification differentially, depending on types of situations. Forty 6-year-old kindergarten children were asked to predict the target object's reaction in each of three types of situations. Each type of situation contained two questions. One of the three types was almost the same as the similar situation used in Study 1, that is, a situation concerning biological phenomena in which the animal or the plant reacts in a functionally similar way to the person (i.e., the inevitable-growth and the too-much-eating situations). For example, the too-much-eating question is as follows: "We usually feed a grasshopper once or twice a day when we raise it at home. What will happen to it if we feed it 10 times a day?" The second type was also the same as the contradictory situation in Study 1, that is, the situation where a person and the target object would react differently.

The third type, called the *compatible situation*, was newly introduced in this study. It concerned situations where the target object and a human being would in fact react differently, but predictions obtained through the person analogy do not seem implausible to young children. An example question (feeling-sad question) is as follows: "Does a grasshopper feel something if the person who has been taking care of it every day dies? [If the child's answer is "Yes"] How does it feel?" Questions for the third type of situation were included to get stronger support for the presence of the feasibility constraint; if it is demonstrated that young children often overpersonify (i.e., use the person analogy and give unreasonable predictions) when the feasibility constraint is supposed not to work, we can reasonably infer its operation. Predictions reached by relying on the person analogy for this type of situation do not seem implausible to young children because of the paucity of their biological knowledge. For example, young children's limited knowledge about "mental properties"

(Inagaki & Sugiyama, 1988) will not enable them to judge predictions like "a tulip will feel happy" as implausible. In addition, they often lack the categorical knowledge that plants do not have such feelings, and the physiological knowledge that an object must have a developed brain in order to have such feelings (C. Johnson & Wellman, 1982). It is thus expected that false predictions generated by the person analogy will be accepted for those situations inducing mental reactions from humans.

How often did these children use personification? In the first type of situation (similar situations), like the children in Study 1, many children used personification; that is, the occurrence rates of personifying responses were 43% of all the responses for a grasshopper and also 43% for a tulip; 60% of the children made at least one personifying response for a grasshopper, and for a tulip, 50% did so. It should be noted that most of the personifying responses were not mere generalizations of the likely human reactions to the other animal and plant, but were modifications based upon mappings between a human and the target object. For example, though their predictions of the object's reactions identified as implicit personifications were by definition very similar at the functional level to the corresponding predictions of human reactions, they were often adjusted in terms of expressions (e.g., using "wither" for a tulip instead of "die" for a person), modified in the agent and/or patient (e.g., whereas a human baby "drinks milk," a tulip "is given water"), or assigned different salient features (e.g., "comes into flower" for a tulip in place of "becomes an adult" for a person). To put it differently, most of these predictions were based on functional similarity rather than physical similarity; for example, physiologically food for a person is not analogous to water for a plant, but functionally both are necessary for survival.

In the second type of situation (contradictory situations), the children seldom used personification. The occurrence rates of personification were 15% for a grasshopper and 5% for a tulip. In contrast, in the third type of situation (compatible situations), the occurrence rates were 73% for a grasshopper and 53% for a tulip; 19 out of the 20 children made at least one personifying response for a grasshopper and 15 did so for a tulip.

Individual response patterns confirmed that children used person analogies discriminately. We examined whether an individual child made a personifying response to either or both of the two questions for each type of situation. Table 3.1 shows the number of children in each response pattern thus classified. Out of the 40 children (for a grasshopper and tulip combined), 16 (40%) showed a PNP pattern; that is, they used personification for both the similar and compatible situations, but not for the contradictory situations. Thirteen other children (33%), who were either NNP or PNN, also refrained from applying it for the contradictory situa-

TABLE 3.1. Individual response patterns to questions about either a grasshopper or a tulip in three types of situations

Response patterns	PPP	NPP	NNP	PNP	PNN	NNN
Grasshopper (N = 20)	3	2	4	10	0	1
Tulip (N = 20)	2	0	7	6	2	3
Total (N = 40)	5	2	11	16	2	4

Note. The first letter (P or N) of the response pattern shows that a child made at least one personifying (P) or two nonpersonifying (N) response(s) to the two similar situations; the second, to the two contradictory situations; and the third, to the two compatible situations. From Inagaki and Hatano (1991).

tions, while using it for either, but not both, of the similar or the compatible situations. There were only five children (13%) who used personification in all three types of situations (PPP) indiscriminately. There were also a few who used no personification at all in any type of situation.

We give below an example for a grasshopper and a tulip to illustrate how discriminately the children used knowledge about humans, depending on the types of situations.

M. K. (6 years, 3 months), for the "too-much-eating" question of the similar situation: "The grasshopper will be dizzy and die, 'cause the grasshopper, though it is an insect, is *like a human* (in this case)."

For the "left-behind" question of the contradictory situation: "The grasshopper will be picked up by someone, 'cause it cannot open the cage." [Interviewer: If someone does not pick up the cage, what will the grasshopper do?] "The grasshopper will just stay there." [Why doesn't the grasshopper do anything? Why does it just stay there?] "*It cannot* (go out of the cage and) *walk, unlike a person.*"

For the "feeling-sad" question of the compatible situation: "The grasshopper will *feel unhappy.*"

Y. S. (6 years, 0 months), for the "too-much-eating" question of the similar situation: "The tulip will go bad." [Why?] "If we water the tulip too much, it *cannot drink water so much,* so it will wither."

For the "left-behind" question of the contradictory situation: "The *tulip doesn't speak.* . . . Someone will bring the (potted) tulip to the police office, as a lost thing." [If there is no one who does such a thing, what will the tulip do? Is there anything the tulip can do?] "*The tulip cannot move, because it has no feet.*"

For the "feeling-sad" question of the compatible situation: "The tulip will surely *be sad. It cannot say 'sad,' but it will feel so inside.*"

Constrained Personification Generates Educated Guesses

As illustrated by the above examples, young children's personification is likely to produce reasonable predictions. In both Studies 1 and 2, children's responses were coded in terms of the reasonableness of the prediction (reasonable, unreasonable, or no prediction) for each object. To obtain criteria for reasonableness of the predictions, about 30 college students were given the prediction questions for each object in a paper-and-pencil form. All types of predictions made by more than a quarter of the students were considered reasonable. Therefore, "reasonable" in these studies means adult-like. For a tulip in the "too-much-water" situation, for example, children's predictions implying some damage (e.g., die or any other ill health) were classified as reasonable, whereas those suggesting no damage or a beneficial effect, like "Giving it glass after glass of water will make the flower bigger and bigger, prettier and prettier," were classified as unreasonable.

Results from both studies indicate that for the similar situations, the children who used personification tended to generate reasonable predictions more often than the children who did not use it. In Study 1, for the rabbit, the mean percentage of reasonable predictions was 89% for the personifying responses, and 71% for the nonpersonifying responses; for the tulip, the mean percentage was 85% for the personifying responses and 75% for the nonpersonifying ones. In Study 2 the percentage of reasonable predictions in nonpersonifying responses was unexpectedly high, and thus did not statistically differ from the corresponding percentage in personifying responses. However, all the personifying responses were accompanied by some reasons, whereas about a half of the nonpersonifying reasonable predictions had no reasons (i.e., "I don't know" or "No" answer) or tautological reasons. When excluding implicit personifying responses, which were accompanied by nontautological explanations by definition, the percentage of reasonable predictions with nontautological reasons was 100% (13/13) for (explicit) personifying responses and 44.4% (20/45) for nonpersonifying responses. Thus it seems that the person analogy was helpful for this type of situations in the sense that it enabled the children to offer reasons for their predictions. For the contradictory situations, very few children used personification and most others produced reasonable predictions in both studies.

For the compatible situation in Study 2, as expected, the children produced unreasonable predictions, because relying on the personification was clearly misleading in this situation: Because the children at this age were supposed to have no adequate knowledge (e.g., about the relation between the brain and feeling), they could not check the plausibility of products of person analogies in this situation. For the two objects combined, percentages of reasonable predictions were 2.0% (1/50) and 92.3% (24/26) for the personifying and nonpersonifying responses, respectively.

A typical personifying answer was as follows: "If the caretaker dies, the tulip will feel lonely and will fall down and wither because nobody takes care of it." Ten nonpersonifying respondents gave a total of 13 reasons why the target object feels nothing. About half of these referred to the fact that the target object had no brain, and the other half concerned the difference between the target object and a person (e.g., "Because the tulip has no mouth/no hands" and "The grasshopper doesn't speak").

The above findings from Studies 1 and 2 clearly support our idea of constrained personification or the constrained person analogy. Other replication studies from our laboratory, using less familiar animals, such as a porcupine, a snail, or a tortoise as the target, corroborated the results of the Studies 1 and 2. Thus, when young children do not have enough knowledge to generate predictions for the target animate object's behaviors or attributes, they can make educated guesses, relying on person analogies in a constrained way. This is partly because many of the nonhuman living things share some structural and functional properties or processes with humans.

☐ Acquisition of the Concept of Living Things Through the Mediation of the Person Analogy

We assume that personification as analogy plays an important role in the construction of naive biology, including the acquisition of a concept of living things, which is one of the core concepts in naive biology. As mentioned in Chapter 2, recognition of commonalities between animals and plants is generally difficult for young children because of both cognitive (or perceptual) and linguistic factors. However, as revealed by our experiment dealing with the effects of contexts described in Chapter 2, if children are given contextual and linguistic help, they are likely to recognize commonalities between animals and plants, more accurately, they could extend human properties that all living things share from humans to both animals and plants. Thus, it would be plausible that these inductive projections in biological contexts help children notice that animals have some human properties and that plants also have some human properties, and as a result they recognize commonalities between animals and plants, even though it is not sure whether they consciously grasp the commonalities.

In this sense, the above experimental results suggest that children's recognition of commonalities between animals and plants is enhanced through the person analogies, which serve as a bridge. In the other experiment using the forced analogy from animals to plants, which dealt with children's conscious grasp of the commonalities, about half the children failed to recognize the commonalities between animals and plants for properties except for growth and taking of food/water (see Chapter 2). Thus, in another experiment (Inagaki & Hatano, in press), we examined whether children's conscious recognition of commonalities between animals and plants would be enhanced through the mediation of person analogies, using properties the commonality of which was hard for children to recognize in the previous study. We assumed that, after recognizing that (a) animals have some human properties and (b) plants have the same human properties, the children could then infer that (c) animals and plants share some other properties.

First, twenty 5-year-olds were given a task of inductive projection from humans to varied living and nonliving things with biological contexts. That is, they were given a short, vitalistic description about the property that people possessed (e.g., "A person becomes bigger and bigger by taking in energy from food and water"), and then required to attribute that property (e.g., growth) to varied animals, plants, and nonliving things. The properties used here were taking food/water, becoming bigger, and being taken ill. These were adopted because when given vitalistic descriptions, they were attributed to both animals and plants (but not to nonliving things) in the previous study. It was expected that this inductive projection with appropriate contexts would activate the use of the person analogy for both animals and plants. Immediately after this inductive projection task, the children were given the same forced analogy task as that described in Chapter 2. They were directly asked whether plants or nonliving things would manifest certain phenomena similar to those observed for animals. Biological phenomena used here were overfeeding, being ill-fed, breathing, and growing in number. Note that for all of these phenomena 50% or fewer of the children recognized commonalities between animals and plants in the previous study, and none of these phenomena were used in the prior induction task of the current study. Example questions in the forced analogy task are as follows:

> *Overfeeding:* A squirrel or an alligator becomes ill when it eats too much food. Do you think anything similar to this occurs with a tulip or a pine tree/with a chair or a pay phone?
>
> *Growing in number:* Squirrels or Alligators gradually increase in number by having babies or laying eggs. Do you think anything similar to this occurs with a tulip or a pine tree/with a chair or a pay phone?

Table 3.2. Percentages of admitting to applying animal analogy to plants or nonliving things

	Ill-fed		Overfeed		Breathe		Grow in number	
	P	N	P	N	P	N	P	N
Preceded by projection task	95	0	60	0	60	0	45	2
Not preceded by projection task	50	0	33	3	45	0	50	5
Differences	**		*					

Note. P means plants, and N means nonliving things. **shows $p < .01$; * $p < .05$.

Table 3.2 shows performances on the forced analogy task for the children who were given this task immediately after the inductive projection task and for those who were given the forced analogy task only. The children who had been given the induction task in advance grasped commonalities between animals and plants significantly more often than those who had not for being ill-fed and overfeeding, and to a lesser extent, for breathing. For growing in number, such a tendency was not found at all. In other words, through the mediating person analogies, which activated the recognition of commonalities between humans and plants as well as between humans and animals in inductive projection, the children recognized some functional equivalence between animals and plants for still other properties. This suggests that the person analogy can work as a learning mechanism. However, we must add that this effect of a mediating person analogy was essentially limited to the phenomena related to taking nutriment. This may have been because young children's first biology emerges around taking nutriment and individual growth, or because the contexts given to the children in this study emphasized the biological nature of taking food/water and growing in size only.

☐ Expansion of Biological Knowledge Through Personification as Analogy

How do children expand their knowledge about biological phenomena and entities, which is also essential for the development of naive biology? As many people think, children expand biological knowledge through their direct experiences, such as raising animals and plants, and their indirect experiences, such as reading picture books, watching TV, conversation with their parents or preschool teachers, and so on. Personification as analogy plays an important role in knowledge acquisition or expansion through such direct and indirect experiences. More specifically, personification enables children to incorporate directly observed or indirectly transmitted facts about a variety of animals and plants meaningfully, by connecting these facts to the core of their biological knowledge, which concerns *human* bodily processes.

As we have seen in this chapter, young children sometimes can, based on personification, predict behaviors of and attribute properties to unfamiliar animals and plants when asked to do so. However, their responses are no more than educated guesses because these animals and plants may be different from humans and their mapping between the target animal or plant and the source human cannot be optimal. The biological world is full of variations and exceptions, even for biologists. Personification as analogy must be less powerful than biologists' reasoning based on the sophisticated taxonomy of living things.

However, personification can almost always help young children interpret the given information regarding behaviors and properties of animals and plants. As revealed in the preceding sections, young children are good at relying on partial analogy (e.g., "That animal is similar to a human in that respect"). Young children may connect the information to humans even when it does not hold with humans ("Unlike people, a tulip cannot walk"), to make it more meaningful. Therefore, personification serves as a learning heuristic even more than a reasoning strategy. We will examine how it actually works.

Expansion of Knowledge Through Direct Experience

It is possible or even likely that children expand biological knowledge using personification in the process of raising animals at home or at preschool. In the process of taking care of animals, children often predict their pet animals' behaviors or interpret biological occurrences using person analogies. Motoyoshi (1979) reported such attempts observed in her daycare center, for example, the 5-year-old girl's remark, "Flowers are like people . . . ," quoted at the beginning of this chapter. We give other episodes from her daycare center below.

Episode 1

Children examined rabbits' preference for food over a month. This was originally initiated by discussion between two children who loved the rabbits: One child insisted that the rabbits liked lettuce better because they ate lettuce ahead of carrots, but the other disagreed with him for the reason that when he fed the rabbits the other day, they ate carrots first. After a month they discovered that the rabbits liked carrots best and lettuce second, but that the rabbits ate lettuce first when they were given carrots for 10 consecutive days. One of the boys, aged 5, said, "If we continue to eat only our favorite food, we get tired of it. Rabbits are the same (as people), aren't they?"

Episode 2

When children, who had believed that a tortoise did not excrete because (unlike humans) it lives in the water, discovered that the tortoise raised in their daycare center excreted yellow watery feces on the white paper, one of them cried, "The tortoise poops too!"

The above episodes illustrate well that young children try to understand (or interpret) biological phenomena that occur during their animal-raising activities using person analogies. Such attempts would contribute to the expansion of their biological knowledge. In fact, Inagaki (1990a) provided experimental data to support this possibility. She interviewed eighteen 5-year-olds who had raised goldfish at home for an extended period and eighteen children who had never raised any animal, and asked varied questions about goldfish and other animals. Each goldfish-raising child was individually matched, in terms of chronological age, with a child who was not raising any animal.

The children who had raised goldfish had acquired a greater amount of factual and procedural knowledge about goldfish than the "non-raising" children. The former children showed not only a larger amount of procedural and observable factual knowledge (e.g., a goldfish is fed once a day) but also a greater deal of factual knowledge about unobservable properties of goldfish (which are often shared with humans), for example, having blood, having a heart, and breathing, than their counterparts. In addition, the goldfish-raising children acquired a greater amount of conceptual knowledge than their counterparts. Conceptual knowledge was assessed through responses to prediction questions such as, "Does the goldfish poop if it is not fed for a number of days? Why do you think so?" and responses to questions requiring children to explain about the raising procedure, such as, "Is it okay not to change the water in a fishbowl for fresh water? Why do you think so?" Goldfish-raising children not only made reasonable predictions for goldfsh's responses more often but also explained the raising procedures more accurately than non-raising children. For the four prediction questions, 94% (17/18) of the goldfish-raising children used at least one person analogy, whereas 61% of the non-raising children did so. For example, one 6-year-old boy with experience in raising goldfish answered for the too-much-feeding question, "If people eat too much, even they will have trouble with their tummy. The goldfish is weak, so it will die." Since it was confirmed that these two groups of children did not differ in factual knowledge about other animals than goldfish, assessed through their responses to questions about mammals, such as, "Does a monkey lay eggs?" or "Does a panda have nails?", the above results can be attributed to the difference in their experience concerning raising goldfish.

From these findings, we can infer that animal-raising children possibly acquire a mental model for that animal by transferring their knowledge about humans through the person analogy, with some modifications based on observations they have made of the animal. Since "human beings have an intrinsic motivation to understand" (Hatano & Inagaki, 1986, p. 263), it is likely that animal-raising children try to understand the meaning of the procedures they are applying and of remarks sometimes made by adults, such as, "Don't feed them too much," by constructing a mental model. They have to borrow knowledge about a human, in order to form a tentative model, because they cannot see the internal bodily structure of the animal. Moreover, as they gain experience in the course of raising the animal, they may recognize that the animal and people are considerably similar in terms of ways of living, though they may be quite dissimilar in appearance, and thus comfortably apply the person analogy to the animal.

Expansion of Knowledge Through Indirect Experience

Let us consider the possibility that children often use person analogies in incorporating new information coming through reading picture books, watching TV, conversation with their parents, and so on. Inagaki and Kasetani (1994) examined how much forty 5-year-olds ($M = 5;1$) and forty 6-year-olds ($M = 6;0$) learned when they were read a picture book about how to raise squirrels. Each child individually listened to a story describing procedures for raising a squirrel, including an episode on diarrhea, while watching pictures depicting each step of the procedure. Half of the children in each age group (hereafter called the "hint group") were given additional short sentences as hint to activate knowledge about humans for descriptions about making a cage for a squirrel, preparing food, cleaning the cage, and treating diarrhea and other illnesses. In the other half (hereafter called the "no-hint group") the children were not given such hints. What follows are example descriptions given to the hint and no-hint groups. Underlined sentences were given only in the hint group.

Description about food: Squirrels' food includes seeds of sunflowers, chestnuts, fruits, and vegetables. Squirrels like chestnuts very much. Give fresh water every day. Mixed food might be given to the squirrels. <u>You do not eat favorite food only. You eat a variety of food, don't you?</u>

Description about diarrhea: The squirrel looks like something is wrong today. There were pieces of bad carrots and old water in the food box. The squirrel's feces are watery today, which is unusual. "What happened to the squirrel? <u>If I eat something bad, I will have a tummyache. I wonder, how about the squirrel?</u> The squirrel does not look lively," said Fuyuo (a child raising a squirrel).

After listening to the story, the children were given tests of comprehension and prediction. The comprehension test, consisting of four items, was given to examine children's understanding of the raising procedures, which had been given in the description. The children were asked to choose one from among three alternatives with pictures and to give the reason. Example questions are as follows: "What kind of food shall a caretaker give the squirrel? (a) favorite chestnuts only, (b) chestnuts, seeds, and vegetables mixed, or (c) an ice cream?" and "A squirrel excretes watery feces, which is unusual. Why are its feces so loose? Is it because (a) it ate something bad, (b) it played in the swimming pool, or (c) it drank some fresh water?"

As shown in Figure 3.1, the 5-year-olds in the hint condition made correct choices more often than the 5-year-olds in the no-hint condition, while there were no such differences due to the hints among the 6-year-olds. In other words, the effect of giving hints to use knowledge about humans tended to be larger among younger children than among older children at least for recognizing correct procedures. With regard to the comprehension score (correct choices plus adequate reasons), the hint group children, irrespective of age, gave more adequate reasons for their correct choices than the no-hint ones, and older children gave more than younger ones.

The hint group children also tended to use person analogies or explanations referring to a human as a reference point more often than the no-hint group children. Examples of responses using person analogies were as follows: "After we eat food, we poop. So does the squirrel" (a boy aged 6 years, 4 months); "If he always eats the same food, the squirrel gets tired of it too" (a boy aged 6 years, 4 months); "Don't feed just the chestnuts. You must give the squirrel various seeds and a carrot, because a person will die if he eats the same kind of food only, and so will the squirrel" (a boy aged 5 years, 2 months).

Some of these person analogies led children to erroneous choices. For

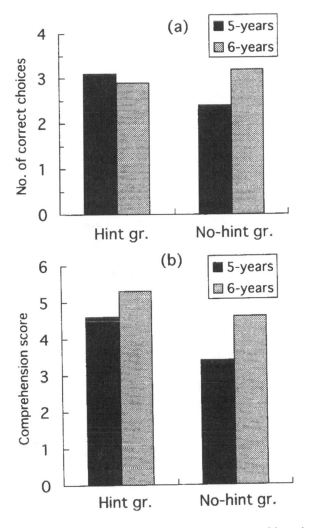

FIGURE 3.1. (a) The number of correct choices among 5-year-olds and 6-year-olds in groups with and without hints. (b) Comprehension score (number of correct choices plus adequate explanation) among 5-year-olds and 6-year-olds in groups with and without hints.

example, many of the children, irrespective of the conditions, chose the alternative of "playing in a swimming pool," not "eating bad food," as the cause of the squirrel's water-like feces, and justified the choice by referring to their own experience of having diarrhea due to getting chills in the tummy from playing in a pool.

These results strongly suggest that giving hints to use knowledge about humans enhances young children's comprehension, which in turn produces reasonable justifications. But children may try to understand the presented story about animals using person analogies even without hints. We show below an interesting case about constrained personification found in the no-hint group. One girl strongly believed that diarrhea was caused by a cold, because recent influenza had caused diarrhea for her. For the diarrhea question, she answered, before being presented with the three alternatives, "'Cause it has caught cold" that is, she applyied knowledge about humans to a squirrel. The experimenter gave the three alternatives and asked her to choose one. She was at a loss, because the alternative of having caught cold was not presented, and she knew the squirrel couldn't play in the pool. She said, "Let me see. The squirrel can't play in a pool . . . Well, let me see. . . . " She finally chose the alternative of the squirrel having played in a pool, ignoring available specific knowledge about squirrels; in other words, she gave up on satisfying the feasibility constraint. She justified her choice by saying, "'Cause it can't catch cold by eating bad food, nor by drinking fresh water." This example illustrates that even when children were not given information referring to humans, they made an inference about the squirrel using knowledge about humans (including themselves).

Young children (and probably lay adults, too) can learn novel facts about animals that are consistent with their knowledge about humans readily and easily, because they rely on the person analogy when they try to incorporate the facts meaningfully. This is true even when given "facts" are false for the target animals, which actually behave differently from humans in those situations. Let us present another of our experiments which reveals young children's heavy reliance on personification as a learning strategy.

Inagaki and Hatano (1999b) found that young children could learn new facts about animals readily when these were consistent with the knowledge that the children already possessed for humans. Here seventy-two 6-year-olds from a kindergarten learned about animal behaviors and their consequences, being randomly assigned to one of the four matierals: a connected list about humans, a connected list about animals, a swapped list about humans, or a swapped list about animals. The children were auditorily presented with a list consisting of six sentences about either animals or humans and asked to remember them. In each sentence, a behavior and its outcome were paired either for a moderately familiar animal or for a person. In the connected list of humans, the behavior and the outcome were causally connected in the sense that the cause naturally induces the outcome in humans. In the connected list about animals, although the behavior and the outcome were apparently causally connected, what was described there was false for the target animal.

Example sentences used in the connected list about animals are as follows (square brackets show words used in the list about humans; italicized words show the animal's behaviors, and the others, their outcomes):

1. A *blue frog* [Hanako] *fell down into the water and* was choked to death.
2. A *wolf* [Taro] *ate rotten meat and* had diarrhea.
3. A *mole* [Jiro] *ate food many times a day and* had something wrong with its [his] tummy.

In the swapped lists about humans and animals, behaviors and their consequences in the connected list were re-paired. Example sentences are as follows:

1. A *blue frog* [Hanako] *fell down into the water and* had something wrong with its [her] tummy.
2. A *wildcat* [Keiko] *rubbed itself [herself] against medical herbs and* had diarrhea.
3. A *mole* [Jiro] *ate food many times a day and* was choked to death.

After two practice items, an experimenter read to the child all six sentences (items) in the list slowly and asked him or her to remember them, saying, "Now, I am going to read a short story about various animals/friends. Later I will ask you what the animals/friends in the story did. So, I'd like you to listen to the story carefully." Immediately after reading all six sentences in the list, the experimenter read again the initial part of the sentence describing an animal's or a human's behavior and asked the child to recall the subsequent part describing its consequence.

Results indicated that the children given the connected lists, irrespective of the kinds of the target, recalled the sentences correctly more often than those given the swapped lists. It is not surprising that the children given the connected list about humans recalled better than those in the swapped list about humans, because the former children were given true facts. However, it should be noted that the children given the connected list about animals performed equally better than those given the swapped list about animals, in spite that the contents in the list about animals were false for the target animal.

In addition, considering that the full-recall score for the six sentences was 12 (two points were given for complete recall for each of six items), the mean score of 8.6 among the children given the connected list about animals indicates that these children correctly recalled 72% of the given facts. These findings suggest that the children learned new facts about animals readily, even if these were false, when the facts were plausible in light of their knowledge about humans.

Although most recall failures were either "No" responses or "I forget" responses, one-third of all erroneous recall responses in the swapped list about animals and a quarter in the swapped list about humans were responses consistent with the children's human-centered biological understandings. About 60% of the children given the swapped lists made such incorrect responses at least once. For example, when given the sentence, "*A mole ate food many times a day and* was choked to death," the children recalled, "had tummyache," or "had diarrhea" instead. For the sentence, "*A blue frog fell down into the water and . . . ?*", the children recalled with the ending, "died" or "caught cold." This suggests that children's attempts to remember facts in relation to their knowledge about humans may sometimes lead to personifying, erroneous recall, especially in situations where children are given too little information to do a factual check.

☐ Positive Features of Personification in Biological Understanding

Let us summarize the positive features of personification in young children's understanding of biological phenomena in relation to the previous claims by Piaget (1929) and Carey (1985). Unlike Piaget, we do not consider young children's personifying or animistic responses as a sign of their general intellectual immaturity. We agree with Carey that personifying or animistic responses reflect children's inadequate biological knowledge. However, we disagree with Carey concerning whether personification or inference based on the comparison-to-people model is exclusively a psychological mode of inference.

Carey seems to think that, because young children regard nonhuman living entities as behaving beings, these children make many underattribution errors for animate objects phylogenetically far from people, such as worms, as well as animistic responses or overattribution errors for plants and nonliving things, such as the sun. In contrast, we consider personification or the person analogy as possibly a sort of biological inference and as adaptive in nature. Young children use personification in a constrained way so that they can generate reasonable predictions without many errors. Children's under- and overattribution errors may be caused by their limited biological knowledge, which prevents them from checking personification-based inferences as well as by an inappropriate similarity metric rather than by the "psychological" nature of personification. In addition, young children are able not only to explicitly grasp commonalities between animals and plants through personification, but also to expand their biological knowledge, relying on personification.

CHAPTER

The Distinction Between Biological and Psychological Processes/Properties

[Interviewer: Taro falls down and hurts his knee. He feels pain, so he says to the pain, "Pain, Pain, go away quickly!" When he says so, can he stop feeling pain on his knee?]

Girl (5 years, 11 months): "No, he can't. He can recover if he puts the medicine on it, but he can't recover just by stroking it (together with saying so)."

Boy (4 years, 9 months): "Yes, he can if he puts a Band-Aid on it." [If he says, "Pain, Pain, go away quickly" without putting a Band-Aid on it, can he stop feeling pain?] "(If so) the pain doesn't fade away!"

Can young children distinguish biological from psychological phenomena? More specifically, can young children apply different causal devices to biological and psychological processes? Can they attribute biological and psychological properties differently to a set of entities? The biology/psychology distinction is more difficult than classifying observable entities in the world, which we have focused on in Chapter 2, because both biological and psychological phenomena are observed among a *subset* of living things—only human beings and some nonhuman animals possess minds as well as bodies. Because of its difficulty, people often assume that young children lack an understanding of this distinction. In Japanese society, parents often say such "magical" words as, "Pain, Pain, fly away," to their 2- to 5-year-old children when they have a minor injury. The excerpts from our interviews quoted at the start of this chapter illustrate children's responses to such words for dispelling pain.

Carey (1985) claimed that children under around age 10 could neither distinguish biological from psychological phenomena nor recognize that biological processes (e.g., those producing growth or death) are autonomous in the sense of being relatively outside psychological control. According to her, for example, young children would see the origin of babies only in terms of mother's intentional behavior, such as going to a store to buy a baby; or, young children would understand death as a sort of sleep or behavioral departure (Carey, 1985). Psychologists inspired by Piaget's ideas also have claimed that young children would consider illness to be caused by social or moral factors, not by biological factors (e.g., Bibace & Walsh, 1981). In short, Carey as well as the Piagetian researchers have claimed that young children did not yet have any biological framework to interpret and explain biological phenomena; instead, according to them, these phenomena were assimilated into the psychological framework that children already possessed.

However, an increasing number of recent studies have challenged this claim. In recent decades, there has been heated debate concerning whether young children possess an autonomous domain of biology, and the issue of whether young children distinguish between biological and psychological processes and properties has been the focus of this debate. In this chapter we describe what young children know about the distinction between biological and psychological processes and properties, and more specifically, about internal bodily processes, inheritance of properties, and illness versus health, all of which are biological phenomena concerning the survival of individuals and species.

☐ Young Children's Understanding of Bodily Phenomena

Psychological Framework Versus Multiple Frameworks for Living Things

As one of the bases for her claim that preschool children did not yet have a biological framework and thus could not distinguish between psychological and biological phenomena, Carey (1985) pointed out the fact that the children in her studies did not attribute biological properties (e.g., eating, having a heart, etc.) to animals (and plants) that are phylogenetically far from people. If children regarded only advanced animals as behaving beings like humans, they would fail to attribute to those animals dissimilar to people some "human" properties that were needed for any animals to survive. Indeed, when asked to attribute biological properties to varied animals from humans to other entities using simple questions such as, "Does X have a property Y?", many 4-year-old children did not attribute these properties (Carey, 1985); for example, 40% of the 4-year-olds failed to attribute "having a heart" to fish and 70% failed to do so for flies; 60% denied "eating" for flies. Thus, it seemed plausible to claim that young children possessed only a psychological framework for living things. Similar underattributions were reported by Inagaki and Sugiyama's (1988) study, though they also pointed out that attributional patterns were different between biological and psychological properties.

However, recent studies have challenged this claim that young children lack the biology/psychology distinction; these studies suggest that preschool children already have a biological framework for living things as well as a psychological one and that they can differentiate biological from psychological phenomena, given proper contexts. Gutheil et al.'s (1998) experiment is one of such studies. Gutheil et al. examined effects of contexts on the inductive projection task used in Carey's (1985) study. A group of 4-year-olds, prior to the standard inductive projection, were briefly given information about a biological property (e.g., eats, has a heart) for a person; for eating, for example, "This person eats because he needs food to live and grow. The food gives him energy to move. If he doesn't eat, he will die." Results indicated that the children in this biological context condition attributed the properties that they had been taught people possessed to even a fly or a worm more often than those who had not been given such information prior to the inductive projection.

It is interesting that Gutheil et al.'s (1998) 4-year-olds who were given biological contexts showed similar attribution patterns to the 7-year-olds without any context in Carey's experiment. This suggests that the 4-year-olds with context relied on a biological framework to guide their inductive judgments. Moreover, it was also confirmed that the observed findings under the biological context were unlikely to be due to a simple response bias, because the extended attribution occurred only for biological properties.

Based on these findings, Gutheil et al. (1998) claimed that preschool children possess multiple frameworks for thinking about animals and can use them to constrain their inductive inferences. Unlike adults, the psychological framework seemed to be the default option among the 4-year-olds, because there was no significant difference in attribution patterns between giving no context and giving psychological contexts describing the property in terms of its effects on a person's mental state or his or her interactions with other people (e.g., "This person has a heart that pounds when he is happy and excited. The pounding helps keep him more excited when he plays with his friends"). However, if given simple relevant biological contexts, children could surely use a biological framework to guide inductive projection.

Coley (1995) also asserted that young children possess multiple frameworks for living things. He presented kindergarten children of age 6 years (and 8-year-olds and adults) with pictures of predatory animals (tiger, hawk, alligator, and shark) and docile domestic animals (guinea pig, parakeet, turtle, and goldfish) and asked whether each animal has biological properties (e.g., has blood, has bones, etc.) and psychological properties (e.g., can think, can feel angry, can feel happy, etc.). Results from group data and individual response patterns revealed that children as young as 6 years of age showed distinct attribution patterns for biological versus psychological properties. The children attributed biological properties equally to the predatory and domestic animals, but attributed "gentle" psychological properties (e.g., can feel happy or can feel scared) to domestic animals more often than to the predatory animals. Thus, for example, the children judged that both a tiger and a guinea pig had blood but that the guinea pig was more likely to feel happy than the tiger.

Mind's Inability to Control Internal Bodily Processes

Inagaki and Hatano (1993) provided evidence against Carey's (1985) claim that young children could not recognize that biological processes are autonomous. In one of their experiments, children 4 and 5 years of age were asked whether organic activities, involuntary or physiologically needed, could be controlled by their intention or desire. For example, the children were asked questions such as, "Can you stop breathing for a couple of days?" or "Suppose Taro becomes sleepy while watching an interesting TV program. Can he continue to watch TV for several more hours?" Results revealed that a majority of the 4- and 5-year-olds recognized that the stopping of breathing is beyond their control, and that they cannot resist drowsiness for a long time even when an interesting TV program is on. In addition, these children were required to choose between one's desire and her daily diet as the determinant of the body weight by the following question, "Haruko and Akiko are twin sisters, so they are the same in weight and height. Haruko wants to become fatter, while Akiko wants to become slimmer. Haruko eats only a little, while Akiko eats a lot. Who will become fatter?" More than 90% of them chose the latter—the girl who eats more food. All participants but two 4-year-olds gave the reason that eating a lot would make her fatter.

Inagaki (1997) extended this controllability task to include 3-year-olds as participants and to ask about more items, including fillers meant to prevent the children from responding "No" automatically. Moreover, relationships between children's awareness of bodily processes and their recognition of the mind's inability to control them were also examined. Children aged 3–5 years were given an awareness task first and then a new controllability task.

The awareness task, which consisted of five items, concerned children's awareness of internal bodily processes, such as respiration, heartbeat, feeling pain, and so on. For example, "Do you breathe? Can you show me how you breathe?", "Is your heart beating or not? Where is your heart?", and so on. It was found that the awareness of bodily processes developed markedly between age 3 and 4; the awareness score of the 3-year-olds was significantly lower than that of the 4-year-olds, and there was no significant difference between the 4- and 5-year-olds. The 3-year-olds had relatively good awareness of sensations such as pain, whereas their awareness of the workings of internal bodily organs, like the heart, was very poor. In contrast, a majority of the 4- and 5-year-olds were aware of heartbeat and respiration as well as sensation.

The controllability task consisted of 10 items: 6 critical items and 4 filler items dealing with voluntary acts, 2 of which concerned voluntary acts to satisfy biological needs. Example questions on critical items were as follows: "Suppose Taro wants to stop his heartbeat. Can he do that?" or "Suppose Taro gets his arm bitten by a mosquito. He feels itchy, so he says to the itch, 'Itch, Itch, go away quickly!' When he says so, can he stop feeling the itch on his arm?" Examples of the filler items were: "Suppose Taro plays in the sandbox and his hands get dirty. Can he get his hands clean again if he washes them in water?" or "Suppose Taro gets very thirsty because he has been running. Can he slake his thirst if he drinks a glass of juice?" The latter was an item asking about a voluntary act satisfying a biological need.

Results indicated, first, that almost all children at each age group correctly answered the filler items; the mean percentage correct ("Yes" responses) for the four items was 86% among the 3-year-olds and 94% among both the 4- and 5-year-olds. This means that the participating children knew well that voluntary acts can be controlled by children's intentions.

Table 4.1 shows the percentages of "unable-to-control" responses for each critical item of the controllability task in each age group. The children's performance varied considerably from item to item and depending on their age. For the heartbeat and the respiration, which represented typical involuntary acts, both the 4- and 5-year-olds gave significantly more "unable-to-control" responses than chance, while the 3-year-olds showed such a tendency only insignificantly. However, the 3-year-olds, as well as the 4- and 5-year-olds, showed a significantly larger number of "unable-

TABLE 4.1. Percentages of "unable-to-control" respondents

Items	3 years (N = 20)	4 years (N = 20)	5 years (N = 20)
Heartbeat	55	85**	95**
Respiration	70	85**	90**
Urination	50	70	90**
Working of stomach	20*	55	85**
Feeling pain	35	60	70
Feeling itch	35	65	70

Note. *$p < .05$; **$p < .01$, above or below chance ($P = .5$).

to-control" responses to the heartbeat and the respiration questions than to the two filler "biological" items (i.e., the removal of thirst by drinking juice or removal of hunger by eating food). In other words, even many 3-year-olds have recognized that biological or bodily phenomena, such as the heartbeat and respiration, are less controllable than hunger or thirst, though they tend to overestimate the mind's ability to control bodily processes.

Although the 5-year-olds correctly recognized that they could not control the workings of the stomach nor the urinary process by their desire, the 3- and 4-year-olds did not show such recognition as clearly as the 5-year-olds. Even a larger number of the 3- and 4-year-olds accepted the mind's ability to control feeling pain and feeling itch. However, it was found that some of the children answered "Yes" with reservation for the pain/itch questions, for example, "Yes he can (stop feeling pain), if he puts medicine or a Band-Aid on the hurt," and in these cases most of them changed their answer from "Yes" to "No" when they were asked further whether the pain could be removed only by their verbal command without medicine (though these responses were not classified as "unable-to-control" in Table 4.1). This suggests that the children's failure on these items was, at least in part, due to the fact that they were imagining other treatments accompanying attempts to mentally control sensation, which could indeed mitigate pain or itching.

Inagaki (1997), conducting an auxiliary experiment with additional groups of 3- and 4-year-olds, investigated this possibility. To test whether they would think that a purely mental (and verbal) act could remove pain or itching, follow-up inquiry questions were provided. Let us briefly describe them, using the item of feeling pain as an example. When a child answered "Yes" to the initial question, "Suppose Masao falls down and hurts his knee. He feels pain, so he wants to stop feeling pain. Can he do that?" and justified his or her response referring to biological or physical means, such as, "put medicine on it" or "put a Band-Aid on it," he or she was next asked an auxiliary question to clarify the response, such as, "If he says to the pain, 'Pain, Pain, go away quickly!' without using medicine [or putting on a Band-Aid, depending on the child's previous response], can he stop feeling pain on his knee quickly?" If the child answers "Yes" to this auxiliary question, he or she was required to choose between direct mental control and physical means to remove the bodily trouble: "Suppose Taro and Jiro fall down and hurt their knees. Taro puts medicine and a Band-Aid on the hurt, while Jiro says to the pain, 'Pain, Pain, go away quickly!' without putting on medicine or a Band-Aid. Who will stop feeling pain more quickly?" (This was called a choice question.)

Results indicated that almost all children in each age group who answered "Yes" to the initial question referred to physical means, such as medicine to remove the bodily trouble in their justifications; in other words, they seldom spontaneously gave a mental strategy for getting rid of the trouble. A majority of the children who asserted that the mind could control the trouble for the auxiliary questions chose biological means as more effective than the mental ones for the choice questions. Taken together, 60–77% of the 3-year-olds and 92-100% of the 4-year-olds considered mental strategies to be ineffective (or less effective than the physical ones) in eliminating the bodily trouble.

Is the recognition of the mind's inability to control organic activities related to children's growing awareness of bodily processes? Significant and nearly significant correlations between the awareness score and the mind's uncontrollability score were found in the main experiment (.39) and the auxiliary experiment (.27), respectively. These correlations indicate that the more the children were aware of their bodily processes, the more often they recognized that bodily processes are independent of their intention. In neither study, however, was the partial correlation, with the effect of the age partialled out, significant, because the awareness score was highly correlated with age.

Preschool children can, we conclude, distinguish what belongs to the body from what belongs to the mind. When asked questions in a more or less general way, 3-year-olds and some 4-year-olds apparently do assume that the mind can control some bodily processes. But when asked more specific questions, such as about strategies for affecting bodily processes, even 3-year-olds refer to biological (physical) strategies but not to mental ones. We believe that as the awareness of internal bodily processes develops markedly around 4 years of age, children's judgments of the controllability of bodily processes may become more independent from psychological causal variables.

Differential Application of Causal Devices to Human Actions

The preceding subsection concerns whether young children know that intentional causality is not applicable to bodily processes that are involuntary or that are physiologically needed. To examine their distinction between biological and psychological phenomena, we could use other research strategies, for example, asking young children to predict or explain how a variety of human actions occur, that is, whether the target action occurs as intended, by mistake, or due to a biological constraint.

Wellman, Hickling, and Schult (1997; see also Schult & Wellman, 1997), used this strategy; more specifically, they examined young children's understanding of causes of human actions and movements. They exploited the fact that human actions can be caused not only by psychological states (e.g., desires and beliefs) but also by physical forces (e.g., gravity) or biological processes (e.g., reflexes). In a series of experiments, 3- and 4-year-olds heard four to nine stories about a character who wanted and intended to do something and could or could not do so, along with the presentation of several line drawings as aids. Then, they were asked the explanation question, "Why did that happen? Why did the character do that?" Let us give some examples from stories used in their experiments.

> *Mistake:* It's time for breakfast, so Jimmy gets the cereal out of the cupboard. Now Jimmy has an idea. He wants to pour milk on his cereal. Jimmy takes a pitcher out of the refrigerator and pours it on his cereal. He pours orange juice on his cereal.
>
> *Biological constraint:* Robin is climbing a tree in her backyard. She is hanging from a branch, not touching the ground. Now she has an idea. She wants to hang on that branch forever and never let go. Robin drops to the ground.
>
> *Physical constraint:* Bobby is playing in his bedroom. He climbs on top of his stool. Now he has an idea. He wants to step off the stool and float in the air, up off the floor. Bobby steps off the stool and comes right down to the floor.

Of particular interest here was to compare children's responses to mistakes with their responses to biologically impossible and to physically impossible actions. Wellman et al. (1997) classified the children's explanations into psychological, biological, or physical explanations, or others including "Don't know." They found that the 4-year-olds consistently (across three experiments) gave different explanations for the three kinds of human actions; they gave psychological explanations most often for the mistakes, such as "She just didn't know it was ketchup" or "He thought it was milk"; biological explanations most frequently for the biologically impossible actions, for example, "His arms got hurting" or "He gets tired and has to sleep again" and physical explanations most often for the im possible physical actions, such as "He's too heavy to float in the sky" or "Planes can fly and people can't, 'cause they don't have wings" (p. 11).

The 3-year-olds consistently gave psychological explanations for the psychologically caused human actions and physical explanations for the impossible physical actions. But for the impossible biological actions they gave as many psychological explanations as biological ones. However, when asked to judge whether the desired actions, psychological, physical and biological, were possible (before offering explanations), 3- and 4-year-olds consistently said that psychological actions *were* possible but that the physically-constrained or biologically-constrained actions were *not* possible. This indicates that the 3-year-olds, like the 4-year-olds, clearly made different predictions for human actions with psychological and biological impetus.

Wellman et al. (1997) further examined young children's explanations that appeared in their conversations with parents, siblings, and occasional visitors in the home, using the Child Language Data Exchange System (CHILDES)(MacWhinney & Snow, 1985, 1990). Focusing on explanations of human actions, they analyzed more than 100,000 conversations recorded at home from four children aged 2 to 5. They found that these children applied psychological, biological, and physical reasoning to people in everyday situations, basically confirming the results from the laboratory study described above. With regard to psychological explanations, for example, a boy 3 years, 4 months of age said, "I (am) talking very quiet because I don't want somebody to wake up." Another child aged 3, years 2 months said, "He never eats spinach 'cause he don't like the taste." For biological explanations, for instance, a child of age 2 years, 11 months said, "I got medicine because it makes my fever go away." Another child aged 4 years, 8 months said, "He'll eat his food, because to be alive." For physical explanations, a boy aged 3 years, 3 months said, "I pushed it because I got knocked down." Another child 4 years, 3 months of age said, "He got a bad tooth because he fell off his bike on his face" (p. 21). It should be noted that they differentially apply these three modes of explanations to different aspects of human actions. These remarks suggest that young preschoolers possess a rudimentary, biological explanatory framework distinct from the psychological one.

Differential Modifiability Judgments

Yet another research strategy to investigate whether young children distinguish between the biological and the psychological is to study how differently they characterize biological and psychological properties that humans and other living things possess, for instance, their judgments of how stable or easily changed they are. Inagaki and Hatano (1993), in one of their experiments, examined whether young children would understand the biology/psychology distinction in terms of modifiability of bodily versus mental characteristics. Children 4 and 5 years of age were asked whether each of the six characteristics was modifiable, and, if modifiable, by what means. Items for hereditary (unmodifiable bodily) characteristics concerned a child's color of eyes and gender; items for (modifiable) bodily characteristics, the running speed and the body weight; items for mental characteristics concerned forgetfulness and a quick-tempered nature. Example questions from each of the three kinds of characteristics were as follows: "A boy, Taro, has black eyes. He wants to make his eyes blue like a foreigner's (a Caucasian's). Can he do that?" (hereditary characteristics); "Taro is a slow runner. He wants to be a fast runner. Can he do that?" (modifiable bodily characteristics); "Taro easily forgets things. He wants to get rid of this tendency. Can he do that?" (mental characteristics).

As shown in Table 4.2, not only 5-year-olds but also 4-year-olds differentiated the three types of characteristics in terms of their modifiability. While a great majority of the children correctly denied the modifiability of the hereditary characteristics of eye color and gender, many of them answered that they could modify the other bodily characteristics, and about half of them admitted the modifiability of the mental ones.

TABLE 4.2. Frequences of responses to the modifiability task

| | Characteristics | | | | | |
| | Unmodif-bodily | | Modif-bodily | | Modif-mental | |
Response	4yr	5yr	4yr	5yr	4yr	5yr
Unable to modify	36	35	10	12	25	18
	(17)	(17)	(2)	(3)	(9)	(6)
Justification for able-to-modify response						
Physical practice	0	0	25	28	0	0
Mental practice	0	0	0	0	0	3
Volition (effort)	0	0	1	0	3	9
External force	4	5	0	0	3	3
No explanation	0	0	4	0	8	6
Don't know	0	0	0	0	1	1

Note. Unmodif-bodily means unmodifiable bodily characteristics, modif-bodily, modifiable bodily ones, and modif-mental, modifiable mental ones. The total number of responses for each age group is 40 (20 subjects with 2 responses per subject). Figures in parentheses show the number of participants who gave two "Unable" responses. From Inagaki and Hatano (1993).

Justifications for "able-to-modify" responses also revealed that both the 4- and 5-year-olds recognized that different means are needed for modifying bodily characteristics and mental ones. A majority of the children who recognized the modifiability of the bodily characteristics asserted that the modifications could be brought about by physical practice, such as more exercise, diet, and so on, whereas nobody accepted such practice as a means of modifying the mental characteristics. In order to modify the mental characteristics, nine 5-year-olds replied that one needed effort or determination, saying, for example, "He must try not to lose his temper," and three referred to mental practice (i.e., concrete strategic means), as shown in one girl's answer; "(We can remove the tendency to forget easily) if we rehearse *such and such* in our mind." This suggests that the children thought that mere effort or determination may play a role in modifying the mental characteristics, but that it is useless for modifying the bodily characteristics.

These findings—not only modifiability judgments but also justifications—were confirmed by Miller and Bartsch's (1997) study in which the modifiability task from the Inagaki and Hatano (1993) study was used. Lockhart, Stegall, Roberts, and Yip (1997), who dealt with more varied physical and psychological traits, also reported that young children regarded the physical traits as less changeable than the psychological characteristics, although these children tended to overestimate the changeability of negative traits over time. In other words, the children revealed general optimism, but they were less optimistic about the physical traits than the mental ones.

☐ Young Children's Understanding of "Inheritance"

Phenomena regarding inheritance have been at the center of the debate concerning children's acquisition of a naive theory of biology. More specifically, the issue of whether young children understand that parents and their offspring share unobservable as well as observable biological properties has attracted researchers' attention. When do children recognize that the parent–offspring relationship has not only social but also biological foundations? When do they understand that biological parents and adoptive parents are different in terms of types of characteristics that they share with their offsprings? When do they realize that some properties are fixed at birth, whereas others are formed more gradually and thus are modifiable?

"Inheritance" of Biological Versus Social Properties

Contrary to Carey's claim (1985), studies from several laboratories have indicated that preschool children can distinguish between the biological and social domains in inheritance (e.g., S. Gelman & Wellman, 1991; Hirschefeld, 1995; Springer, 1992; Springer & Keil, 1989). For example, Springer and Keil (1989) showed that children from 4 to 7 years old believed that features leading to biologically functional consequences for animals are inherited, while other sorts of features, such as those leading to social or psychological consequences, are not, although these children showed poor understanding of the inheritance of inborn traits.

Springer (1992) provided evidence suggesting that preschool children judged parentage to share biological properties more often than friendship would. After being informed that a target animal possessed biological properties (e.g., a target horse has hairy ears) or behavioral properties (e.g., a target horse has scrapes on legs), 4- to 7-year-old children were asked whether each of two other animals (the target horse's baby with dissimilar appearance and the target horse's friend with similar appearance) would share the property or not. Not only the 6- to 7-year-olds but also the 4- to 5-year-olds judged that the dissimilar looking offspring shared biological properties more often than the similar looking but unrelated animal from another family. Moreover, this tendency was not found in attributing behavioral (nonbiological) properties; the children attributed these nonbiological, acquired properties equally to both the target's offspring and the target's friend.

Solomon, Johnson, Zaitchik, and Carey (1996) doubted the results that preschoolers understand the inheritance of biological properties from parents to their offspring. They asserted that since parentage is not only a biological but also a social relationship, we need to examine whether young children recognize that inheritance, that is, the biological origin of an animal's biological properties, must be causally linked to birth. Thus, they investigated young children's understanding of phenomena regarding which offsprings resemble their parents, using an experimental design that can assess distinctions between biological and nonbiological parentage (e.g., adoption).

In one of their experiments 4- to 7-year-old children were read a fairytale-style story in which a girl is born to a shepherdess (or princess) and adopted by a princess (or shepherdess). The children were then asked which the girl would resemble when she grew up, the shepherdess or the princess. The biological parent was described as having one of a pair of features, and the adoptive parent as having the other. The pairs of features consisted of three physical traits (e.g., short/tall), two beliefs (e.g., believes that a lion has 32 teeth/believes that a lion has 36 teeth), two preferences (e.g., likes dogs/likes cats), and two temperamental characteristics (e.g., laughs a lot/cries a lot). When Solomon et al. computed the occurrence rates of a differentiated pattern, which was defined as responses that attributed to the girl all three of the biological mother's physical traits but none of the biological mother's mental traits, 19% of the preschoolers, 38% of the 6-year-olds, and 63% of the 7-year-olds showed this pattern. Based on this and other results from their experiments, Solomon et al. (1996) concluded that children younger than 7 do not understand birth as part of a process mediating the biological resemblance to parents and nurturance as mediating the acquisition of mental properties.

However, a number of studies dealing with "adoption" or a "switched-at-birth" situation provide data against Solomon et al.'s (1996) conclusion. Hirschfeld (1995) examined preschool children's understanding of inheritance of race, using a "switched-at-birth" task. Children 3–5 years of age heard a story about two couples, one Black (Mr. and Mrs. Smith) and one White (Mr. and Mrs. Jones), whose babies were switched at birth and grew up with the nonbiologically related couple. Color-wash line drawings of each couple were presented as aids. An example story was as follows: "Mr. and Mrs. Smith had a baby girl. That means that the baby came out of Mrs. Smith's tummy. Right after it came out of her tummy, the baby went to live with Mr. and Mrs. Jones. The baby lived with them and Mr. and Mrs. Jones took care of her. They fed her, bought her clothes, and hugged her and kissed her when she was sad." After that, children were shown two color-wash drawings, one was a drawing of a White school-aged child and the other, a drawing of a Black school-aged child, and asked to predict which of these girls was the baby grown into school age. Hirschfeld found that although the 3-year-olds did not show a clear tendency, both the 4- and 5-year-olds expected skin color to be fixed at birth; about three quarters of the 4- and 5-year-olds chose the girls whose race matched the birth parents on both items concerning skin or hair color and one third of them justified their response in terms of birth parents' bodily characteristics. In another experiment, Hirschfeld used stories in which the babies of two couples were accidentally switched at birth in a hospital, and he found similar results.

Springer (1996) provided evidence favoring the claim that preschoolers can distinguish between biological and adoptive parentage, by examining the possibility that the discrepancy between Solomon et al.'s (1996) and Hirschfeld's (1995) results might result from the materials and questions used. He presented the same children, 4–7-year-old, with the story used by Solomon et al. (fairy tale type) and the story used by Hirschfeld (switched-at-birth), and asked them to attribute two physical properties, two beliefs, and two preferences that the biological parents possess to the adopted or switched children. Analyses based on the mean proportions of judgments that the baby would resemble its biological parent revealed that although both the 6- and 7-year-olds expected the baby to resemble the biological parent more for physical properties than for nonphysical properties for both types of stories, the preschoolers aged 4 and 5 showed such responses for the switched-at-birth story but not for the Solomon et al. story. In addition, when children's individual responses were analyzed, half of the preschoolers showed the adult pattern (a baby resembles its biological parent for the two physical properties and the adoptive parent for nonphysical properties) for the switched-at-birth stories, whereas only 23% did so for the Solomon et al. story. The preschoolers who knew where a baby grows before birth showed the adult pattern more often than those who did not, and this tendency was found more clearly for the switched-at-birth story.

Hirschfeld (1995) also pointed out the possibility that the array of properties used in the Solomon et al. (1996) study is so skewed toward nonbiological properties that preschoolers have many more opportunities to deny the hereditability of biological properties than to affirm it. In the study described above, Springer (1996) indicated that many of the preschoolers who showed mixed patterns in the Solomon et al. story showed adult patterns for the switched-at-birth stories. Considering that more than half of the preschoolers in Solomon et al.'s (1996) study showed the mixed pattern, it is possible that these preschoolers also possessed frameworks that enabled them to differentiate biological from nonbiological parentage.

In any case, evidence so far seems to favor the claim that children as young as 4 years of age can distinguish between biological and adoptive parentage, and more specifically, that they can apply multiple causal devices to phenomena for which an offspring resembles its parent, taking into account a baby's birth or knowledge about where a baby grows.

Do Preschoolers Know About Biological Mechanisms for Inheritance?

We would like to emphasize that the above summary does not mean that preschoolers understand uniquely biological mechanisms for inheritance. All that children recognize is the role of birth as a causal link in inheritance of physical properties, and this may only imply that they expect some properties to be fixed at birth and others to be changeable after birth. The data do not offer any biologically definitive explanation about inheritance. In a sense, children's understanding assessed by the adoption or the switched-at-birth task is almost equivalent to that assessed by Inagaki and Hatano's (1993) modifiability task, though the former task gives a richer context and is more complex. It seems plausible that Springer's (1995) naive theory of inheritance, which young children construct based on factual knowledge that a baby grows inside its mother, may work as a causal mechanism of inheritance at the very initial stage. However, that naive theory is limited in that it cannot explain the role of the father in inheritance.

We assume that true understanding of inheritance and reproduction is beyond young children's capability, because neither do they engage in activities concerning reproduction nor are they encouraged to know about them publicly in many societies. They may have an intuition that an offspring resembles its parents from an early age, because it is essential for their survival. However, this intuition may be somewhat different from the one based on purely biological understanding. Specifically, young children may in part understand inheritance from mothers to their offspring based on Springer's (1995) model, or they may recognize that some biological (physical) properties cannot be modified by their intention or efforts. However, they would regard the resemblance to father either as unexplained or as a kind of social "transmission" as a result of shared life experience until they are taught the mechanism of reproduction at school, or get information about it, say, from books. The following example illustrates that an offspring's resemblance to its father is puzzling for many children for a long time. One of the third-graders (9-year-olds) who learned the mechanism of fertilization in humans through a video at school wrote in her essay as follows: "I am often told, 'You are very like your father.' I wondered why I resemble my father, even though I was born from my mother. By watching the video and listening to the explanation, I understand where eggs and sperms are produced and how a sperm reaches an egg. A sperm inside my father met an egg in my mother's tummy, which resulted in me being here. This is why I resemble my father. . . . Today, the puzzle I have had was solved" (Murakawa, 1993).

Inheritance is probably a good example of a topic that is very important in scientific biology but that is marginal at best in young children's naive biology. Young children may intuitively grasp the distinction between the biological and the psychological-social without understanding how biological characteristics are inherited—certainly not at the level of genes and probably not even at the behavioral level (except for a baby's growing inside the mommy's tummy).

☐ Young Children's Understanding of Illness and Health

Biological Versus Psychological Understanding of Contagion and Contamination

Although illness is one of the important biological phenomena relating to the survival of individuals and the human species as a whole, it is not very easy to grasp illness as a phenomenon caused by biological variables. Describing how a particular person gets a particular disease at the biological level is not always possible even by contemporary medical science. Ordinary people sometimes feel that, except for highly contagious, acute diseases, whether one falls ill is almost a matter of good or bad luck.

In both industrialized and indigenous societies, people possess two competing sets of beliefs about illness (see Maffi, 1996; Siegal, 1997). On the one hand, they have a set of more or less "rational" beliefs representing their practically useful know-hows about how to minimize the risk of being taken ill: avoiding too much contact with patients, eating a variety of foods, etc. These beliefs potentially belong to the domain of biology. On the other hand, people have another set of "metaphysical" beliefs that often lead them to attribute illnesses to supernatural power. The latter set of beliefs belongs to the domain of psychology including morality and religion.

From Carey's (1985) position that children before around age 10 do not have an autonomous domain of biology, young children would be expected to consider illness to be caused by psychological-social variables including immanent justice. Results reported by psychologists inspired by Piaget's idea are consistent with Carey's position. For example, Kister and Patterson (1980), who did research based on the Piagetian account of Bibace and Walsh (1981), reported that 4- and 5-year-old children tended to regard not only colds but also even a toothache and a scraped knee as contagious and to interpret illness as a punishment for naughtiness.

Siegal (1988) criticized the direct, prolonged questioning used by the Piaget-inspired researchers on the basis that it could lead children to misinterpret the task requirements. To illustrate this, he examined children's understanding of contagion and contamination as causes of illness, using simpler questioning and more familiar settings. In the contagion task, children aged 4–8 were asked to evaluate others' explanations for illness. They were shown videotaped segments of puppets suffering from colds and toothaches. In each segment the puppets explained their ailments in terms of contagion or immanent justice, that is, saying that they caught the ailment when playing with a friend who had an ailment or that they caught the ailment through misbehavior, such as playing with forbidden scissors. After each segment, the children were asked whether the puppets' explanations were right or wrong. In the contamination task, the children were told stories, with demonstrations, in which a cockroach, a used comb, and a spoon (used as a control) fell accidentally to the bottom of a glass of milk just as a hypothetical child (the same age and gender as the participating children) was about to drink. The children were asked whether the hypothetical child would get sick if he or she drank some of the milk. After viewing the experimenter removing the object from the milk, they were asked the same question again.

Results indicated that the children at all ages accepted the explanation that colds are contagious and rejected the explanation that colds are caused by immanent justice. This tendency was not clearly found for the toothache, which, Siegal (1988) interpreted as due to the children's lack of personal experience with toothaches. With regard to the contamination, a majority of the preschoolers judged that drinking the contaminated milk, even after the removal of the contaminant, would make a child sick, but drinking it where a clean spoon had fallen in would not.

Springer and Ruckel (1992) also demonstrated that preschool children may reject immanent justice as a cause of illness. When given information that a boy had stolen an apple from someone before eating it (called social items), or that the boy had dropped cheese in the dirt before eating it (biological items), and asked whether he would get sick from eating it, the 4- and 5-year-olds affirmed the likelihood of illness for biological items more often than for social items. A great majority of the children who accepted the possibility that eating dirty or old food would make the boy sick justified their responses by referring to germs. When asked further why the boy would get sick, many of the children who accepted the existence of immanent justice (e.g., those who judged that eating the stolen apple would make the boy sick) revealed that they in fact had assumptions about material contamination; they usually referred to germs (e.g., the stolen food had germs on it) and sometimes alluded to a visible source of contamination (e.g., the original owner licked the food, the food had been coughed on by someone, etc.). Compared with adults, these children over-estimated the likelihood of being taken ill for the mild forms of contamination used in this study; whereas only 30% of the adults predicted that the boy would get sick, all the preschoolers did so.

To examine which of the biological and social mechanisms preschool children were predisposed to accept, Springer and Ruckel (1992) further presented to another group of 4- and 5-year-olds pairs of "mechanisms" involving a biological (material) cause and a social or intentional cause, expressed in the form of immanent justice, and required them to choose one from among these two. The biological mechanisms involved poison, contamination, and such, while the social mechanisms involved revenge, failure to carry out an intention, and so on. For example, the children were asked, "Did the boy get sick because of poison in the worm (in the apple), or because the worm got angry?"; "Did the boy get sick because germs got inside him, or because he forgot to make a sandwich?" and so on. It was found that these children preferred biological mechanisms significantly more often than social (immanent justice) mechanisms. This clearly indicates that preschoolers distinguish between biological and social causes for illness.

Kalish (1997) examined whether preschool children would distinguish between the effects of contamination on the mind and the body. The children listened to stories about a character who did or did not eat some contaminated food and who did or did not know if the food was contaminated. Take two examples from stories used there: "Sam ate an apple he found on the table. After he ate the apple, his friend told him it was from the garbage. Sam ate an apple from the garbage by mistake" (Knows/Eats); "Sally was eating some cheese. She didn't know it, but a sick kid sneezed on her cheese and got germs all over it. Sally didn't know and she ate the cheese" (Doesn't Know/Eats). The children were asked to predict whether or not the character in the story would get sick (i.e., biological responses) and whether the character would think the food was yummy or yucky (i.e., emotional responses). Results indicated that the children distinguished between bodily and mental reactions to contamination in that knowledge determines mental reactions to contamination, but physical contact determines bodily reactions.

Kalish further examined whether preschool children would consider biological reactions to contamination to be different in speed from psychological (emotional) reactions to it. Adults would consider that an emotional response is often an immediate reaction to contamination, whereas suffering from illness based on contamination is a delayed reaction. Children aged 3 and 5 years heard stories, each of which consisted of three parts: (a) the children were reminded of the connection between the action and the outcome (e.g., "People can get sick if they share food with sick friends" or "People get sad when their food gets dirty"); then (b) the antecedent activity was described (e.g., food getting dirty); and (c) the children were asked when the character would experience the outcome (e.g., be sick, be sad). For example, "Right now, just when they are sharing food, will Alice be sick? Will she be sick right now or not until later?" or "Right now, just when his apple falls in the garbage, will Joe be sad? Will he be sad right now, or not until later?" It was found that all but a few older preschoolers generally failed to recognize that illness is a delayed response to contact with contaminated food; they thought that both bodily (illness) and mental (emotion) reactions to contaminated food would occur immediately. Kalish (1997) suggested that although preschoolers do distinguish bodily from mental reactions to contamination, they have a poor understanding of the actual bodily processes involved. We will return to this issue again later.

Children's Understanding of Germs as Causal Mechanisms of Illness

Previous studies have reported that young children often refer to germs as causes of illness (e.g., Springer & Ruckel, 1992; Wilkinson, 1988). Do young children, like adults, consider germs to be the mechanisms involved in illness causation? Do children regard germs as living things that eat, grow, reproduce, die, etc., inside the body? The debates concerning whether young children have a theory of biology distinct from a theory of psychology have dealt with these issues as well.

On the one hand, a number of researchers claim that young children see germs as causal mechanisms. For example, Springer and Ruckel (1992), as described above, reported that preschoolers mention germs when they are asked why eating contaminated food makes the boy sick. Kalish (1996), who systematically examined preschool children's understanding of the role of germs in contamination and contagion, also reported that young children regard germs as an underlying mechanism for illness. Here, children 4 and 5 years of age were told stories about characters who performed dangerous actions that might be thought to lead to illness (e.g., eating an apple that has fallen in the garbage) or who performed benign actions that would not normally be seen as leading to illness (e.g., eating cheese that has fallen in water). There were two conditions for stories: In the standard condition, the children were not told explicitly about germs in the story. In the explicit condition, the children heard in the story whether or not germs were present. Each child was given six benign stories and six dangerous stories and asked to predict whether the character in the story would get sick or not. Results indicated that the preschool children were likely to predict that the character would get sick when the presence of germs was explicitly mentioned, and that the character would not get sick when there were no germs involved, irrespective of whether the action was dangerous or benign.

Like the result from Springer and Ruckel (1992), here too the children tended to overestimate the likelihood of illness, especially for the contamination items. It was also found in an additional study that children consider illness to be caused not only by germs but also as a consequence of a wide variety of behaviors, such as getting out in the cold, getting all wet and cold, eating some soap, and so on. Similar results were reported by McMenamy and Wiser (1997). Sigelman and Alfred-Liro (1995) re-vealed that even among adults, a substantial number of them gave cold weather and fatigue as potential risk factors for getting a cold when asked open-ended questions.

From the perspective that young children who have less experience rely on abstract biological principles, Keil (1992) examined whether chil-dren aged 5–10 years would distinguish biological agents such as germs and viruses from nonbiological agents such as poisons and toxins as causes of illness. In a series of studies, the children were shown various amor-phous micropic objects that were introduced sometimes as poison pellets and other times as germs or viruses. Since the children did not know what a virus was, they were given simple descriptions of its functional role, for example, "A virus is something that has to get inside people's bodies and use parts of their bodies, or it won't last long." The children were asked to attribute biological properties, such as "moving on its own," "being alive," or "changing size inside the human body," to biological agents and nonbiological agents. Keil found that children as young as 5-years-old distinguished between biological and nonbiological agents in that they attributed to the former such properties as being alive, moving, size-changing, and being contagious more often than to the latter. This indicates, Keil claims, that the children see different mechanisms for the nonbiological and biological agents.

On the other hand, Solomon and Cassimatis (1999) doubted the claim that young children see germs as part of a uniquely biological causal pro-cess. They assert that the above results on contamination simply indicate that children understand the pragmatics of utterances involving germs (e.g., "Don't eat that cheese, it has germs on it"), that is, that germs are something that makes a person sick. In a series of their experiments chil-dren 4–10 years of age (and adults) were asked to attribute both biologi-cal properties (e.g., eating, having babies, etc.) and psychological properties (e.g., thinking, feeling sad) to not only germs and poisons but also people, ants, trees, and rocks, in answer to simple attribution questions such as, "Can an X eat?" Results showed that younger children's attribution judg-ments for germs were not different from those for poisons but were dif-ferent from those for animals. These children seem to have regarded germs as neither animate entities nor psychological beings; germs, to them, some-thing like poisons: nonbiological (chemical) objects. It was also found that younger children, unlike adults, judged as equally contagious ill-nesses caused by both germs and poisons. In other words, the children under age 7 did not differentiate the effects of symptoms caused by germs from those by poisons.

Taplin, Finney, and Gelman (1998) confirmed Solomon and Cassimatis's (1999) findings in that 5–6-year-olds in their study saw germs as more like nonliving than living matter. These findings make us suspect the claim, as Solomon and Cassimatis suspected it, that preschoolers understand germs as a uniquely biological mechanism of contagion and contamination.

As Au, Romo and DeWitt (1999) pointed out, knowing that germs are things *that* can cause illness is very different from knowing *how* germs make one sick. Remember Kalish's (1997) study, in which most preschool children failed to recognize that becoming ill was a delayed effect of contact with germs, suggesting that young children may not understand the biological roles of germs in human bodies. Indeed, Au and Romo (1999) demonstrated that children from kindergarten through the sixth grade generally lack an inherent biological understanding of germs; only 6% of these participating children mentioned that the "incubation of germs" explains why it takes time for germs to multiply or reproduce inside the human body. Au and Romo (1999) concluded that it is difficult for children (and probably lay adults too) to acquire and use knowledge about uniquely biological causal mechanisms without being taught scientific biology. Reviewing recent studies, Kalish (1999) also claimed that the conservative conclusion is that young children do not consider germs to be a special biological kind of mechanism and suggests that they may have a physical (i.e., material), but not biological, conception of infection.

Alternative Views of Illness Causality

The above conclusions by Au and Romo (1999) and Kalish (1999) seem reasonable because, considering that germs were discovered as causes of illness as recently as in the 19th century, it is unlikely that young children easily understand germs as uniquely biological causal mechanisms, or even as abstract biological entities. However, it is also unlikely that children have no biological knowledge about causes of illness, because the understanding of illness causality (or prevention of illness) is important from an evolutionary perspective. Although the previous studies (e.g., Springer & Ruckel, 1992; Kalish, 1997) reported that young children are overly sensitive to contamination and contagion as causes of illness compared with adults, this result is, in a sense, adaptive from an evolutionary perspective. Rozin and his associates (Rozin, 1990; Rozin, Millman, & Nemeroff, 1986) interpreted their findings that even adults tend to be overly careful and avoid seemingly noxious or disgusting food as adaptive evolutionarily. Thus, it seems plausible that young children have a substantial understanding of illness phenomena from perspectives other than germ theory. But these other perspectives are not *non*biological. Keil,

Levin, Richman, and Gutheil (1999) claimed, based on reviews of the history of knowledge about disease and on observations of traditional cultures, that ancient people (represented by Hippocrates of Greece) and people from traditional cultures possessed numerous folk theories of medicine that are biological in nature. One of these, the imbalance theory, indicates that disease or poor health is a result of difficulty in maintaining balance in a person's humors.

Vitalistic explanations of disease, which will be described in detail in Chapter 5, seem to be a variant of this imbalance theory and continue to exist as an interpretation for susceptibility (or resistance) to illness. Whether or not a person who is exposed to germs and other direct causes of illness gets sick often depends on his or her susceptibility to illness. Since the imbalance theory has not been developed very much in Western medicine, naive biology researchers who are strongly influenced by germ theory tend to ignore the role of bodily or psychological factors contributing to susceptibility to illness in determining whether a person gets sick (e.g., Kalish, 1998).

Understanding of Susceptibility to Illness

Human bodily conditions are often affected by daily activities. For example, the less balanced a person's diet, or the less regular their daily routines, the more susceptible they will be to illness. Inagaki (1997) examined whether young children recognize that bodily and social/psychological aspects of daily activities contribute to susceptibility to illness, and if so, to what degree.

In her study, kindergarten children aged 4–6 were presented with pairs of drawings of two characters, and asked which of the two was more likely to catch cold with the question, "When these two boys, X and Y, play with a child who has a cold and is coughing a lot, who is more likely to catch cold, or are both equally likely?" The two characters were allegedly different in terms of the bodily/biological or social/psychological factors in their daily activities. The bodily/biological factors included imbalanced diet, insufficient food, insufficient fresh air, and irregular daily routines. The social/psychological factors involved telling a lie and misbehaving.

A majority of the children in each age group (with the exception of the 4-year-olds' responses to the fresh air item) chose the character who engaged in biologically bad activities as being more likely to catch cold. More specifically, the character who ate only a little every day, who ate few vegetables, who stayed up late watching TV, or who did not air out the room by opening windows was more likely to catch cold than the character who ate a lot, who ate a lot of vegetables, who went to bed early, or who aired out the room.

Although the 4- and 5-year-olds could give few reasons for their choices, about half of the 6-year-olds justified their responses for the items involving eating little and eating few vegetables. For example, one 6-year-old child said, "(A boy who has) little nutriment does not have energy, so germs easily enter his body." Another 6-year-old child similarly justified his choice, saying, "When this boy X eats a lot, his throat is full of nutriment. This boy Y eats little, so his throat is not full of nutriment, and so the coughing can pass through his throat." Very few children could give reasonable explanations why the boy who didn't air out the room was more likely to catch cold. However, one of the 6-year-olds justified his choice, saying, "Old air makes this boy weaker, and when he plays with a child who has a cold, he will be even weaker and catch cold." Another said, "We cannot take in nutriment without airing out the room." Since the choice patterns of the 4- and 5-year-olds were very similar to those of the 6-year-olds, it is strongly suggested that the 4- and 5-year-olds, like the 6-year-olds, considered that the lack of energy or vital power due to, for example, eating little, would make the protagonist susceptible to illness.

These children believed that social/psychological factors would also influence susceptibility to illness. A majority of not only 4- and 5-year-olds but also 6-year-olds answered that the boy who often hit and pinched a friend or who told a lie was more likely to catch cold than the boy who was a good friend or who never lied. None of the 4- and 5-year-olds gave any reasons for their choices. Only 30% of the 6-year-olds justified their responses by referring to something like immanent justice. There were very few who chose both alternatives or rejected both alternatives, that is, responses indicating that telling a lie or misbehaving was irrelevant to catching cold. An additional experiment revealed that the response that social/psychological factors would increase one's susceptibility to illness was not due to the experimental artifact of children's failure to make "equally likely" responses, because there was no difference in choice between two alternatives that had no specified or implied behavioral difference (e.g., the boy named Taro and the boy named Jiro). In short, most children recognized that physical aspects of daily activities would affect one's susceptibility to illness, but at the same time they believed that social/psychological factors also contributed.

Do children believe that the contributions of psychological factors are the same as those of biological factors to becoming ill? To examine this issue, Inagaki (1997) devised a task combining three physical factors and three social/psychological ones so that these combinations were in con-

flict, and investigated whether children would differentially apply biological factors (e.g., nutrimental) to illness and moral factors to social
phenomena (i.e., being invited to a party).

Children 4 ($M = 4;1$) and 5 ($M = 5;1$) years of age were presented with
a pair of drawings (see Figure 4.1) and asked to choose between a child X
who engaged in biologically good activities (e.g., eats a lot at meals) but
behaved badly (e.g., often hits and misbehaves) and a child Y who engaged in biologically bad activities (e.g., eats only a little) but behaved
well (e.g., is a good friend) in terms of who was more likely to catch cold.
For example, "When playing with a child who has a cold and is coughing
a lot, who is more likely to catch cold (or are both equally likely), a boy
who often hits and pinches his friend on the back but eats a lot at meals
every day, or a boy who is a good friend but eats only a little?" After
finishing the six biological items, they were also asked, as social items,
which of the two would be more likely to be invited to a birthday party
by a classmate.

The children's responses were classified into three categories for both
the biological (i.e., catching cold) items and the social (i.e., being invited
to a party) items: (a) biological-cue dominant response: making a choice
by relying more on the biological condition than the moral one; (b) social-cue dominant response: making a choice relying less on the biological condition than the moral one; (c) equivalent response: choosing both
or neither alternatives.

Figure 4.2 shows the percentages of the three types of responses for the
biological (cold) items and the social/psychological (party) items. The 5-
year-olds made biological-cue dominant responses more often than social-cue dominant responses for the cold items. They justified their choices
by referring to biological factors for the cold questions and to moral factors for the party questions. In contrast, the 4-year-olds showed almost as
many social-cue dominant responses as biological-cue dominant responses
for the cold questions, although they made social-cue dominant responses
much more often for the party questions. This suggests that the 4-year-
olds' reasoning for biological phenomena was more influenced by psychological considerations than was the 5-year-olds' biological reasoning.
However, not only the 5-year-olds but also the 4-year-olds clearly differentiated biological phenomena from social/psychological phenomena in
causality.

In sum, we can conclude from the above studies that young children
recognize that physical aspects of daily activities affect susceptibility to
illness. At the same time, they believe that morally bad behaviors make
some additional contribution to illness susceptibility, though they recognize biological factors as more important for illness.

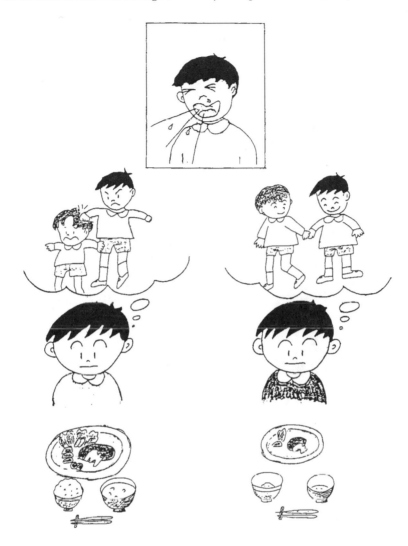

FIGURE 4.1. An example stimulus card used in the study on susceptibility to illness.

Are Mind and Body Completely Separable or Interdependent?

In the debates concerning whether young children have acquired an autonomous domain of biology, the complete differentiation of biological from psychological phenomena seems to be used as an important crite-

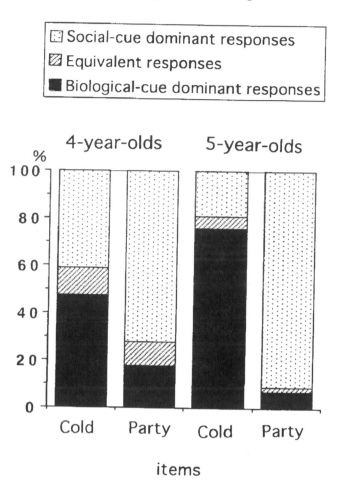

FIGURE 4.2. Percentage of responses for the biological (cold) and social/psychological (party) items.

rion. However, we wonder if mind and body are completely separable. Rather, psychological phenomena and bodily phenomena may be interdependent to some degree in human beings, as Eastern medicine claims. These interdependent relationships may be reflected in beliefs held by older children and adults, unless it is denied in science education. Research heavily influenced by the idea of mind/body dichotomy might fail to capture children's understanding of mind/body relationships. As we will describe in detail in the next chapter, vitalistic biology assumes that the mind and the body are always interdependent to some degree, say, in illness causality; not only psychosomatic but also contagious illnesses are partly psychological in nature. To highlight this point, we now describe non-Western adults' responses to susceptibility to illness.

When (Japanese) college students were asked the same questions as those that the preschool children were asked in the experiment described above, some of them chose the same alternative that young children did, although a majority answered that telling a lie or misbehaving was irrelevant to catching cold. More specifically, 3 (out of 20) students responded that the character who often told a lie was more likely to catch cold than the character who did not, and another 4, though they first made "equally likely" responses, added notes that it was probable that the character telling a lie was more likely to catch cold; for the misbehavior item such students were 2 and 2, respectively. These students provided explanations, such as, "Psychologically anxious states, such as telling a lie, may influence health," or "The child who is not fine in both mind and body may be more likely to catch cold."

Inagaki and Hatano (1999a) asked (Japanese) college students what factors they thought contributed to getting dysentery, a cold, or a duodenal ulcer, and found that a substantial proportion of the students (30–45%) believed that psychological factors (e.g., depression), as well as physical factors (e.g., imbalanced diet), would make some contribution even to infectious diseases such as dysentery or a cold.

These data on adults seem to suggest that there exists a public belief, at least in Japan, that the mind and the body are not totally independent but interdependent to some degree. If so, the children's responses admitting some contribution of social/psychological factors to illness may reflect in part such a public belief. We could claim that, even if preschool children fail to understand germs as biological mechanisms, they may have good understanding of illness causality in terms of susceptibility to illness.

☐ Summary

From the findings described in this chapter, we can tentatively conclude that preschool children can distinguish biological from psychological phenomena, applying different causal devices to them, at least in understanding internal bodily processes, inheritance of biological properties in parentage, and illness and health. By age 4, children seem to possess some sort of biological framework for living things.

At the same time, however, the review in this chapter clearly indicates limitations of young children's biological knowledge. For internal bodily processes, they know nothing about physiological or biochemical mechanisms. They understand almost nothing about how human genes given by both parents jointly determine the biological layout of children, nor about how germs and viruses cause illness after a period of incubation. They clearly reject explanations in terms of intentional causality for these biological phenomena, but their own explanations are far from scientific. Young children have some understanding of causality for biological phenomena, but what they possess seems to be an abstract biological framework rather than pieces of detailed biological knowledge about mechanisms. We will discuss this issue in the next chapter.

Vitalistic Causality

The experimental evidence presented so far enables us to conclude that young children have a coherently organized body of knowledge applicable to biological phenomena. This body of knowledge can be called a naive theory, as a causal explanatory framework is included in it. Children as young as 4 years of age can make consistent and plausible predictions for a set of biological phenomena, and slightly older children can offer justifications for their predictions referring to certain causal devices. How to characterize these causal devices is critical for determining the nature of a theory and has been an issue of debate.

In this chapter we discuss the causal explanatory framework that young children use for understanding biological phenomena, including especially human bodily processes. More specifically, we claim that the causality that young children apply to biological phenomena is nonintentional in nature, and also different from mechanical causality. We call this causality vitalistic; it is in between intentional and mechanical causality. First, we propose vitalistic causality as a necessary notion for understanding the nature of young children's naive biology. We then present some experimental data on vitalism in three sections. Finally, we elaborate the notion of vitalism and discuss relationships between vitalism and other competing and compensatory notions proposed in this research area.

☐ **Nonmechanical, Nonintentional Causality**

As mentioned in Chapter 1, Carey (1985) claimed that children under age 10 base their explanations of biological phenomena on an intentional causality because they are ignorant of the physiological mechanisms involved. In fact, previous studies using open-ended interviews have indicated that young children cannot give physiological or mechanism-based explanations when asked to explain biological phenomena (e.g., bodily processes mediating input–output relations). For example, Gellert (1962) reported that, when asked in open-ended interviews to describe the function of internal bodily organs, most children under the age of 11 or 12 years could not refer to the physiological mechanisms involved in the workings of those organs, such as blood circulation for the heart, or transformation of food for the stomach. Contento (1981) also pointed out that, though young children have some knowledge about input–output relations, they do not understand the mediating processes. Carey (1985) seemed to regard these findings as evidence supporting her claim that children under age 10 did not possess a theory of biology differentiated from psychology.

Based on the above findings, however, it is premature for us to conclude that young children know almost nothing about internal processes mediating input–output relations and thus have to rely on intentional causality for bodily functions. There are two reasons. First, these studies only investigated children's explicit understanding (Greeno, 1983) as assessed by their answers in open-ended interviews. Many recent studies indicate that young children have significant receptive or implicit understanding of what the world is like much earlier than they reveal explicit understanding of it (R. Gelman, 1979). More specifically, they may be able to choose the most appropriate explanation from among presented alternatives or to make consistent and differentiated predictions for a set of situations, some of which they have not experienced (probably using a particular causal device).

Inagaki and Hatano (1990) found that children aged 5–8 have some implicit understanding of bodily functions, such as blood circulation. Although most of them could not explain functions of the heart verbally when they were asked, "What does the heart do inside the body?", about half of 7- and 8-year-olds could predict, in response to a question such as "What will happen if the blood does not come to your hands/brain?" that the halt of blood circulation, an input they had never encountered, would cause as an output damage to the hands (or the brain). Some of them justified their responses, saying as follows: "If blood does not come to the hands, they will die, because the blood does not carry energies to them," or "We cannot move our hands, because energies fade away if blood does not come there." We assume that these children could verbalize what others understood implicitly.

Second, although Carey (1985) assumed only mechanical causality as opposed to intentional causality, we may assume an intermediate form of causality. We propose that young children who are reluctant to rely on intentional causality for bodily phenomena but cannot yet use mechanical causality would often rely on this intermediate form of causality, which might be called *vitalistic causality*.

Intentional causality means that a person's intention causes the target phenomenon, whereas mechanical causality means that physiological mechanisms cause the target phenomenon. For instance, a specific bodily system enables a person, irrespective of his or her intention, to exchange substances with its environment or to carry them to and from bodily parts. In contrast, vitalistic causality indicates that the target phenomenon is caused by the activity of an internal organ, which has, like a human, "agency" (i.e., a tendency to initiate and sustain behaviors). The activity is often described as a transmission or exchange of the "vital force," which can be conceptualized as unspecified substance, energy, or information. Vitalistic causality is clearly different from person-intentional causality in the sense that the organ's activities inducing the phenomenon are independent of the intention of the person who possesses the organ.

We will elaborate young children's versions of vitalistic causality later in this chapter. Here we indicate that, although young children do not know physiological and biochemical mechanisms of bodily processes, they may have developed something similar to the forms of indigenous biology that our ancestors possessed when they did not enjoy the benefit of modern science. Vitalistic causality played a key role therein.

☐ Young Children's Explanations for Biological Phenomena

In Inagaki and Hatano (1990) described above, the children aged 5–8 gave explanations referring to something like vital force as a mediator when asked novel questions about bodily processes, but only 20% of them did so. Hence, we attempted to obtain further evidence on vitalism. Inagaki (2000) conducted an experiment, devising questions that would help children offer their explanations for eating and its related bodily phenomena that interest young children. A pilot study by us and studies by others (e.g., Estes, Wellman, & Woolley, 1989) suggested that first asking simple judgment questions and then asking for justifications could help children produce their explanations, rather than asking explanation questions alone. Thus, children in this study were first asked judgment questions and then asked for relevant explanations.

Twenty 5-year-olds (M = 5;7) and twenty 6-year-olds (M = 6;7) from a kindergarten were given six questions, one of which concerned eating itself; three of which dealt with relationships between eating and susceptibility to illness, recovery from the injury, and living long, and the remaining two concerned other important bodily phenomena: breathing and the workings of the heart. What follows are questions used in this study. In each question except for (1b) and (5b), the children were asked to justify their prediction. When the children used the word "nutriment" in their justifications or explanations, they were asked to specify it by questions, such as "What is the nutriment?" or "What does the nutriment do?"

(1a) What will happen if you eat nothing every day? (1b) What do you take in from food inside your body?

(2) (Using a line drawing as aid) Haruko always eats a little, while Akiko eats a lot. When a cold is going around, who is more likely to catch cold, Haruko, Akiko, or are they both equally likely?

(3) Natsuko got her leg injured in a traffic accident. Will she recover quickly from her injury if she eats a lot?

(4) Taro's grandpa is aged and now 80-years-old. Will he live long, say to 100- or 200-years-old, if he eats a lot?

(5a) You breathe, don't you? What will happen to you if you stop breathing for several hours? (If the child gave no answer) Would you still be alive? (5b) What do you take in through breathing?

(6) What happens to your heart after you run? (If the child gave no answer) Is your heartbeat quicker, or the same as usual? (If the child answers, "Quicker") The quicker heartbeat tells that the heart works harder. Why do you think your heart works harder after you have run?

Each child's responses were tape-recorded and then transcribed. Vitalistic explanations were identified when the child's justifications included words referring to "power," "energy," "vigor," and unspecified substances (e.g., "something good for the body"), even if they did not explicitly refer to the activities of internal organs, for example, "Power comes out from eating food." When the child used the word "nutriment" and specified it in follow-up inquiries as referring to energy-related words (e.g., "something like the source for becoming vigorous") or words implying unspecified substance, his or her justifications were judged as vitalistic. When he or she could not specify the nutriment or explained it using "scientific" words such as "vitamin" or "calcium," his or her justifications were not judged as vitalistic. The child's justifications for the illness question were judged as vitalistic when they implied the existence of something that would help a person resist being taken ill, even if they did not contain energy-related words; for example, "Eating a lot makes a film at the throat and so the cold can't enter (the body)."

It was found that a substantial proportion of the children (30% of the 5-year-olds and 50% of the 6-year-olds) used the word "nutriment" in their justifications for the eating and other related questions. Thus, we first describe how they specified it for the follow-up inquiries. Whereas only two of the 5-year-olds could explain nutriment as "something for becoming vigorous," most of the 6-year-olds could specify it, and half of them paraphrased it with their own words, such as, "something making the body not dull," "something giving (us) power," "something like the source for becoming vigorous," and so on.

For the question, "What will happen if you eat nothing every day?", almost all the 5- and 6-year-olds predicted that a person would die. Although most of the 5-year-olds could not justify their responses, about half of the 6-year-olds gave explanations referring to the lack of energy or nutriment, such as "If we don't eat food, we lose energy and die." One of the boys, aged 6 years, 10 months, explained, "(A person) will die, because (his) tummy suffers from the decrease of nutriment."

As shown in Table 5.1, a majority of the 5- and 6-year-olds predicted that the child who ate little would be more susceptible to illness. The 5-year-olds gave six vitalistic explanations, and the 6-year-olds gave 11 vitalistic explanations. Typical examples are as follows: "The child eating little is easy to catch cold. 'Cause power doesn't come out from eating little," "Vigor is lost from eating little," "The child eating little doesn't have something to get rid of the cold."

About half of the 5-year-olds and 70% of the 6-year-olds considered that eating a lot would lead to quick recovery from the injury. The 6-year-olds gave six vitalistic explanations. One of the children explained, "If the nutriment in the tummy travels to her leg, (she) may recover." Another 6-year-old girl said, "Nutriment is sent to different parts. The nutriment comes out from the tummy."

Table 5.1. Frequencies of predictions for eating-related items

| | Who is more susceptible to catching cold? | | | Does the girl who eats a lot recover from the injury? | | Does the grandpa who eats a lot live long? | |
	Eats little	Same	Eats a lot	Yes	No	Yes	No
5 years	15	2	3	11	9	13	7
6 years	18	1	1	13	6	17	3

Note. N = 20 for each age group, but one 6-year-old child was not given the recovery question.

A majority (85%) of the 6-year-olds predicted that eating a lot would make the grandpa live long, which they justified as, for example, "Power comes out from eating food" or "(If the grandpa) has the nutriment, (he) may live long."

For the question on respiration, almost all the children predicted that stopping breathing would lead to death, but they could seldom justify their responses. However, for the question, "What do we take in through breathing?", three of the fourteen 6-year-olds who answered "air" specified the working of air inside the body with their own words (i.e., "something needed for living," "it makes us comfortable inside the body," and "it makes us healthy.") The other 6-year-olds could not specify the working of air. A majority (14) of of the 5-year-olds could not understand what this intake question meant. In short, the children seemed to have difficulty explaining respiration, though a few 6-year-olds considered something like "vital force" (unspecified substance) to be taken in through breathing.

For the question about the working of the heart after running, 40% of the 5-year-olds gave either a "don't know" answer or incorrect predictions, whereas most 6-year-olds correctly predicted the quicker heartbeat. However, these 6-year-olds could not justify their responses. One of the 6-year-olds gave the following vitalistic explanation refering to an intention, but an intention of the relevant organ *not* the person as a whole being: "Because running uses energy, (a heart) must work hard." Another gave a personifying explanation: "(When this person is running, a heart thinks) *'He is now running, so I have to work hard'* and the heart beats fast." (This 6-year-old boy changed his tone of voice at the italicized part.)

Table 5.2 shows frequencies of vitalistic and other explanations offered by the children who gave expected predictions for each question. The frequencies of vitalistic explanations observed across questions indicate that the 6-year-old children tended to offer vitalistic explanations to eating and other related phenomena, especially resistance to illness, and to a lesser extent, respiration. For the six questions used here, 14 (70%) of the 6-year-olds gave vitalistic explanations at least once, and 2.2 times on average (range, 1–3). Only 6 (30%) of the 5-year-olds gave a vitalistic explanation, predominantly for the resistance-to-illness question. There were only two organ-intentional, or personifying, explanations among the 6-year-olds. Contrary to Carey's (1985) claim, there were no intentional explanations (i.e., those referring to a *person's* intention) at all for these six questions among either age group. With regard to "physical" explanations that Au and Romo (1999) claimed children would be likely to rely on, we observed only two cases, in a form such as, "Broken bones would stick to each other by boiled rice."

In sum, a substantial portion of the 6-year-olds gave vitalistic explana-

Table 5.2. Frequencies of vitalistic and other explanations offered by children who gave expected predictions for each question

Ages Predictions	Eating		Resistance to illness		Recovery from injury		Living long		Breathing		Working of heartbeat	
	5 yrs [18]	6 yrs [19]	5 yrs [15]	6 yrs [18]	5 yrs [11]	6 yrs [13]	5 yrs [13]	6 yrs [17]	5 yrs [17]	6 yrs [19]	5 yrs [11]	6 yrs [19]
Types of explanations												
Vitalistic explanation	0	7	6	11	1	5	0	4	0	3	0	1
Other explanation	0	3	3	0	2	4	2	3	0	4	0	6
Unexplained	18	9	6	7	8	4	11	10	17	12	11	12

Note. "Vitalistic" explanations are justifications referring to energy-related words; "Unexplained" includes not only "don't know" answers but also tautological, incomprehensible, or phenomenological answers; "Other" explanations include comprehensible justifications except for vitalistic ones. Figures in the square brackets show the number of children who made correct predictions.

tions for eating and other related bodily phenomena; they tended to consider that energy or power taken in through eating would help people resist to being taken ill, recover quickly even from the injury, and live long. Although many of the results supporting children's preference for vitalistic causality, as will be reviewed in the next section, came from studies in which children were asked to choose one from a number of explanations presented (Au & Romo, 1999), there are several biological phenomena, such as eating, growing, and being taken ill, for which vitalistic explanations are readily generated by children themselves. In contrast, these children had difficulty with explaining respiration or the workings of the heart. It is suggested that early naive biology seems to be established around the notion of eating.

☐ Young Children Choose Vitalistic Explanations Most Often

Evidence of Young Children's Preference for Vitalistic Explanations

To examine whether young children would prefer vitalistic explanations for a wide variety of bodily phenomena to other types of explanations presented, Inagaki and Hatano (1993, Experiment 2) ran a forced choice experiment. It was predicted that even if young children could not apply mechanical causality, and if they could not generate vitalistic causal explanations by themselves for the "why" questions, they would prefer vitalistic explanations to intentional ones for bodily processes when asked to choose one from among several possibilities.

Twenty 6-year-olds from a kindergarten (along with twenty 8-year-olds and twenty college students) were asked six questions concerning biological phenomena; they were first asked for an explanation, and then required to choose one from among three possible explanations for each. The six phenomena were eating food, blood circulation, respiration, feeling pain, urinating, and having a baby.

The three explanations represented intentional, vitalistic and mechanical causality, respectively. Let us give two example questions with three alternative explanations.

On eating food: Why do we eat food every day?

1. Because we want to eat tasty food. [intentional]
2. Because our tummy takes in vital power from the food. [vitalistic]
3. Because we take the food into our body after its form is changed in the stomach and bowels. [mechanical]

On respiration: Why do we take in air?

1. Because we want to feel good. [intentional]
2. Because our chest takes in vital power from the air. [vitalistic]
3. Because the lungs take in oxygen and change it into useless carbon dioxide. [mechanical]

As can be seen, the intentional explanation ascribed the phenomenon to the intention of a person, and thus took the form of a sentence with "we" as the subject. The vitalistic explanation explained the phenomenon by referring to the agency of a relevant bodily organ, more specifically, active and/or effortful engagement in activity, which is the giving and/or taking of unspecified material, energy, or information (vital force). The subject of the sentence was a specific bodily organ, or bodily part when the name of the organ was not familiar to young children. The mechanical explanation was the children's version of the scientific (physiological) causation, and thus each sentence, the subject of which was usually a bodily organ, was constructed by consulting an illustrated reference book on the human body written for primary school children (Koizumi, Miyahara, & Muramatu, 1990). Although boundaries among them are not always clear, these three types of explanations were constructed based on distinct operational criteria.

The children were required to answer the first question in an open-ended form, that is, without being presented with the three options, and then given the same question in a multiple-choice form. They were presented with the three causal explanations as three fictitious children's answers and asked, "Whose explanation sounds best of the three?" This procedure was repeated for the remaining five questions.

How did the 6-year-olds respond to these questions? First, we examined what kind of causal explanations the children generated on their own for the biological phenomena before being presented with the three causal explanations to choose from. The children's explanations were transcribed and coded as being nonbiological, biological, or "no explanation." Nonbiological explanations were coded when there was no reference to bodily processes, such as, "Because we eat food every day to grow bigger" or "Because the blood comes out from the hurt part, I feel pain." Biological explanations were identified when there was a reference to bodily processes, such as referring to functions of nutrition or oxygen to sustain life (e.g., "Because the food has nutrition and the nutrition becomes material for moving our body") or functions of a specific internal organ (e.g., "Because the heart works [to circulate the blood]"). This category included explanations based on vitalistic causality as well as mechanical ones. No answer or an "I don't know" answer was classified as no explanation. Uncodable answers were also included in "no explanation."

More than half of the children's spontaneous explanations were nonbiological, and there was a substantial percentage of "I don't know" answers or no answer. These findings suggest that young children have difficulty generating biological causal explanations explicitly when asked to (without preceding judgment or prediction question), and thus they are likely to rely on nonbiological explanations (including psychological or intentional ones), which are easy to give. Such results are consistent with the previous studies concerning children's explicit understanding of bodily functions reviewed by Carey (1985).

None of these 6-year-olds offered an explanation that met the above definition for vitalistic causality (even for the eating question). However, when asked to choose a causal explanation from among the three, the children chose vitalistic explanations as the most plausible most often; they chose them 54% of the time. They showed much smaller percentages for the mechanical and intentional explanations (21% and 25%, respectively). It should be noted that the 6-year-olds preferred nonintentional (vitalistic plus mechanical) causalities 75% of the time.

Data analyses of individual responses showed that out of the twenty 6-year-olds, only one chose four or more intentional explanations of the six items (we call them intentional responders), whereas nine chose four or more vitalistic explanations (vitalistic responders). None of the 6-year-olds selected four or more mechanical explanations. These marked differences in individual response patterns were partly due to the different consistencies across items.

In order to investigate whether those who chose a certain type of explanation for an item tended to choose the same type for another, 15 tables of 3 × 3 distributions were constructed for all pairs of the six items. These were then collapsed into 2 × 2 tables, in three different ways, for statistical analyses because of the small number of respondents. When dichotomized into Vitalistic versus Nonvitalistic, 10 of the 15 cross-tables showed a positive association, and 4 of them were significant or just short of significance at .10 by the Fisher exact probability test. For the Intentional versus Nonintentional dichotomy, 10 were positive and 2 fell just short of significance. For Mechanical versus Nonmechanical, out of the 10 pairs, both items of which had some mechanical responses, 4 were positive but none was significant. Thus we can conclude that, though they may not have been aware of it, the 6-year-olds applied vitalistic and intentional causality, but not mechanical causality, more or less consistently. The 6-year-olds may have chosen mechanical explanations primarily based on local cues, for example, the use of difficult words. These results suggest that there exists a period in which children may rely on vitalistic causality as the basis for acceptable explanations before coming to rely on mechanical causality.

Some readers may wonder if it is possible for 6-year-olds to compare three answer alternatives and choose the most plausible one reliably, though the above findings suggest that the children did not respond randomly. To exclude the possibility that the children made random choices due to lack of memory, they were asked to recall the option they had chosen on every other item, and, if they did not recall any identifiable phrase, they were required to recognize the option, by giving an answer of "Yes" or "No" for the series of three questions, "Was the answer you had chosen such and such?" (recall and recognition questions). The option the child had chosen was always presented last of the three.

Since the 6-year-olds did not reproduce an identifiable phrase of the alternative that they had chosen 95% of the time, they were given the recognition questions. Of the total of 60 responses to the recall and recognition questions, the 6-year-olds gave 9 "inconsistent" responses (in that their responses were different from their original choices), and 3 "forget" responses (in that they could not answer at all due to forgetting). In other words, 80% of the 6-year-olds' responses were consistent, suggesting that the children made few random choices due to lack of memory.

Although the above experimental findings strongly suggest that young children prefer vitalistic causal explanations for bodily functions, the forced choice procedure has a few methodological problems. First, comparing multiple explanations and choosing the most plausible one imposes a heavy processing load, especially when three explanations are presented as in the above experiment. The procedure adopted there may not be used for still younger children. Second, young children's preference for vitalistic causal explanations does not necessarily mean that they are committed to vitalistic causality. It is not easy to provide different types of causal explanations comparable in all the aspects that might influence children's plausibility judgments. Explanations belonging to the same type may differ considerably in plausibility, for example, depending upon which organ or bodily part is referred to. In the above experiment we chose the most persuasive explanation of each type that we could think of. Then we examined whether the phrases and expressions sounded natural and appealing to children through several pilot testings. Yet, as Carey (1995) pointed out, it is very difficult to make different explanation types comparable with respect to the informativeness of the explanation and familiarity with the information it contains.

Thus, instead of relying just on the forced choice procedure, it is very important to consider children's ideas expressed in their own words as well, as was done by Inagaki (2000). The findings reviewed so far strongly suggest that vitalistic explanations may spontaneously be applied to several bodily phenomena only, including eating, growing, and being taken ill. Young children often fail to offer any biological explanations for other bodily phenomena, such as urination, though they seem to prefer vitalistic explanations when presented with them.

Vitalistic Explanation by Children in the West

There have been at least three studies that investigated whether children living in "Western" countries also like vitalistic explanations. In those studies, different types of explanations were evaluated by children. First, Olguin (1995) examined whether 4-year-olds as well as 6- and 8-year-olds would judge intentional, vitalistic, and mechanical explanations as either *good* or *silly* when presented one explanation at a time. She found that whereas the 4-year-olds showed no consistent pattern of preferences among the explanations, both the 6- and 8-year-olds showed a marked preference for both vitalistic and mechanical explanations. She argued that those mechanical explanations presented by developmental psychologists and chosen by children could be characterized as reflecting a vitalist biology in which more details of the bodily processes were supplied.

Miller and Bartsch (1997) examined whether Inagaki and Hatano's (1993) finding that 6-year-olds were vitalists would be confirmed among American participants. By presenting pairs of vitalistic versus intentional and vitalistic versus mechanical explanations, they found that American children also preferred vitalistic causal explanations to intentional ones for biological phenomena. The children liked vitalistic and mechanical explanations almost equally. At the same time, they found that, contrary to Inagaki and Hatano (1993), college students were also vitalists; that is, these students chose vitalistic explanations for biological phenomena as often as the 6- and the 8-year-olds did. (We will discuss this result later, in Chapter 7.)

Finally, Morris, Taplin, and Gelman (2000) systematically investigated Australian children's use of vitalistic causality. They not only translated and refined the original questions but also tried to differentiate two components of vitalism, that is, the processing of energy and organ intentionality. They clearly demonstrated that Australian 5-year-olds share with young Japanese children the reliance on vitalism in naive biological reasoning. They also found that the former component of vitalism (i.e., the processing of energy) is much more important than the latter (i.e., organ intentionality), but the latter plays some additional role. More specifically, the children preferred the energy transfer explanations over the organ-intentional explanations, when forced to choose. However, when they were asked to endorse energy transfer explanations and the organ-intentional explanations independently, they were positive to both, though they again showed a stronger preference for the former. The authors suggested that vitalistic causality serves universally as a causal placeholder in naive biology until more precise mechanisms are known, but the two components of vitalistic causality proposed by Inagaki and Hatano seem to be separable, at least in the West.

☐ Vitalistic Causality Is Applied Only for Biological Phenomena

Do young children rely on vitalistic causality only for biological phenomena? As alluded to above, we assume that vitalistic causality is applied only to organisms. Moreover, we assume that young children seldom attribute social/psychological behavior, which is optional and not needed for survival, to the agency of a bodily organ or part. We present some experimental data concerning these issues in turn.

Causal Devices Differ Between Living Things and Artifacts

How is vitalistic causality different from the mechanical causality that refers to physiological mechanisms for biological phenomena? A possible difference is that, whereas mechanical causality is applied to both living and nonliving entities without distinction, vitalistic causality is only applied to organisms. Another possibility is that, among young children at least, vitalistic causality is applied to living things, whereas mechanical causality is applied to nonliving entities. We believe that the second is more likely, because, as many investigators (e.g., Atran, 1998; S. Gelman & Hirschfeld, 1999; Keil, 1995) have asserted, human minds interpret behaviors of living entities differently from those of nonliving things, and it is appealing to rely on different modes of explanation for living and nonliving things (including artifacts).

However, an interesting alternative idea has been offered by Au and her associates (Au & Romo, 1996, 1999; Au, Romo, & DeWitt, 1999). According to them, young children's conception may not lack mechanical causality for biological phenomena. The authors believe that the term "mechanical causality" needs to be unpacked. If the term refers to physiological causality, then few people will dispute the claim that children generally do not understand mechanical causality very well. However, if this term is used to refer to causality in the domain of mechanics (e.g., how things and stuff interact and move around in space and the gravitational field), then there is plenty of evidence that children starting from age 5 or so favor mechanical causality in explaining biological phenomena as described below.

Au and Romo (1996, 1999) asked over 300 children from ages 5–14 to explain in their own words a range of biological phenomena: food spoilage, incubation of an infectious disease, inheritance of hair color, and HIV/AIDS transmission. Their results suggest that mechanical causality is the mechanism of choice for children in their attempts to make sense of various biological phenomena. Their review of the medical anthropological literature also uncovered, they claim, reports that adults (who do not have the benefit of science education) commonly use mechanical causality to explain illness and treatment (Au & Romo, 1999). Moreover, their finding on explanations generated by these children is consistent with research in which children were asked to choose among several explanations. In explaining how, for instance, a baby flower may get its blue color, Springer and Keil (1991) found that 6- and 7-year-olds favored mechanical causality over other kinds of causal mechanisms (e.g., genetic, intentional).

Au and her associates (Au & Romo, 1999; Au et al., 1999) seem critical of the notion of vitalistic causality that young children use for explaining biological phenomena. From their perspective, most investigators on naive biology have focused almost exclusively on the strength of vitalistic causality and the weakness of psychological causality as a candidate for what children use in thinking about causality in the biological world. "Mechanical causality" has not been considered as a viable candidate. They also point out that virtually all of the results supporting children's preference for vitalistic causality come (so far) from studies in which children were offered several explanations (e.g., psychological, vitalistic, physiological). As Carey (1995) indicated, it is difficult to make different explanation types comparable. So, when children chose one type of explanation over another, it was not always clear why they did so. That is why it is so important, as we did in the preceding section, to get children to explain biological phenomena in their own words, rather than putting words in children's mouths.

We trust the findings by Au and her associates (Au & Romo, 1999; Au et al., 1999), but we believe that the findings are not incompatible with our emphasis on vitalistic causality as the core of young children's naive biology. First, we assume that different biological phenomena may induce different types of explanations including mechanical ones: even for bodily processes some phenomena (e.g., the role of teeth in the digestive process) may be explained mechanically. Moreover, as their studies showed, inheritance in terms of genes and spoilage and infection in terms of germs or viruses are beyond young children's imagination. And, as they claim, even ordinary adults, who have not received intensive science education, may not understand causal mechanisms involved in these phenomena. However, all of these points do not exclude the possibility of young children's intuitive understanding of such bodily processes as digestion, growth, and resistance to illness in terms of vitalistic causality.

Second, although their coding is precise and reasonable, some of what they refer to as "explicit movement of unspecified entities (e.g., sickness, it)" reasons may be what we call vitalistic ones; even when children use the term "germs," they may not grasp that germs are micro-organisms (Solomon & Cassimatis, 1999), but treat germs as a kind of bad vital power. For example, when the child answered, "He got sick because it went into his neck" or "The cough went all through his body and made him sick" (Au & Romo, 1999, p. 375), it would be fitting if the words "it" or "the cough" were replaced by bad vital force.

Third, their studies focused on older children than our children, who had been taught about science if not directly about biology. Answers of the participating children in their studies may have been based on "synthetic models" (Vosniadou & Brewer, 1992). Unlike models spontaneously constructed by children, synthetic models may often be physical or mechanical, because they are acquired in the context of science education, which emphasizes mechanical causality and/or mechanisms.

Au (personal communication, May 27, 1999) indicates that in her pilot data, she noticed that children sometimes talked about the soul leaving the body in answering a question such as, "Why would a grasshopper die?" (She set up the task by saying, "See this grasshopper. Can it live forever?" If a child said, "No," then she asked, "Why would a grasshopper die?" Some children would say because its soul went to heaven.) She believes that if "soul" in this context is regarded as being in the same category as vital energy, this might be a way to elicit more talk from children about vitalism. It is interesting to note that some Asian Americans who know much about the historical roots of vitalism tend to regard vitalistic and related causality as close to spiritual or magical (see also Nguyen & Rosengren, 2000). We assume, as far as young children's vitalistic causality is concerned, that it is induced from an serious attempt to make sense of biological phenomena; if it is applied to magical or metaphysical reasoning, it is done later in development, and after vitalistic explanations for biological phenomena are partially replaced by mechanical explanations.

Living Things Versus Artifacts in Recovery

As will be discussed later in this chapter (pp. 118–119), it may be misleading to emphasize a commonality between young children's version of vitalism and historical ideas too much; in the case of the former, it is possible that children make conceptual distinctions even when they use the same terms, such as energy, for both living things and complex artifacts. This is illustrated by our recent study, which will be described in the following paragraphs.

Inagaki (2001b) examined whether young children would distinguish living things from complex artifacts in terms of differences in recovery processes from trouble. In vitalistic causality, the internal organs are supposed to work to take in vital force from the external physical world through food or air and exchange it, so that all parts of the body can function well. However, taking in some form of energy from the outside for activity (or function) can be observed among some complex artifacts, such as automobiles or various electrical appliances. If children focused on this aspect alone, they would not distinguish between living things and complex artifacts in terms of their internal processes. In contrast, if vitalistic causality is specific to biology, children would differentiate the operations of living things from those of such complex artifacts.

In Experiment 1, Inagaki (2001b) investigated whether young children would recognize that the speed of recovery processes differ between living things and complex artifacts. Forty-four kindergartners aged 5 and 6 were asked whether the target object would recover from trouble (e.g., illness/breakdown) immediately after some treatment was given. If the child answered "No" to this question, he or she was further asked whether it would recover from the trouble in a couple of days. The target objects were complex artifacts (i.e., a vacuum cleaner, an electric fan, and a TV set), humans, nonhuman animals, and plants. Three items each were asked about recovery from different types of troubles. Example questions are as follows:

> *For an artifact:* Wind doesn't come out of an electric fan, even though the switch is on. The switch is out of order. Will wind come from the fan immediately—say, before counting 1, 2, 3—after a repairman has replaced the switch with a new one? [If the child answers "No"] Will wind come out in a couple of days?
>
> *For a person:* Taro falls down and hurts his leg. Will he recover from the hurt immediately—say, before counting 1, 2, 3—after he puts medicine on it?
>
> *For a nonhuman animal:* A rabbit hurts its paws because it walks on pieces of broken glass. Will the rabbit recover from its hurt immediately—say, before counting 1, 2, 3—after you put medicine on the hurt place?
>
> *For a plant:* A rose is not healthy. It has a lot of worm-eaten leaves. Will the rose become healthy immediately—say, before counting 1, 2, 3—after you remove hairy caterpillars from the leaves?

As shown in Figure 5.1, both the 5- and 6-year-olds recognized that the recovery process inside the "body" proceeded slowly among humans,

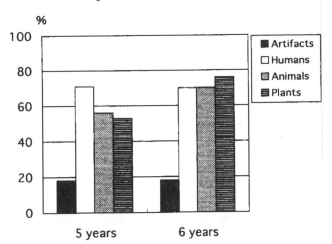

FIGURE 5.1. Percentages of slow-recovery responses for each entity.

nonhuman animals, and plants, whereas it was quick for complex artifacts. When frequencies of "slow recovery responses" (i.e., an "unable"
response for the "immediate" question and an "able" response for the
"couple-of-days" question) were compared across the four types of target
objects for each item, the differences were highly significant.

In Experiment 2, another group of twenty 5- and 6-year-old children
were required to give justifications following their predictions for another
set of recovery questions. Example questions are as follows:

For an artifact: Can a car continue to run for hours when a small amount
of gas is in it? [If a child answers "No"] How can you get the car to
continue to run for hours? Why do you think so? [If a child answers
"Yes"] Why do you think so?

For a person: Can Taro run fast when he has eaten nothing from day
until night except for a small breakfast? How can he run fast? Why
do you think so?

For a squirrel: Can a squirrel move around quickly when it is given a
small amount of food? How can the squirrel move quickly?

For a tulip: Can a tulip continue to bloom when it is watered only a
little? How can the tulip continue to bloom?

Results are as follows: Almost all the children predicted that both the
living things and the artifact (car) could not continue to function under
the shortage of food/water/gasoline and answered that in order to recover from the malfunction, the living things need to take in food/water,
and the car, gasoline. However, the children's justifications were very dif-

ferent between the living things and the artifact. For human and nonhumans animals, 65–75% of the children gave explanations relying on the emergence of power or vigor from taking food, such as "Power/vigor comes out (from eating food)." One boy aged 5 years, 9 months explained why eating much led to the recovery from trouble as follows: "Food has much nutriment. [What is nutriment?] Nutriment makes us full of power." For a car, in contrast, the children did not give such emergence-of-power explanations, except for one case where the car was personified such as, "The car needs nutriment like humans. Gasoline is treated as food by the car." Two other children gave explanations referring to some energy without using any words implying "emergence of energy": "The car can move by the working of electricity" and "The car can move by the energy of gasoline." Half of the children could not give any explanations. This suggests that children recognize that living things can use energy internally stored through digesting food, whereas complex artifacts function directly by externally provided energy.

When asked about a possibility of spontaneous recovery from trouble (e.g., fatigue), almost all the children correctly predicted that living things including plants, would spontaneously recover from trouble, but artifacts (e.g., a vacuum cleaner) could not. In addition, a great majority of the children explained that artifacts' recovery from trouble required the exchange of a part or the whole with a new one (e.g., exchange an old battery with a new one), whereas they did not give such explanations for living things, including plants, at all. Instead, one third of the children gave explanations referring to emergence of energy/vigor for humans and nonhuman animals, such as "Power (or vigor) recovers during rest" or "Vigor comes out from eating food or drinking water during rest," whereas such explanations were seldom used for the artifacts.

In sum, the 5- and 6-year-olds recognized that living things and complex artifacts were different in terms of their internal processes, more specifically, the speed and spontaneity of recovery from ill-functioning states, even if these are apparently similar in that they function by taking in some energy from the outside. These children seem to apply vitalistic or "emergence-of-power" explanations to living things alone.

Vitalistic Causality Is Not Applied to Social/Psychological Behaviors

To support our claim that young children have implicit (receptive) causal understanding of bodily processes and thus they apply vitalistic causality selectively for biological phenomena, two experiments were conducted

(Inagaki & Hatano, 1993, Experiments 3 and 3a). We expected that for psychological phenomena, children would choose an explanation based on the acting person's volition or desire, but not an explanation based on the bodily part's agency. In contrast, for biological phenomena, they would prefer an explanation based on the bodily part's (or organ's) agency to that based on the person's intention.

In the first experiment (Inagaki & Hatano, 1993, Experiment 3), twenty 6-year-olds (as well as twenty 8-year-olds and twenty adults) participated. They were individually asked 11 questions, 5 of which concerned biological phenomena, and the remaining 6, psychological phenomena. Each question had two alternative explanations, one of which represented a vitalistic causal explanation (i.e., the phenomenon was attributed to a bodily part's agency), and the other showed intentional causality (i.e., the phenomenon was attributed to a person's intention or desire). The organ was assigned an intentional state for those items dealing with psychological phenomena, so that the resultant vitalistic explanations were, as can be seen below, comparable to their intentional explanation counterparts in this regard (whether this manipulation was problematic was examined in the other experiment). Questions about biological phenomena and their two alternative explanations were the same as those used in Inagaki and Hatano's (1993) Experiment 2, described earlier (p. 102), excluding the item on reproduction. In addition, the explanations representing mechanical causality were excluded and subjects of the sentences describing intentional explanations were changed from "we" to "Taro" (the character's name), and thus some of the phrasings were slightly modified.

Two of the questions about psychological phenomena are as follows:

1. When a pretty girl entered the room, Taro went over to her. Why did he do so? (a) Because Taro wanted to become a friend of hers [intentional explanation]. (b) Because Taro's legs wanted to go over to her [vitalistic explanation].
2. When Taro is served a cake at snacktime, he eats it at once. Why does he do so? (a) Taro wants to eat the cake [intentional]. (b) Taro's mouth wants to eat the cake [vitalistic].

An example of the questions about biological phenomena is as follows:

1. Taro eats meal three times a day. Why does he do so? (a) Because Taro wants to eat tasty food [intentional explanation]. (b) Becuase Taro's tummy takes in vital power from the food [vitalistic explanation].

The questions on biological phenomena and those on psychological ones were mixed together, randomly ordered, and given in a fixed order for all the children. Half of the children were presented the alternative of a person's intention (i.e., intentional causality) first, and the other half, the alternative of a body part's agency and intention (vitalistic causality) first.

Results indicated that the children preferred intentional to vitalistic causal explanations in the case of psychological phenomena. In other words, these children seldom chose vitalistic explanations (i.e., those ascribing the phenomena to the relevant bodily parts) in the case of psychological phenomena. For biological phenomena, however, they preferred the vitalistic to the intentional explanations, like their agemates in the previous experiment. Intentional explanations were chosen a little more often for biological phenomena than in the previous experiment, probably because the children were required to make choices without being presented with "scientific" (mechanical) explanations.

In order to examine individual patterns, we selected those children who (a) made more intentional than vitalistic choices for both psychological and biological phenomena, that is, chose intentional explanations four or more times for the six psychological items and three or more times for the five biological items (I–I pattern); (b) made more intentional than vitalistic choices for psychological phenomena but more vitalistic than intentional choices for biological ones (I–V pattern); (c) made more vitalistic than intentional choices for psychological ones but more intentional than vitalistic choices for biological ones (V–I pattern); and (d) made more vitalistic than intentional choices for both types of phenomena (V–V pattern). If children tended to prefer vitalistic explanations to intentional ones due to the novelty of vitalistic explanations, V–V patterns would have occurred most often. However, this pattern was seldom found. (I–I patterns were not found, either.) Instead, a great majority of the children showed an I–V pattern, that is, choosing intentional explanations for psychological phenomena and vitalistic ones for biological phenomena. The differences in frequencies between the I–V pattern and the V–I pattern were significant by a binomial test.

These results showed that vitalistic explanations were not always attractive to the children. Moreover, the results suggest that the children applied intentional and vitalistic causalities differentially to biological and psychological phenomena. However, many competing interpretations are possible for differential application, because the pairs of explanations (intentional vs. vitalistic) used in this experiment were not comparable between psychological and biological items. It could be suggested, for example, that the vitalistic explanations for psychological phenomena were often rejected because (a) while most vitalistic explanations for biological phenomena described what the body parts do, those for psychological ones described what the body parts "want"; (b) the body parts involved in the explanations for psychological phenomena were external organs, whereas those for biological phenomena were internal organs; and (c) vitalistic explanations for psychological phenomena sounded highly unnatural because of the mismatch between the body part and its allocated activity. In order to exclude these alternative interpretations, therefore, we conducted an additional experiment (Inagaki & Hatano, 1993, Experiment 3a).

In this additional experiment, we examined more systematically whether 6-year-olds would apply causal explanations differentially for psychological and biological phenomena with modified vitalistic explanations for the former. Here vitalistic explanations were designed to be as comparable as possible between psychological and biological phenomena. Major modifications for psychological items were as follows: (a) all the vitalistic explanations, like those for biological items, described what the body parts do, not what the body parts want; (b) the body parts involved in the explanations were sometimes internal, though other times external; and (c) the vitalistic explanations mentioned the target organ's main activity so that they would sound natural.

Participants were forty 6-year-olds from the same kindergarten as the children in the eariler experiment. They were randomly assigned to either the psychological condition or the biological condition. The children in the psychological condition were given five questions about psychological phenomena, and those in the biological condition were given five questions on biological phenomena always in random order for each child.

The five questions concerning biological phenomena and their two alternative explanations were the same as those used in the earlier experiment. The five questions about psychological phenomena were modified as mentioned above, with four of the five phenomena and three intentional causal explanations for them retained. The modified example questions are as follows:

1. When a pretty girl entered the room, Taro went over to her. Why did he do so? (a) Because Taro wanted to become a friend of hers [intentional explanation]. (b) Because Taro's heart urged him to go near her [vitalistic explanation].
2. When Taro is served a cake at snack time, he eats it at once. Why does he do so? (a) Taro likes cake very much [intentional]. (b) Taro's tummy is waiting for the cake to come [vitalistic].

It was found that the 6-year-olds preferred intentional to vitalistic explanations in the case of psychological phenomena, but for biological phenomena they opted for vitalistic rather than intentional explanations. All 20 children in the psychological condition made three or more intentional choices for the five items (we call them intentional responders) for psychological phenomena, whereas 13 children in the biological condition made three or more vitalistic choices (vitalistic responders), and only 7 children were intentional responders for biological phenomena. The difference in frequencies of intentional versus vitalistic responders between the psychological and the biological conditions was significant. This strongly suggests that children applied intentional and vitalistic causalities differentially for biological and psychological phenomena.

☐ Elaborating the Notion of Vitalism

As reviewed above, recent studies, using sophisticated assessments, have revealed that young children's biological reasoning about human bodily processes is arguably based on vitalistic causality, and that, in applying vitalism, they not only distinguish living entities from nonliving ones but also recognize that the functions of the mind and body are distinguishable from each other. Children almost never interpret or explain bodily phenomena or processes in terms of intentional causality. Let us discuss in more detail the nature of the vitalistic causality that young children possess, and that even adults may use as a fallback strategy. We first focus on the functions and dynamics of vital power, the causal device in vitalistic explanations. Then we discuss commonalities and differences between young children's versions and a few historical ideas of vitalistic causality.

Functions and Dynamics of Vital Power

How Vital Power Operates

How do young children assume that vital power operates for living things? Our studies have shown that their reasoning includes at least two very important functions of vital power for an organism's survival. First, young children assume that all other living things, like humans, take in vital power from food and/or water to maintain their vigor. Humans, children believe, can live for 100 years or even longer if they take in a sufficient amount of vital power (Inagaki, 2000). In contrast, if they are not provided with vital power for an extended period of time, children believe humans, and other living things, will die. This sort of reasoning is applied not only to organisms as a whole (Inagaki & Hatano, 1996, Experiments 2 and 3) but also to their parts (e.g., hands no longer supplied with blood in Inagaki & Hatano's, 1990, study). Second, young children assume that living things can grow in size by using a surplus of vital power. Therefore, if animals are fed little or plants are watered little, they will not become bigger (Inagaki & Hatano, 1996, Experiments 2 and 3).

Vital power also seems to function in children's understanding of illness causality. Young children assume that, as discussed in Chapter 4, vital power prevents living things from getting ill. In other words, a body full of vital power is unlikely to fall ill, even when its owner comes in contact with a person suffering from the illness. Moreover, a person who has a great deal of vital power can recover rapidly even when he or she becomes ill or injured (Inagaki, 2000). Such responses by young children may reflect the Japanese culture: Many Japanese people, both adults and children, believe in folk preventive medicine that advocates the importance of one's susceptibility or resistance to illness and that offers various specific recommendations for improving resistance. This folk medicine refers, at least implicitly, to ingesting and sustaining vital power.

How Vital Power Is Ingested

Vital power has to be taken in from the outside, and the obvious sources for ingesting it are food and water. In more elaborated forms of vitalism, some additional sources like air (taken through breathing) and other people's vital power (taken through sympathy) are also included, but in young children's biology, food and water are far more salient than other sources, as the study by Inagaki (2000) revealed.

Do some kinds of food involve more vital power than others? Because the notion of vital power corresponds in part to that of nutrition, those foods that are considered to be better for one's health (e.g., vegetables) are believed to contain more vital power than those that are not particularly healthy (cakes or candies) or are too luxurious (marbled beef). This point was also discussed in Chapter 4 in relation to susceptibility to illness. Young children are often asked by their parents to eat certain healthy foods (e.g., carrots or spinach) for both biological and moral reasons. These parental attempts may be based on the notion of vital power; although parents cannot always explain which components in the food that they recommend are good for health, they believe that their recommendation is correct because the food seems to possess a lot of vital power.

Because food is the most salient source for vital power, young children's vitalistic biology is established around eating or nutrition. Although preserving the species or one's own genes is probably the supreme goal of living entities, and even young children have an intuition that offspring resemble their parents (Solomon et al., 1996; Springer, 1992), we do not believe that they readily understand the biological nature of inheritance, as we discussed in Chapter 4.

How Vital Power Is Sustained or Lost

An organism has to spend more vital power to be active and lively than just to survive. Thus it has to take in food and water more or less regularly. However, whether vital power is conserved or lost quickly depends on internal bodily conditions. For example, many lay adults in Japan assume that people who are old and/or physically weak tend to promptly lose vital power taken from food, so they need to be especially careful to choose food that has a lot of vital power.

As we have seen, young children (adults as well) believe that vital power can be lost quickly if a person experiences stress, either physical or psychological. The former (i.e., physical stress) includes extremely cold or hot weather, unseasonable weather, continuous engagement in hard exercise, and lack of sleep. The latter (i.e., psychological stress) includes difficulties in human relations, financial problems, and anticipated or actual failure in work or study. This implies that some psychological variables influence people's susceptibility to illnesses, even when the illnesses are caused by specific entities like germs and viruses (Inagaki, 1997). Recall the college students' responses to illness causality described in Chapter 4: A substantial portion of the students considered that psychological factors would make some contributions even to infectious diseases such as dysentery or a cold (Inagaki & Hatano, 1999a). In other words, they believed that not only psychosomatic but also contagious illnesses are partly psychological in nature. In other words, vitalistic biology insists that the mind and body are always interdependent to some degree in illness causality.

Vitalistic Causality in Young Children's Minds and in History

In this book we have focused on vitalistic causality in young children's naive biology. Needless to say, the use of this term is based on the assumption that their biological reasoning is similar to that of our ancestors, who did not enjoy the benefit of modern science and who thus did not know much about physiological and biochemical mechanisms of bodily processes. In fact, an elaborate mode of vitalistic explanation can be found in the Japanese endogenous science before the Meiji restoration (and the beginning of Japan's rapid modernization), which had evolved with medicine and agriculture as its core (Hatano & Inagaki, 1987). This endogenous science, which had been strongly influenced by Chinese ideas of vitalism, was not mechanical and atomistic, but vitalistic and holistic. Bodily functions were interpreted in terms of vitalism, often as exchanges of unspecified "vital power" (*ki* in Japanese). For example, "The internal organ X works hard to produce such and such effects, sending vital power."

Needless to say, there was a parallel line of thought in the West. Western vitalism, which survived until the late 19th century in one form or another, indicated that "there are processes in living organisms which do not obey the laws of physics and chemistry" (Mayr, 1982, p. 52).

It is very interesting to note similarities in biological reasoning between young children growing up in contemporary society and some scholars in the history of biological thought, but we should be very careful not to confuse these different forms of vitalistic causality. The prominent scholars referred to in the history of science or medicine had to explain everything, and their explanations had to be persuasive. In contrast, young children may leave many phenomena not explained at all or be satisfied with identifying causal devices only, though they are also theory builders in the sense that they seek understanding of phenomena in terms of explanatory schemas (Keil & Wilson, 2000). As a result, various aspects or components of "vitalism" are found only among scholars in history. For example, a number of Japanese scholars in the Edo period assumed that good and bad vital forces operate. However, young children may tend to reason in terms of the increase and decrease of a single vital power, which is considered positive. Unlike the scholars, young children may not extend vitalistic explanations very far beyond the basic triangular relationships of eating/watering—being active and lively—growing.

Another example is the organ agency in vitalistic causality. Because vital power is an unspecified substance or energy, there must be a machinery which handles it. Thus a number of Eastern scholars, seeking a detailed and persuasive explanation, attributed some agency to bodily organs, so that they can "spontaneously" engage in life-sustaining activities such as taking in or distributing vital power. They relied on a general mechanism of personification: Since they had no means for observing the opaque inside or details of the organs, they tried to understand them in a global fashion, by assuming them to be human-like (but noncommunicative) agents (see Ohmori, 1985), though organs were seldom given such mental states as "want" or "be aware of" (Hatano & Inagaki, 1994b). In contrast, young children may use "vital power" just as a causal device, without specifying its operation.

☐ Vitalism and Other Related Notions

We compare vitalistic causality with other forms of biological causality as well as relate these notions each other. First, we consider teleology and essentialism as potentially competing and compensatory causal shemas with vitalistic causality. Then we consider life-theorizing as a mediating notion between these three causalities.

Vitalism and Teleology

Teleology is the view that any enduring property of an entity has some functions for it or for other related entities. When teleology is applied to biological properties of living things, it offers plausible intrinsic explanations such as "Plants are green because it helps there be more plants" (Keil, 1992).

Are young children's teleological-functional explanations biological? Keil (1992, 1994) believed that, although the teleological-functional explanation is applicable to both living things and artifacts, it can characterize young children's biological reasoning because (a) it is more readily used for living things than for artifacts during early childhood, and (b) the children believe that a living object or its part functions for itself, whereas an artifact functions for others. However, based on a couple of recent experiments, Kelemen (1999b) argued against Keil. Her data (Kelemen, 1999a, 1999c) generally show that whereas adults use teleology selectively for living things and artifacts, young children apply it almost indiscriminately, even to nonliving natural kinds (e.g., "a mountain is there to climb"). She asserts that young children's teleological explanation for body parts of animals cannot be taken as evidence for their possession of naive biology, because their teleology is promiscuous. Her observation is potentially very important, but has to be checked by using different methodologies, because the participants in her experiments may have been led to the play mode by being asked a series of peculiar questions with queer drawings.

A possible way to coordinate Keil's and Kelemen's assertions is to divide teleology into two subtypes, intrinsic (parts or properties are for the sake of their owners) and extrinsic (parts, properties, or even the whole entities are for the sake of others, most often for humans). Teleology, intrinsic and extrinsic combined, may be promiscuous during early years, as Kelemen asserts, because young children live in a highly protective environment and thus most artifacts and nonliving natural kinds there are useful for them. However, intrinsic teleology seems to be limited to living things, even in her data. A version of intrinsic teleology, which might be called life teleology, applied to bodily organs (i.e., they exist to sustain life), is closely related to vitalism. It provides vitalistic explanations with some foundation; for example, because the heart exists to sustain the life of its owner, it works hard to send vital power through the blood to all bodily parts so that they can function well. However, how early children understand the distinction between life teleology and other forms of teleology is yet to be demonstrated.

Assuming that older preschoolers and kindergartners can offer life-teleological explanations for biological properties, what is the relationship between the vitalistic explanation for biological phenomena and the teleological-functional explanation for biological properties? Both are certainly in-between the intentional and the mechanical; both seem to afford valid perspectives on the biological world. One interpretation is that they are essentially the same idea with different emphases—the teleological concerns more the why or the cause, whereas the vitalistic is concerned more with the how or the process. Another interpretation is that, because the vitalistic explanation refers to activity of the responsible organ or bodily part (implicitly for sustaining life), it is closer to mechanical causality than is the teleological one, which refers only to the necessity. Still another interpretation, which we now prefer, is that whereas vitalism is basically for biological processes (bodily processes among others), intrinsic teleology is primarily for parts or properties. In other words, even young children may choose one or the other depending upon the type of question. In any case, it will be intriguing to examine these characterizations of young children's "biological" explanations in concrete experimental studies.

Vitalism and Psychological Essentialism

Psychological essentialism means a folk belief that there is an underlying essence for a set of observed facts, and as long as this essence is preserved, the entity maintains its identity, and also as long as the essence is shared, entities that seem perceptually very different actually constitute a single kind (S. Gelman, 1999). Essentialism's important aspect is that it serves as a causal mechanism, the essence causally gives rise to those observable properties, for example, characteristic features of animals and plants (S. Gelman & Hirschfeld, 1999). It is clear that everyday biological taxonomy presupposes essentialism (Atran, 1998). In this biological essentialism (more accurately, psychological essentialism about living things), essence is a generative structure or genetic layout, which produces observable characteristics of animals and plants. It must be especially important in children's distinction between animals (or plants) and artifacts, as suggested by experiments by Keil (1989) and by S. Gelman and Wellman (1991), because only living things are assumed to possess their essence as genetic layout.

What is the relationship between essentialism and vitalism? A very strong version of vitalist theory may assume that vital power is the essence and that specific bodily functions are embodiments of the vital power. However, it is doubtful that young children commit themselves to such a position. Our interpretation is that, although early essentialism is also promiscuous (e.g., young children may say, "A variety of cakes have common essence as long as they are called a cake," see Carey 1995), biological essentialism is another, potentially competing biological mechanism to vitalism, and children adopt this or that depending upon situations and contexts. We speculate that when the target's overt behaviors or characteristics are to be connected to its internal structures, explanations in terms of essentialism tend to be induced; in contrast, vitalistic causality is, like teleology, basically for explaining in a global fashion how those behaviors or characteristics function.

Vitalism and Life Theorization

Vital power is for maintaining life. Vitalistic causality is applied only to living things, and thus there must be some close relationships between vitalism and the understanding of life. This prediction has been supported by a series of studies by Jaakkola, Slaughter, and others. Jaakkola (1997; cited in Slaughter, Jaakkola, & Carey, 1999) discovered that between the ages of 4 and 6, children begin to spontaneously refer to life as the purpose of bodily functioning. She asked children, for example, what their heart or blood was for, as well as where the heart or blood was located. About a third of the 4-year-olds and all but one of the 6-year-olds were life-theorizers; that is, they referred to life, staying alive, or not-dying as the goal of bodily functioning.

Slaughter et al. (1999) indicated that there were differences in a wide range of biological understanding between life-theorizers and non-life-theorizers. Non-life-theorizers asserted that not everyone would die, dead people needed food, water, and air, and dead people could be brought back to life. The authors interpreted these assertions as showing that non-life-theorizers lack a biological concept of death, in other words, they do not locate death in the life cycle of living things. Non-life-theorizers conceptualized death as extended sleep or living in different locations (e.g., under the ground). In contrast, the life-theorizers seemed to understand death in biological terms, that is, as the cessation of bodily functions and the end state of the irreversible life cycle. That the conception of death between these two groups of children was so different suggested to Slaughter et al. (1999) that there must be conceptual change before vitalistic biology emerges.

Slaughter and Lyons (in press) further investigated the developmental shift to a vitalistic biological theory by conducting a training experiment. They found that the short-term teaching of the biological concept of life in relation to functions of body parts (e.g., "We need clean blood to keep us alive") helped some non-life-theorizer children construct a vitalistic theory, and that such children then revealed increased biological understanding of the human body and of death. They claim, based on these results, that children's naive biology is a vitalistic theory, with the abstract concept of life as its central causal device.

We would like to offer a slightly different interpretation of these findings, however. In these studies, whether a child is a life-theorizer is determined operationally by his or her spontaneous reference to life in the structured interview on body. Thus being a life-theorizer means having not only the concept of life (serving to make the living-nonlivinng distinction) but also *awareness* of the bodily structures and processes as directed to sustain life. In this sence, being a life theorization implies commitment to a central essentialist-teleological-vitalistic belief that the organs of the human body consitute essence, function to support life, and incorporate and exchange vital power. Life theorization is not a causal mechanism, but may help children differentiate general causal mechanisms such as teleology and essentialism into those that operate for maintaining life and those for other goals, and draw attention to when life sustaining mechanisms can be applied. Needless to say, life-theorization is completely compatible with mechanical causality as well, because bodily mechanisms are primarily for maintaining and enhancing the life of the body owner.

It will be intriguing to study whether the enhanced awareness of life increases children's interest in bodily processes or mechanisms through which life is sustained, either global ones like the exchange of vital power or specific physiological ones. It will also be interesting to investigate whether this awareness of life can connect teleology, essentialism, and vitalism together to form an extended basis for naive biology.

Let us summarize the discussion in this section. Because both teleology and essentialism are domain-general mechanisms, they must be specialized to living things or the domain of biology before they serve as a biological causal mechanism. In particular, their specialization for biological reasoning may be based on life-theorization or awareness of the bodily structures as life-sustaining devices. In contrast, vitalism is applied only to living things (including humans) from the start, and thus requires as its prerequisite the recognition of living things alone. Thus, though "biologized" teleology and essentialism (life teleology and biological essentialism) also play an important role in naive and intuitive biology later, vitalistic causality is, we may claim, the first causal schema of naive biology. Even young preschoolers may have the basic vitalistic intuition that they can obtain something from food/water that energizes their body. We will examine this issue in the next chapter.

Construction of Naive Biology Under Cognitive and Sociocultural Constraints

In Chapter 1 we indicate that our "working criterion" of the acquisition of a naive theory is whether children can make coherent, reasonable, and differentiated predictions (probably based on proper causal devices in the domain), although we admit that a stronger criterion is that children can offer appropriate causal explanations for relevant phenomena. When we examine the research findings so far reviewed in light of the above working criterion, we can tentatively conclude that children as young as 5 years of age have acquired naive biology. Two justifications can be offered for this conclusion.

First, many of the studies described in Chapter 4 reported that 4- and 5-year-old children can differentiate human biological properties and phenomena from psychological ones. With regard to bodily functions, for example, children aged 4 and 5 recognize that internal bodily processes cannot be controlled by their desires or intentions (Inagaki & Hatano, 1993; Inagaki, 1997). They also differentiate hereditary, other bodily, and mental characteristics of humans in terms of their modifiability (Inagaki & Hatano, 1993; Miller & Bartsch, 1997). As to the understanding of inheritance, preschool children apply multiple causal devices differentially for an offspring's resemblance to its parent, depending on whether target properties are biological or social-psychological (Hirschfeld, 1995; Springer, 1992, 1996). At the least, 5-year-old children consider illness to be caused (Siegal, 1988), or susceptability to illness to be influenced (Inagaki, 1997), primarily by biological factors, not by moral factors. In addition, these children consistently distinguish between bodily and mental reactions to contamination (Kalish, 1997).

Young children's biological understanding may go beyond humans, although this has been less systematically studied. By about 5 years of age, children can distinguish living entities, including animals and plants, from nonliving things, and begin to recognize more or less consciously commonalities between animals and plants, two sorts of things that are perceptually very different (Inagaki & Hatano, 1996; see Chapter 2).

Second, as we have seen in Chapters 4 and 5, children as young as 5 prefer biological explanations when choosing from among a number of alternative causal explanations for biological phenomena. The children aged 5 (Morris et al., 2000) opted for a vitalistic explanation as the most reasonable one, when choosing from intentional, vitalistic, and mechanical causal explanations for internal bodily processes. The children aged 4 and 5 preferred biological (material) causes to social or intentional causes when asked to choose one of two presented causes for illness (Springer & Ruckel, 1992). Some studies even showed that young children can offer biological explanations themselves. For instance, in the Shult and Wellman (1997) study, 4-year-olds gave causal explanations differentially for human movements and actions that require biological, psychological, or physical reasoning; these children offered biological explanations (referring to bodily states and processes) for biologically caused human actions, whereas they gave psychological explanations for psychologically caused movements and physical explanations for human physical movements. In Inagaki's (2000) study, 30% of the 5-year-olds and 70% of the 6-year-olds gave vitalistic explanations at least once for the six questions concerning eating and other related bodily phenomena, and the 5-year-olds' prediction patterns for these phenomena were very similar to those of the 6-year-olds. Jaakkola (1997; cited in Slaughter et al., 1999) reported that 33% of 4-year-olds and 92% of 6-year-olds were judged as "life-theorizers" (who spontaneously referred to the life-sustaining character of bodily processes) when given a series of structured interviews about the human body. If we interpolate from these figures, we can infer that a majority of 5-year-olds would be "life-theorizers."

From the above findings, we conclude that naive biology is surely established within 5 years after birth, and children may have acquired it to some degree a few years earlier.

☐ How Children Acquire Naive Biology

This early acquisition of naive biology is not surprising from the perspective of human evolution, because it has been essential for our species to have some knowledge about animals and plants as potential food (Wellman & Gelman, 1992) and also knowledge about our bodily functions and health to protect ourselves (Inagaki & Hatano, 1993). However, how is it possible, in reality, for children to acquire naive biology so early in life and apparently without systematic teaching?

Our answer to this question can be summarized as follows: Children (a) construct biological knowledge based on their experiences, (b) using a powerful learning mechanism of selective analogy with knowledge about humans as the source, (c) helped by innate constraints, and (d) helped by sociocultural constraints. Like most investigators of conceptual development, we adopt a constructivist stance as in (a), in other words, an assumption that children as well as adults are not only active learners but also theory builders (Carey, 1985; Wellman, 1990).

We have emphasized (b) above throughout the preceding chapters. Although personification is a domain-general learning procedure, it is particularly effective in the development of naive biology. Young children know pretty much about humans (including their own bodily reactions), whereas they are necessarily ignorant of most other entities. This enables them to rely readily on the person analogy in order to understand the life processes of other animals and plants. Children develop an abstract schema of living things through analogically comprehending behaviors of other animals and plants as directed to sustain their life, relying on their knowledge about human bodily processes. As indicated in the preceding chapters, this schema is vitalistic and consists primarily of the triangular relationship apparent in humans between taking food and water, being active and vigorous, and growth. We assume that this schema is extended to nonhuman animals and plants. However, personification concerns the extension of the vitalistic principle to nonhuman living things. Personificiation cannot explain how the vitalistic principle is acquired by young children for human beings, nor can it indicate how children accumulate promptly knowledge about animals and plants and come to regard them as entities similar to humans. Here we need the notion of constraints, both cognitive and sociocultural (as in (c) and (d)). It is true that in everyday life, children have some opportunities to observe animals and plants, and also their own bodily processes, but it is constraints, we assume, that enhance children's construction of core pieces of biological knowledge.

In the sections below we first consider what innate constraints are involved and how they work in the construction of naive biology, and we then review those studies that suggest the operation of innate constraints for naive biology. We assume that humans are endowed with domain-specific constraints for acquiring naive biology and that it is thus acquired early and without difficulty in cultures all over the world. Certain innate constraints should serve to control and direct attention or coding, while others restrict the range of the hypothesis space to be explored. Next, we discuss the role played by sociocultural constraints in the construction of naive biology. We present some examples of cross-cultural and within-cultural variations in naive biology that seem due to the operation of constraining sociocultural variables and contexts. We claim that culture influences children's biological understanding by enabling them to obtain access to a variety of animals and plants. Moreover, young children may be encultured in their modes of biological thought through discourse (e.g., parental talk) about aspects of the world. Sociocultural constraints also serve to enhance or inhibit children's particular attention and interpretation interactively.

☐ What Innate Constraints Are Involved and How They Work

Early and universal acquisition of naive biology is assisted, we believe, by a group of innate constraints that direct developing individuals' attention and coding, and another group of constraints that restrict the range of children's interpretations of observed connections between phenomena. Our discussion here, unlike that in the previous chapters, is not based on firm empirical evidence but is speculative, for two reasons. First, there have been very few studies on precursors of naive biology during infancy, where the operation of innate constraints should be most clearly observed. This may be due just to the short history of naive biological research, or due to the later emergence of naive biology than naive physics or naive psychology. Second, even in young childhood, there have been almost no experimental studies focusing on constraints in the acquisition of naive biological concepts or conceptions comparable to those experiments on constraints in word learning (Markman, 1992; Tomasello, 1992).

However, we can predict, based on an evolutionary perspective, which particular aspects of the environment young children tend to pay attention to and which particular interpretations of the observations they tend to entertain, so that they can readily conceptualize the biological world. In the next section we will examine, using the best available findings, whether these predictions are feasible.

Generally speaking, virtually every investigator assumes some innate constraints to operate in conceptual development and learning. However, the exact nature of the constraints is yet to be specified and has been the target of heated debates, because this is exactly the test case for different accounts of the mind by nativists versus emergentists (a modern version of empiricists). Nativists (e.g., Spelke, 1994) assume that there are innate constraints in the form of pieces of knowledge or representational contents that constitute the core of the knowledge system in each domain. In contrast, emergentists (e.g., Elman et al., 1996; Munakata, McClelland, Johnson, & Siegler, 1997) claim that any domain-specific knowledge, which serves as prior constraints on further learning, is a product of the interactions between such domain-general features as architectural and temporal constraints coupled with patterns of inputs or learning tasks in a particular domain. In other words, emergentists admit certain innate domain-general constraints but do not believe that there can be innate representations.

Our position is intermediate between these two poles. As indicated above, we believe that innate constraints operating in core domains should be tendencies and biases serving to control and direct attention or coding, and restrict the range of hypothesis space to be explored. Because a unique set of constraints in each core domain draws attention to relevant aspects of the target objects or phenomena, even young children can distinguish those that should be interpreted within the domain from those that should not. Also, because another set of constraints enables humans to search for an interpretation or hypothesis highly selectively, they can find, in most cases, a reasonable one promptly, and thus can accumulate pieces of knowledge constituting a core domain of thought.

Our fundamental assumption is that innate constraints for the acquisition of naive theories including biology are tendencies and biases that humans have acquired for their survival in the evolution of millions of years. More specifically, the tendencies and biases, now serving for the acquisition of naive biology, allowed our ancestors to survive (e.g., avoid dangers from other animals, find food). To put it differently, those who had such dispositions tended to survive and leave their offspring better off.

This basic assumption implies, first, that humans tend to pay attention to those aspects of animals that distinguish them from nonanimals, because, in the "wild environment" (Toda, 2000), animals are more problematic for humans than are nonanimals (they may attack humans, steal stored foods, etc.). The aspect that differentiate animals from nonanimals include such features as whether entities spontaneously move or do not move by themselves. As will be shown in detail later, there is evidence indicating that even infants have the animate/inanimate distinction, paying attention to these aspects. Humans also have tendencies to attend to some features, states, and behaviors of animals. They classify animals based on the size and ferocity (Atran, 1998); they pay attention to whether animals are active, hungry, and so on; and animals' eating and excretion are often eye-catching—all these seem adaptive for humans in the "wild environment." For example, because a potential predator will not attack humans when it is eating another thing or it is fully fed, paying attention to such behaviors or states must have been useful.

Human attention may be directed to plants as well in order to find food. It would be important for hunters-gathers to be able to use subtle cues by which they could distinguish plants and their products (that are potentially edible) from nonliving natural kinds (e.g., pieces of clay or rocks). Even today, it is important for farmers to pay attention to some states of plants, such as whether they are lively and healthy, have fruits and seeds, are catching a disease, and so on. These innate constraints make all of us fine amateur biologists even today (Pinker, 1997).

It must also be highly beneficial to classify into distinctive categories a variety of properties and processes that can be observed in important entities, most notably humans. Thus humans may have a tendency to be interested in properties' stability, controllability, and modifiability, which could be useful for predicting the future. Those properties that are stable and not modifiable may be associated with the essence of the entity. Controllability also serves as the basis for differentiating processes, as the mind/body distinction is based on the recognition of the uncontrollability of bodily processes. Remember that preschool children not only differentiate bodily characteristics from mental ones in terms of modifiability but also recognize the uncontrollability of internal bodily processes.

Humans also have some preferences in causal attribution, in other words, a sct of constraints that serves to eliminate in advance a large number of logically possible interpretations or hypotheses. Whereas some of these constraints work in highly specific situations, others work for a variety of observations. An example of highly specific constraints is a tendency to search among a variety of foods for a cause for diarrhea.

In contrast, vitalistic causality is preferred for a large number of situations such as "eating or drinking makes one vigorous and energetic" and "feeding or watering makes an animal or a plant lively and all right"; in its general form it indicates that "something is taken from food or water, and it makes a living thing vigorous and active," and this something can be called vital power or energy. It cannot be any specific material, because a great variety of foods that do not seem to share any features provide us with strength in a similar way.

We point out in passing that, likewise, there are preferences for a particular causal attribution for a class of observations relevant to other domains. Various human behaviors are interpreted in terms of intentionality, for instance, attributed to a person's belief that the target behavior will satisfy the goal. Various situations in which a moving object hits a stationery object and launches induce contact causality: The first object gives physical force to the second object through the contact. These causalities become the core of the core domains of thought, naive psychology, and naive physics, respectively.

These constraints may seldom take a form of specific knowledge. They can best be described as a general, abstract principle, just guiding the acquisition of more specific, and immediately useful, pieces of knowledge through concrete experiences. This is probably because the progression of evolution is so slow that possessing specific pieces of information may be highly detrimental when ecological environments change (Hatano & Inagaki, 2000).

☐ Cognitive Bases of and Universals in Naive Biology

Although we believe that humans are endowed with some constraints for conceptual development in core domains genetically, we agree that this is at present an assumption, and it is almost impossible to show that they are undoubtedly innate in any strict sense. These constraints do not operate at birth. It is possible to explain the time lag in terms of either maturation or early experience. However, if a knowledge system deals with aspects of the world important for human species' survival and thus it is shared by most adults both within and between cultures, if the knowledge system is acquired early and without difficulty, and if it is difficult to attribute its acquisition solely to experiential factors, we can reasonably hypothesize that humans possess innate domain-specific constraints for acquiring that knowledge system.

In what follows we present the evidence we have for claiming the early, uniform, and easy acquisition of naive biology and cross-cultural universality of folk and naive biology. After that, we present some emerging findings that strongly suggest that there are dedicated neural mechanisms for processing information about living things. Although this last set of results does not guarantee that innate constraints are operative in the acquisition of naive biology, it at least suggests that humans are endowed with the neural as well as cognitive basis for acquiring a knowledge system for dealing with living things.

Early, Uniform, and Easy Acquisition of Naive Biology

As described at the beginning of this chapter, the experimental findings we have reviewed indicate that naive biology is established by age 5, and possibly acquired to some degree a few years earlier. The findings also suggest that the early "biology" that 4-year-olds may possess is fragile in the sense that their reasoning is easily influenced by contexts (Gutheil et al., 1998) and by the types of questions asked (Inagaki, 1997). Since the studies to date show that 3-year-old children's responses have similar tendencies (though often at a statistically insignificant level) to 4-year-olds', we expect that future studies, devising ingenious questions that satisfy young preschoolers' conversational rules (Siegal, 1997), may reveal that 3-year-olds have acquired a rudimentary form of naive biology.

How about biological knowledge of children younger than 3 years of age? They already possess some precursors to naive biology. An increasing number of recent studies has indicated that infants seem to make the animate/inanimate distinction from early on. For example, Bertenthal (1993) found that 3-month-old infants showed a longer looking time for a display of moving dots specifying a walking motion of a human than the one in which the same dots move randomly. Rochat, Morgan, and Carpenter (1997) also found that 3-month-old infants showed enhanced visual attention to a "chase" display, in which two discs moved as if one had chased after the other, compared to a display in which the two discs moved randomly. These findings could be interpreted as that infants discriminate animate-biological motion from mechanical, random motion.

A number of studies have indicated that infants distinguish humans from inanimate objects in terms of self-initiated movement versus movement caused by external force. For example, Poulin-Dubois and Shultz (1990) revealed that when presented with events in which a person (female stranger) or an inanimate object (ball or chair) moves without any force acting on it, 13-month-old infants decreased their fixation time in the person-as-agent condition, but not in the object-as-agent condition. Moreover, Poulin-Dubois, Lepage, and Ferland (1996) found that 12-month-old infants showed negative effects, such as crying and fussing, more often when a radio-controlled robot was "spontaneously" moving around the room than when the same robot was stationary. When a human stranger was moving around and when she was standing still, these infants did not show such differential reactions between the conditions. These findings indicate that infants as young as 12 months old seem to regard an inanimate object's, but not a person's, self-propelled movements as anomalous. Spelke, Phillips, and Woodward (1995), using a habituation method for videotaped events involving either inanimate objects or people, provided evidence suggesting that much younger infants, 7-months-old, can infer that although inanimate objects do not move unless they contact each other in space and time, people can move independently without physical contact between them.

Mandler and McDonough (1993) examined 7–11-month old infants' conceptual categorization, using an object examination task. Categories of animals and vehicles were used here. Their task included toys of five animals (i.e., horse, bird, turtle, rabbit, elephant) and five vehicles (i.e., motorcycle, train engine, cement truck, school bus, all-terrain vehicle). The infants were familiarized with four of the five exemplars from one category by being allowed to freely explore them one at a time. After the same four objects had been examined twice, the infants were given two test objects one at a time; the first object was the fifth previously unseen exemplar from the familiarized category, and the second, an exemplar (also previously unseen) from the contrasting category.

Results showed that both 9- and 11-month-old infants examined the contrasting test exemplar longer, indicating that the infants treated the animals and vehicles as belonging to different categories. This tendency was found among the 7-month-old infants too, though not at a significant level. It is noteworthy that these infants treated animals as a category and vehicles as a different category, despite the large perceptual variations among the exemplars of animals and vehicles used here. Moreover, categorization of animals and vehicles was not influenced by the surface similarity between categories; more specifically, other 9- and 11-month-old infants treated birds and airplanes as different even when the exemplars from both categories were very similar in shapes, such as the possession of outstretched wings. In their further study (Mandler & McDonough, 1998), 11-month-old infants categorized plants as separate from not only vehicles but also animals, and they also categorized furniture as different from kitchen utensils.

Interestingly, in the Mandler and McDonough study (1993), the 9- and 11-month-old infants did not show subcategorization within the animal category, whereas they did so within the vehicle category. When familiarized with dogs (e.g., poodle, terrier, German shepherd, etc.), the infants did not categorize the dogs as distinct from a rabbit or from a fish. When familiarized with cars, they differentiated the cars from both an airplane and a motorcycle. This tendency was also found in their further study (Mandler & McDonough, 1998). In this latter study, although both 9- and 11-month-old infants distinguished dogs from birds, they did not differentiate the mammal categories of dogs and cats until 11 months. This does not mean that these infants could not see the differences between dogs and cats, or between dogs and rabbits, because Eimas and Quinn

(1994), using the picture-looking task, revealed that even 3–4-month-old infants perceptually differentiated horses from zebra and cats from lions.

Thus, the findings obtained in Mandler and McDonough's (1993, 1998) studies concerned infants' conceptual categorization rather than perceptual categorization, and indicate that the process of global differentiation of animals from nonanimals (including artifacts) has begun by the end of the first year. Mandler and McDonough (1998) claimed that the type of motion is important in infants' initial conceptualization of what animals are like and that the early global conceptualization is differentiated with increasing age. More specifically, infants may conceptualize a class of objects in terms of whether those objects are self-starters or not, which directs infants' attention to such aspects of the objects, ignoring other detailed features.

We have little available evidence concerning how much infants recognize their bodily processes. However, some recent studies suggest that even infants have some sense of body. For example, Rochat (1998) revealed that infants as young as 3-months-old are sensitive to changes in the relative position of their own legs and the featural characteristics of the legs (i.e., the relative bending of the legs at the knees and ankles), using the infant's preferential looking toward different on-line views of their legs. He interpreted this finding as "the early expression of a calibrated intermodal space of the body or, in other words, the early expression of a perceptually based body schema" (p. 106). However, more data are needed concerning infants' recognition of their bodily processes, which is arguably a precursor of the mind/body distinctions.

Cross-Cultural Universality

That innate constraints serve as the bases for acquiring naive biology is strongly suggested also by the universality of adult folkbiology, especially when the universality is observed across diverse cultures. As proposed by Atran (1990), it may be possible to find the "common sense" or core beliefs shared by all forms of folkbiology and even by scientific biology. Although what such core beliefs are is debatable, the taxonomy of living entities or a set of the ontological distinctions is certainly included among them, because all folkbiological classifications reported so far correspond very closely to the scientific one (e.g., Boster, 1991).

Atran (1998) also claims that (life-)teleological schemata, the domain-specific processing apparatus unique to the conceptual module of folkbiology, generate categories of living things that roughly correspond to biological species and higher-order groupings almost universally across cultures. In fact, he and his associates (López et al., 1997) have found that both the Itzaj Maya Indians living in the tropical forest and American college students who had grown up in rural Michigan can classify mammals living in their own territory in good accordance with scientific (evolutionary) classifications. Maya Indians' classification is a little more accurate than American college students' classification. Interestingly, where Itzaj Maya Indian classifications deviated from scientific classifications, American students showed similar deviations. For instance, both groups put together felines and canines, though these two clusters of mammals do not have particular biological affinity. The natural scheme of our mind cannot help forming such a combined category, namely, that of large predators for humans (consisting of tigers, pumas, wolves, etc.).

Regarding the universality of children's biological knowledge, we should be reminded here that much of the research inspired by Piaget has shown parallels in the biological understanding (or naive biology) of children in different cultures (e.g., children's attribution of life status and consciousness to a variety of objects). Distinctions between animals and terrestrial inanimate objects are particularly strong. We also expect, though they have been documented in only several countries, the frequent use of personification (or animism) and reliance on vitalistic causality, important components of naive biology, to be more or less universal. In fact, young children's preference for vitalistic causality is found in the United States and Australia as well as in Japan (see Chapter 5).

More recently, Hatano, Siegler, Richards, Inagaki, Stavy, and Wax (1993) tried to differentiate between universal and culturally specific aspects of children's conceptions of life and understanding of attributes of living things. They compared kindergartners (M = 6;0), second- (M = 8;0), and fourth-graders (M = 10;0) from Israel, Japan, and the United States. The children were asked whether two instances each of four object types (people, nonhuman animals, plants, and nonliving objects) possessed each of 16 attributes that included life status (being alive), unobservable animal attributes (e.g., has a heart), sensory attributes (e.g., feels pain), and attributes true of all living things (e.g., grows bigger). Results illustrate both similarities and differences across cultures in children's biological understanding. Children in all cultures knew that people, nonhuman animals, plants, and nonliving objects were different types of entities with different properties; the children were extremely accurate regarding humans, somewhat less accurate regarding other animals and nonliving objects, and least accurate regarding plants (see Hatano & Inagaki, 1999).

As properly pointed out by Coley (2000), the samples from the three countries in the above study were homogeneous in the sense that they were all from a large city in the technologically advanced society. A more intriguing comparison is reported by Walker (1999) on the Yoruba in western Nigeria. Her study included participants of five different ages from three different socioeconomic groups (rural, urban, and elite). Although the results of the study were complicated, the major finding concerning the universality was that all the groups showed a developmental pattern very similar to that observed in the United States (Keil, 1989). That is, when entities underwent superficial transformations, the participants in older groups gave preservation-of-identity judgments more often than those in younger groups for familiar natural kinds, whereas all the groups, irrespective of ages, judged that artifacts changed their identity.

Dedicated Neural Mechanisms for Biological Entities and Reasoning

Since Warrington (Warrington & McCarthy, 1983; Warrington & Shallice, 1984), a growing number of clinical studies have reported that some patients reveal selective impairment in naming or recognition for living things (represented by animals) or nonliving things (represented by human-made physical tools). Although some researchers wondered if such category-specific deficits were spurious, that is, just a reflection of the fact that whereas detailed visual processing is needed for recognizing living things, artifacts can be identified mostly by their functions, recent detailed reports of several cases have made this sensory-functional interpretation of category-specific deficits less tenable (e.g., Caramazza & Shelton, 1998). For instance, those patients who show much greater difficulty in recognizing animals than artifacts do not necessarily have problems processing complex visual information in general; their difficulty in processing knowledge about animals is not limited to the visual modality; and so on.

However, it is premature to conclude that semantic and conceptual knowledge of living things is localized separately in the brain from knowledge of nonliving things. There are two reasons. First, neuroimaging (for instance, using positron emission tomography, PET) experiments with normal participants for animals versus artifacts "show segregation between categories, but the specific areas involved differ across studies" (Caramazza & Shelton, 1998, p. 23). These studies yielded only partially overlapping results, probably because different members of animal and tool categories were presented in different forms (photos vs. line drawings) for different tasks (naming vs. same/different judgment), and we are not ready to localize the processing of animals and artifacts.

Second, even if we find consistent segregation between animals and tools, it is still debatable what categorical contrast it represents. There are at least three plausible interpretations for the animal/artifact segregation, that is, between things that move spontaneously versus those that move by external force (i.e., animals versus nonanimals), living versus nonliving things, and natural kinds versus artifacts. To choose among the alternative interpretations, Kawashima et al. (2001) brought into the experimental design, in addition to animals and artifacts, plants, which are important members of the living thing category and constitute another ontological class.

How the human brain represents knowledge about plants is an interesting issue, but it has been understudied, except for vegetables and fruits (Hart, Berndt, & Caramazza, 1985; Hillis & Caramazza, 1991). Here is an obvious reason for this neglect. Folk knowledge of plants is not very rich in Western countries (Wolff, Medin, & Pankratz, 1999), so naming or recognition of plants seems too hard for ordinary college students. Kawashima et al. (2001) recruited for a neuroimaging experiment Japanese college students, who are supposedly more knowledgable about plants than their Western counterparts. They investigated brain activities of eight male volunteer participants during the recognition of visual stimuli representing animals, plants, and artifacts using PET. The participants were presented with and required to name silently two different photos each of 15 entities belonging to the three ontological categories, and 30 series of 4 to 6 digits as control stimuli.

Marked increases in regional cerebral blood flow, which indicates the enhanced activation of the region, were found in the bilateral hippocampus and the parahippocampal and right lateral occipital regions for the silent naming of animal, plant, and artifact stimuli, compared with the silent reading of digits. Although differences among the three conditions of the silent naming of animal, plant, and artifact stimuli were smaller than the difference between the three naming conditions and the silent reading of digit condition, there were a few characteristic activations for different categories. The right inferior temporal sulcus was activated only for animals and plants, not for artifacts. In contrast, the left lateral occipital region was activated for plants and artifacts, not for animals. In short, entities belonging to different categories are not necessarily represented in different locations of the brain; rather, they may be represented by different combinations of locations. An important point in the present discussion, however, is that humans have some neural basis for processing living things differently from nonliving things.

☐ How Sociocultural Constraints Operate

The above emphasis on innate constraints does not exclude the possibility of sociocultural factors' operating simultaneously and significantly in the theory construction process of developing individuals. Children's interaction with more mature members and shared artifacts, and also activity-based experiences, in the community or culture surrounding them contribute to the acquisition of naive biology. Such influences can also be interpreted as constraining the developmental process, because they restrict the range of the constructed knowledge while enhancing the knowledge acquisition within the range.

Sociocultural constraints include usable artifacts which are shared by a majority of people of the community or its subgroup, such as physical facilities and tools, social institutions and organizations, documented pieces of knowledge, common sense and beliefs, and more. Children develop not in a given natural environment but in an environment that has been reconstructed by preceding generations. Sociocultural constraints also include the behavior of other people who are concerned with a developing child, interactions with them, and contexts created by them.

Some developmental researchers admit the effect of sociocultural contexts, but only as facilitating or inhibiting the fixed course of the development of an individual mind, especially in its initial phase (e.g., Carey & Spelke, 1994). We, in contrast, claim that other people and tools surrounding the developing individuals are essential constituents of the construction process, serving as constraints in the acquisition of knowledge systems in domains from the beginning. This is because the sort of constraints given genetically at the start of conceptual development are so abstract and skeletal that they can be highly effective only when they are specified and/or supplimented by a set of sociocultural constraints.

Unlike innate tendencies and biases that are by definition universal in the human species, the specific features of many sociocultural constraints vary between and within communities or cultures, though some are also universal in human ways of living. Thus sociocultural constraints arguably produce differently instantiated versions of naive biology. For example, if children are actively engaged in raising animals, it is possible for them to acquire a rich body of knowledge about their raised animals, and therefore to use that body of knowledge, as well as their knowledge about humans, as a source for analogical predictions and explanations for other living things. It is probably an innate and universal tendency to choose knowledge about highly familiar animals as the source for making analogical inferences for living things, but which animals are highly familiar is directly influenced by culture.

In short, thanks to sociocultural constraints, competencies adapted to the community or culture can readily be acquired. Innate constraints change extremely slowly compared with the tempo of cultural-historical changes and thus can enhance only some universal aspects of human development. Within the limit of innate constraints, sociocultural constraints often provide developing individuals with the specific opportunities for learning. In other words, sociocultural constraints are more specific than the innate ones, but, when needed, they can be modified fairly quickly. For instance, if fear of poisonous snakes is shared by members of the community, it serves as a specific sociocultural constraint that directs children's attention to snake-like objects or movements interactively (e.g., through joint attention); however, this constraint will disappear in just a few generations if poisonous snakes are all extinguished.

In this section, we discuss the exact roles played by sociocultural constraints in the acquisition of naive biology. We assume that sociocultural constraints operate mainly in three different ways in the construction and revision of naive theories in core domains. First, sociocultural contexts (hierarchically organized from everyday activity situations through historical, technological, and economic conditions of the world) greatly influence what are accessible for each child in the course of development. In other words, sociocultural constraints restrict children's access to resources; to put it differently, "the environment and culture provide the 'material' upon which constructive mental processes will work " (Resnick, 1987, p. 47). That a number of activities are culturally organized means that children growing up in a culture can participate much more readily and easily in those activities than others. In this sense, sociocultural constraints start to operate very soon after the birth. Many cross-cultural differences in naive biology and other core domains can be attributed to cultural differences in access to the biological world and its representations.

Second, children's accumulated experiences in sociocultural contexts are represented in the form of domain-specific knowledge, which operate as acquired cognitive constraints in further learning and development; these constraints probably operate to a greater extent later in conceptual development. We believe that much of the "prior knowledge" in human development and learning has a sociocultural origin, in other words, is an "internalized" form of sociocultural constraints. The growth of the human mind is achieved by incorporating experiences accumulated in earlier generations in the form of culture (Hatano & Inagaki, 2000; Vygotsky, 1978). We thus propose a sociocultural reinterpretation of a well-established finding that domain-specific knowledge enhances new pieces of knowledge within its domain (Chi et al., 1989; Glaser, 1984).

Third, conceptual development is also enhanced by sociocultural factors in interactive ways. Sociocultural constraints such as other people with extensive prior experience and physical, symbolic, and social tools help interactively developing individuals acquire some knowledge with little difficulty. This is a unique feature of sociocultural constraints. When interacting with other people, our cognition and learning in an unfamiliar situation that requires search and exploration are constrained in the following ways (Hatano & Inagaki, 2000; Tomasello, Kruger, & Ratner, 1993): What we observe is not randomly selected out of almost infinite pieces of information but directed by joint attention, what we try is not a randomly chosen chain of responses from our repertory but is often triggered by imitation, and how we interpret a set of observations is influenced by guided comprehension activities. Sociocultural constraints enable us not only to be competent but also to acquire knowledge and skills readily. These constraints are domain-specific, though relying on the above general cognitive mechanisms, because different sets of constraints work in different practices and produce different pieces of knowledge relevant to different domains.

Let us take once again the case in which children raise an animal at home. Children are likely to participate in the raising activity, which is led by their parents or older siblings. Children's choice of procedures is directed by joint attention with more mature partners. They are expected to learn procedures involved promptly, because their learning can be based on the imitation of the partners' activity. In addition, active engagement in raising animals may lead children to acquire a sort of conceptual knowledge or a mental model of the raised animals', often being helped by guided comprehension activities induced for the sake of the raised animals' well-being. Thus, children tend to be more competent when they engage in joint activities than when doing a solitary activity, and they construct and elaborate relevant pieces of knowledge more promptly.

Those tools or artifacts used in the raising activity also serve to direct children's attention and to narrow the range of procedures and interpretations they consider. For example, there is a manual for raising goldfish or other pets, which may include some pieces of information understandable to children. A fish tank or a cage may suggest what kind of care the animal needs. Some special food may be available so that our feeding behavior can readily be standardized. Although the constraints offered by tools are primarily for successfully performing tasks, they tend to enhance the acquisition of knowledge as well.

We assume, as proposed by a number of cultural psychologists (e.g., Goodnow, Miller, & Kessel, 1995), that "participation in practices," which emerges a few years after birth, is a general mechanism by which sociocultural constraints operate interactively in knowlege acquisition. As children begin to learn in a uniquely human way, in other words, as they acquire the ability to mentally represent other people's mental representations (Tomasello et al., 1993), they become able to share goals, methods, and concepts of activities, in short, to participate in practices.

Taken together, sociocultural constraints operate in conceptual development from very early years, at least complementing innate constraints. The role played by prior knowledge that has a sociocultural origin becomes more and more important later. When we solve a problem, understand the target, or learn something new, we do not just solitarily manipulate symbols in our head that represent the external world. Because we continuously interact with other people and artifacts, our competence in these cognitive activities is heavily dependent on them. The acquisition of core domains of thought is no exception.

☐ Cultural Variations in Naive Biology

We examine below whether the available data are consistent with those predictions derived from the discussion in the preceding section on how sociocultural constraints operate. More specifically, we investigate young children's activity-based experiences that are relevant to the acquisition of naive biology and their consequences. We also compare naive biological understandings between groups of children who differ in the relevant activities and sociocultural contexts, in order to show clearly the workings of sociocultural constraints.

Activity-Based Experiences

Naive biology is acquired through exposure to a culturally arranged biological environment and discourse about it, and enriched further through participation in cultural practices. What kinds of practices are most influential in the acquisition of naive biology? As for the acquisition of biological taxonomy, the following three kinds of practices can be considered critical, at least in our industrialized society: (a) raising animals and growing plants, (b) visiting a zoo or botanical garden, and (c) joint reading of picture books (or watching TV programs) on animals and plants. Engaging in these activities provides young children with opportunities to experience the natural world—opportunities that are minimal in industrialized societies. These are not practices in which almost all members of a community engage. However, they are regarded as valuable experiences, especially for young children, because, as people intuitively understand, naive biology is a core domain of thought, and in a technologically advanced society, children do not have many opportunities for contact with the natural world of animals and plants. In addition, children enjoy the activities.

Raising animals and growing plants involves direct contact with animals and plants, though the activity itself is organized culturally. Although children in our society do not engage in the activity to make a living, they tend to make a serious effort to follow correct procedures, because the target is alive. Although this apparently represents a typical situation of learning by doing (Anzai & Simon, 1979), it does not start with an individual search for finding effective strategies. Rather, it starts with prescribed, conventional procedures under an adult's (or more mature peer's) guidance, and a raiser can modify these procedures only after he or she gains expertise. It can better be conceptualized as learning through participation in practice, which involves both incorporation of culture and individual construction.

Imagine a case in which children raise an animal at home. To the extent that children are interested in the raised animal, they are likely to learn procedures involved in the raising activity, and thus to inherit some behavioral tradition promptly. In addition, active, spontaneous engagement in raising animals may lead children to acquire a sort of conceptual knowledge or a mental model of the raised animals, based on which they can produce reasonable predictions for their reactions to novel situations, give explanations about the prescribed procedures, and modify the procedures flexibly.

Visiting a zoo or a botanical garden is also a culturally organized activity, because a zoo or a botanical garden itself is a cultural construction, and taking young children there is recommended in our culture. The visit does not involve learning by doing in the sense that children are not responsible for taking care of animals or plants. However, it enables children to see the target directly (hear, smell, and even touch it). It offers less mediated contact than reading a picture book or watching a television program on animals or plants. Motoyoshi's (1979) observation in her daycare center illustrates the effect of such visits on children's perception of animals. After visiting a zoo, a 2-year-old, who had previously applied the adjective "cute" to all the animals on her picture book, such as, "A doggy is cute, a lion is cute," and so forth, began to use adjectives differentially for those animals, such as, "A doggy is cute, a lion is scary, an elephant smells bad," and so forth. It is often pointed out that many children are impressed with the warmth of a rabbit or a guinea pig when they hold it in their arms at a children's zoo.

Inagaki, Hatano, and Namiki (in an ongoing study, yet to be published) videotaped and audiotaped interactions between young children (apparently 2–5-years-old) and their families when they visited zoos. The observation was made when they were watching conspicuous animals (e.g., elephants, monkeys, or sea lions) or touching highly docile animals (e.g., rabbits, guinea pigs, or goats). Protocols of about 70 families revealed the following.

1. Parents seldom explain. They just draw the child's attention to some feature or behavior of the target animal.

2. They often name the animal, thus indicating that animals are grouped at the level of folk generic-species.
3. They try to share with their child how big the animal is, the sounds the animal makes, and other physical characteristics of the animal.
4. They often refer to the animal's movements, eating, drinking, and being accompanied by a baby. The animal's excretion, when it occurs, also catches the eyes of the child. As a consequence, important shared properties of advanced animals are repeatedly verbalized.
5. The child usually gives a short response to the parents.

We have not yet conducted any systematic study of the children's learning, but we can reasonably assume that they acquire a framework for viewing the animal kingdom by visiting a zoo.

Joint reading of a picture book about living things (or a similar activity such as watching a television program on nature) is an indirect, mediated form of contact with the natural world. By engaging in such an activity, children can incorporate others' experiences constituting the symbolic tradition of the society without much cost.

S. Gelman, Coley, Rosengren, Hartman, and Pappas (1998) observed maternal input when mothers read picture books on animals (and on artifacts for comparison) with their 20- or 35-month-old children. Their results indicated that, although labeling occupied about two-thirds of the mothers' utterances, they often offered verbal information beyond labeling; the mothers often referred to the target animal's behavior and actions. However, like the parents observed in a zoo, they seldom gave an explanation for the unobservable essence of animals (e.g., internal bodily structure). These and other related pieces of parental input can be used as the database for children to develop a naive theory of biology.

Practices that are concerned with bodily processes (e.g., eating and recuperating), in addition to the above-mentioned practices dealing with animals and plants, seem to contribute to the formation and elaboration of naive biology. Moreover, activities appearing in different practices, such as talking about health and illness, may help children internalize cultural models and vocabularies. Inagaki and Oshima (2001) examined whether the joint reading of a book on an atopic disease would help young children understand the disease. Atopy is innate hypersensitivity, and in modern civilized societies, a considerable number of young children are said to suffer from atopic skin disease. Six-year-old kindergarten children with and without atopic disease were individually read a picture book about the atopic skin disease by a female experimenter and given a comprehension test after the reading. Results indicated that a substantial portion of the nonatopic children understood the content of the book fairly well, though their understanding did not tend to be as deep as that of the atopic children.

Cognitive Consequences of Repeated Participation in Practices

A number of studies have in fact revealed that repeated participation in a culturally organized activity may produce a slightly different version of naive biology from the standard one. Inagaki (1990a) compared the biological knowledge of kindergartners who had actively engaged in raising goldfish for an extended period at home with that of children of the same age who had never raised any animal. Although these two groups of children did not differ in factual knowledge about mammals in general, the goldfish-raisers had much richer procedural, factual, and conceptual knowledge about goldfish. More interestingly, the goldfish-raisers used the knowledge about goldfish as a source for analogies in predicting reactions of an unfamiliar "aquatic" animal (i.e., a frog), one that they had never raised, and produced reasonable predictions with some explanations for it. For example, one of the raisers answered when asked whether we could keep a baby frog the same size forever, "No, we can't, because a frog will grow bigger as goldfish grew bigger. My goldfish were small before, but now they are big." It might be added that the goldfish-raisers tended to use person analogies as well as goldfish analogies for a frog. In other words, the goldfish-raisers could use two sources for making analogical predictions.

In another study (Inagaki, 1996; see also Hatano & Inagaki, 1992), it was found that another group of goldfish-raising children tended to enlarge their previously possessed narrow conception of animals. As shown in Figure 6.1 as an example, the goldfish-raisers attributed animal properties that they knew that humans possess (e.g., having a heart, excreting, etc.) not only to goldfish but also to a majority of animals phylogenetically in between humans and goldfish at a higher rate than the corresponding nonraisers. This suggests that the experience of raising goldfish modifies young children's preferred mode of biological inference.

In still another study, Inagaki (2001a) examined effects of raising mammals which are much closer to humans than goldfish. Fifteen 5-year-old children who had raised mammals (9 hamster-raisers and 6 dog-raisers) for an extended period at home were compared with 15 same-aged children who had not raised any mammals. Both groups of children were given an inductive projection task consisting of four novel properties, together with 10 questions each of factual/procedural knowledge about either hamsters or dogs (depending on which they had been raising) and factual knowledge about mammals in general. In the induction task, after being taught about either hamsters/dogs or people, a novel property (e.g., immunity) and its function, the children were asked whether each of

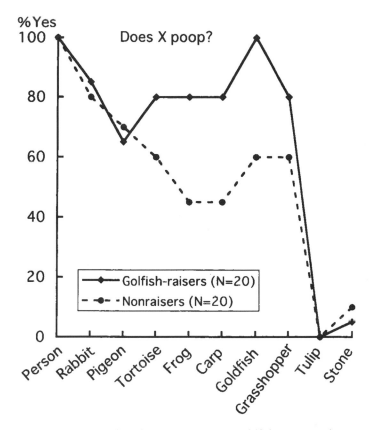

FIGURE 6.1. An example of attribution patterns in goldfish-raisers and nonraisers.

eight other entities (either people or hamsters/dogs, monkeys, squirrels, frogs, carps, grasshoppers, flowers, and stones) would have it.

It was found that the animal-raisers had a greater amount of factual knowledge about hamsters/dogs than nonraisers, though both groups were comparable in factual knowledge about mammals in general. When required to project the novel properties taught about humans to other entities, the raisers extended them to varied animals including grasshoppers (but not to flowers or stones) more often than the nonraisers. When asked to project the given novel properties taught about the raised animal (i.e., the hamster or dog) to other entities, the animal-raisers extended them at least to monkeys on the one hand and frogs on the other more often than the nonraisers. These results strongly suggest that the experience of raising a mammal as a pet also helps children go beyond "human-centered" inference and project biological properties to animals dissimilar to people.

Cultural and Linguistic Variables

The finding that the biological understanding observed in different cultures is not identical strongly suggests that larger cultural contexts of children's lives also influence the construction of naive biology. As mentioned in reviewing studies on cross-cultural universality, Hatano et al. (1993) compared the biological understanding of kindergartners, second-, and fourth-graders from Israel, Japan, and the United States. Although the study revealed a number of commonalities across the three countries, it also showed some interesting differences. As predicted from cultural analyses, Israeli children were considerably more likely not to attribute to plants the life status and other properties that are shared by all living things, whereas Japanese children, whose overall accuracy was comparable to the Israelis, were considerably more likely to attribute to inanimate objects properties that are unique to living things.

These differences are especially interesting because they suggest that children's naive biology is influenced by beliefs within the culture where they grow up. Consider why Japanese children might be more likely than children in the United States or Israel to view plants or inanimate objects as alive and having attributes of living things. Japanese culture includes a belief that plants are like human beings. This attitude is represented by the Buddhist idea that even a tree or blade of grass has a mind. In Japanese folk psychology, even inanimate objects are sometimes considered to have minds. For example, it is at least not a silly idea for Japanese to assign life or divinity not only to plants but also to inanimate objects, especially big or old ones. In addition, linguistic and orthographic factors seem to influence Japanese children's attributional judgments. The *kanji* (Chinese character), which represents life, has a prototypical meaning of "fresh" or "perishable" as well as "alive." Therefore, this *kanji* can be applied to cake, wine, sauce, and other perishable goods.

Similar features of culture and language may account for Israeli children being less apt than American or Japanese children to attribute to plants life status and properties of living things. Stavy and Wax (1989) suggested that within the Israeli culture, plants are regarded as very different from humans and other animals in their life status. This cultural attitude parallels that of a biblical passage (Genesis, 1:30), well known to Israeli students, indicating that plants were created as food for living things including mammals, birds, and insects. Adding to, or perhaps reflecting, their cultural beliefs, the Hebrew word for "animal" is very close to that for "living" and "alive." In contrast, the word for "plant" has no obvious relation to such terms (Stavy & Wax, 1989).

Ross, Medin, Coley, and Atran (under review) investigated inductive projection in not only urban U.S. children but also children from three other cultural groups, that is, rural majority-culture, Menominee (rural Native American), and Yukatek Maya. These children were shown a picture of one base-item (e.g., human, wolf, bee) and taught a novel property X (e.g., andro) about it. Properties were unfamiliar internal substances of the form "has X inside." Then, the children were shown each of 17 targets and asked whether it had X inside. Results revealed very different inductive projection patterns in these three cultural groups of children. That is, the different populations displayed apparently different patterns of reasoning. The authors suggested that these differences appear to be driven by (a) different cultural models and (b) differential access to experiences in nature.

There have been several other cross-cultural studies that revealed adults' characteristic biological understanding and reasoning, probably due to their accumulated cultural experiences and pieces of knowledge derived from them. For example, Coley, Medin, Proffitt, Lynch, and Atran (1999) reported that the Itzaj Maya Indians living in the tropical forest of northern Guatemala prefer to use their rich, specific knowledge about the species referred to in a given question in induction. Unlike Michigan college students who evaluated an argument with more diverse premises (e.g., "tapirs and squirrels have disease X") as stronger (for inferring that "all other animals in the area have that disease") than an argument whose premises are similar ("rats and mice have disease Y"), the Itzaj Maya participants often made the opposite judgment. They explained their reasoning on ecological grounds ("tapirs and squirrels are unlikely to share a disease, unless an ecological agent intervenes, for example, a bat biting them"). Coley et al. attributed this observed difference not to Itzaj Maya's inability to use the diversity principle but to their expert knowledge about the living things in the forest, including their ecological relationships.

Walker (1999) also described interesting adult explanations that seem to reflect their cultural backgrounds. Whereas the Yoruba living in urban Nigeria often showed a tendency not to preserve identity for natural things, those in the rural area generated preservation judgments at an extremely high rate and offered religious justifications (e.g., "because the animal has its own structure from heaven" and "you cannot change the work of God"). The rural Yoruba's high percentage correct may be attributed to their traditional conceptions and values. The author suggests that the urban Yoruba's nonpreservation judgments for natural kinds are due to "harsh and rapidly changing social and economic conditions" (p. 214) in cities in recent years, or their resultant beliefs reflected in such justifications as, "In this world anything can happen."

How culture influences the development of biological understanding has yet to be studied. Culture may provide children with opportunities to engage in activities that lead them to construct some particular biological understanding, as in the case of children raising goldfish, as mentioned above, but this is not the only path through which cultural influence is exerted. Parents, schools, and even mass media may serve to transmit cultural beliefs through discourse and nonverbal behavior (e.g., concerning how to treat living things and bodily phenomena).

☐ A Scenario for the Emergence of Naive Biology

Let us present a scenario about how naive biology is acquired as a summary of the preceding discussion in this chapter. According to our scenario, which is admittedly speculative, the acquisition of naive biology proceeds as young children, as not only active learners but also theory builders, try to connect a preceding event to the following event and causally interpret the observed connection. The observations and resultant rules that we take as most important for the acquisition of naive biology concern connections between taking food/water and bodily states of humans and other living things, such as, "When hungry or thirsty, eating or drinking makes one vigorous and energetic" and "Feeding or watering makes an animal or a plant lively and healthy"; young children as biological beings are almost destined to experience hunger and thirst; and both events, that is, eating/drinking or feeding/watering and lively and healthy, probably draw attention due to innate and sociocultural constraints. Moreover, these observed connections can promptly be interpreted causally. A likely causation is, "Something is taken from food or water, and it makes a living thing vigorous and healthy." This "something" could not be a specific substance, because a great variety of foods that do not seem to share any features provide us with energy in a similar way. Whether or not young children are innately prepared to possess vitalistic intuition, they can apply it quite easily to the above observed connections.

There are some other, additional observations that serve to enhance the acquisition of naive biology. Although knowledge about specific animals and plants in terms of their practical valences (e.g., "If a moving object is like a bear, it could be dangerous" or "If it is a persimmon and is ripe, it is edible and tasty") does not have to be acquired early in our society, young children may still acquire knowledge about familiar animals and plants. Also, some bodily phenomena invite the vitalistic causal linkage to be extended, for example, growth (part or surplus of "something" produces growth), and recovery from illnesses and injuries (more of "something" is needed for fast recovery). Here again, various constraints work in restricting the range of causal connections to be considered; cultural beliefs (expressed, for example, as "You cannot grow bigger if you do not eat enough") are as important as cognitive bases.

A little later, two additional developments occur. First, young children as theory builders try to construct a causal explanatory structure that can explain a set of observations consistently. In this process, such notions as the body and vital power are introduced (and expressed in some verbal forms). Young children become aware that processes are going on in the body that belong to themselves but are not subject to their control and that eating and other activities are to sustain life (keeping us alive as well as making us active and vigorous) by supplying vital power. Combining animals and plants may become possible; both animals and plants are similar to humans in the relationships between taking food/water–being active–growing, as repeatedly referred to in the previous chapters.

Second, children come to reveal explicit biological understanding; that is, they can offer explanations. As indicated in Chapter 1, the minimal requirement to attribute a naive theory is that children can make coherent and basically correct predictions based on given causal devices, but we must admit that this is just implicit understanding. Being able to explain biological phenomena in terms of such biological causal devices as vital power or life teleology is thus an important milestone in the development of naive biology.

CHAPTER

Conceptual Change in Naive Biology

The preceding chapters have revealed that young children, at least older preschoolers, possess a naive theory of biology. Psychologists dealing with other core domains of thought also claim that preschool children have naive theories about the important aspects of the world; for example, they assert that preschool children have naive psychology or a theory of mind (e.g., Perner, 1991; Wellman, 1990). However, that children have naive theories does not mean that their theories are the same as intuitive theories lay adults possess. Because the construction of the initial theory is based on a limited database, it has to be restructured as more and more facts are incorporated into it with increasing age, unless the initial set of observed facts constitutes a representative sample of all relevant facts. Some of the innate or very early tendencies and biases that are helpful at the initial phase may be weakened or given up, as accumulated pieces of prior knowledge come to serve as constraints. This also makes conceptual change or theory change during childhood inevitable.

In this chapter, we discuss conceptual change that spontaneously occurs during childhood, and its mechanisms. More specifically, first, we discuss the nature of conceptual change as a fundamental restructuring of (conceptual) knowledge in general, and we then sketch conceptual change in the course of development of biological knowledge, primarily relying on our experimental evidence. Finally, we return to the general discussion of how conceptual change occurs.

151

☐ Conceptual Change as Fundamental Restructuring

What is Conceptual Change?

The notion of conceptual change in cognitive development has been proposed as an alternative to "enrichment views" (Carey, 1985, 1991). It denotes that conceptual development involves not just enrichment or elaboration of the existing knowledge systems but their considerable reorganization or restructuring. Conceptual change involves change in core concepts, conceptions, or conceptualizations (including rules, models, and theories). To put it differently, it concerns a large-scale restructuring of the existing knowledge system (especially conceptual knowledge in it). The knowledge systems before and after the conceptual change may sometimes be locally incommensurable (Carey, 1988); that is, some pieces of knowledge in one system cannot properly be translated into the other, as exemplified by the shift from children's undifferentiated concept of heat/temperature to adults' separate concepts of heat and temperature (Wiser & Carey, 1983).

It should be noted that conceptual change seldom occurs suddenly, just as it has taken years for concepts, conceptions, or conceptualizations to change in the history of science. The process of conceptual change tends to be slow and gradual, even if its end result is drastically different from its initial state.

Conceptual change often takes the form of theory change, because concepts and conceptions are embedded in theories; changing one core concept in a theory generates changes in related concepts and eventually leads to a change in the whole set of concepts. Theory change involves changes in causal devices or explanations and/or a large-scale change in the range of phenomena or entities that are included. See Keil (1998, 1999) for distinct senses of conceptual change other than theory change.

Types of Conceptual Change

Four types of conceptual change can be distinguished with regard to the relationship between the old, pre-change knowledge system and the new, post-change system. Let us take theory change as an example. First, a new theory emerges from an old theory in the same domain, with the latter being subsumed in, or replaced by, the former. It can be described as A → A', where A and A' denote the old and new theory, respectively.

For example, between ages 2 and 4–5 years, the early theory of mind, which is based solely on desires and perceptions, is transformed into the "representational theory of mind," which includes beliefs as well (Gopnik & Wellman, 1994).

Second, a new theory emerges and develops from an old one within the same domain, and the latter continues to exist with its salience decreased: A → A' & A. Sometimes the old theory is even extended by the new theory. For example, Perner (1991) claims that, although at about 4 years of age, children's understanding of the mind changes from a "situation theory" (where mental states are construed in relation to situations) to a "representational theory" (where mental states are understood as serving representational functions), the latter does not replace the former but merely extends it; even adults may be situation theorists when possible, but they, unlike young children, can take a representational view when necessary. Subbotsky (1997) also proposed a "coexistence model of the development of fundamental structures of mind" by demonstrating that phenomenalistic forms of causal reasoning retain their power in the mind of an educated adult.

Third, a new theory emerges from an old one through differentiation, and new and old theories, representing knowledge systems in different domains, develop separately afterwards: A → A & B. One example is the emergence of a theory of matter from a theory of physics in which objects and materials from which they are made are not fully distinguished (Smith, Carey, & Wiser, 1985). Carey (1985, 1995) argued that naive biology emerges from an intuitive psychology.

Fourth, a new theory emerges through the integration of old subtheories: A & B → C. For example, young Israeli children consider plants as neither living things nor nonliving things, but "growers" (Stavy & Wax, 1989). In contrast, they easily recognize animals as living by attending to their self-initiated movement. In other words, these young children seem to possess different theories for animals and plants. As they grow older, they acquire a theory of living things by integrating these different subtheories of animals and plants.

We consider, in the domain of biology, the second type of theory change as most tenable and the fourth type is also possible at the level of its specific theory. As we will describe in detail later, conceptual change in naive biology takes place approximately between ages 5 and 10 years within the domain. Young children tend to understand biological phenomena by relying on vitalistic causality and personifying inference, whereas older children and adults use mechanical causality and inference based on higher order biological categories. However, vitalistic causality and personifying inference continue to function as a basis of understanding and to be used as a fallback in situations where people do not think they are required to make precise and detailed predictions or explanations based on so-called scientific biology (Hatano & Inagaki, 1997).

Spontaneous Versus Instruction-Based Conceptual Change

Forms of conceptual change can also be distinguished in terms of whether the change occurs spontaneously or is induced by instruction (Hatano & Inagaki, 1997; Vosniadou & Ioannides, 1998). Spontaneous conceptual change is the change that results from children's increasing experience in their physical and sociocultural environment. In other words, it occurs without systematic instruction, though schooling certainly has some general facilitative effects on it. Most of the examples referred to in the preceding section are of this form. This form of change seems to occur readily, because it is commonly found among most children growing up in highly technological societies. An additional example is the change that occurs within young children's belief–desire psychology between ages 3 and 6, that is, from a copy-container theory of mind representing a static mind that 3-year-old children are supposed to possess to an interpretive-homuncular theory representing an active and constructive mind (Wellman, 1990). Cognitive developmentalists have been primarily concerned with this spontaneous conceptual change.

In contrast, researchers who are interested in science education have dealt with instruction-based conceptual change, which occurs by incorporating conceptual devices of science and thereby correcting "misconceptions" (e.g., Vosniadou & Brewer, 1992). This instruction-based conceptual change requires laborious and effortful processes of systematic teaching to be achieved, and even with good teaching, only a limited portion of older children and adults may achieve it (e.g., Clement, 1982).

However, it should be noted that the difference between spontaneous conceptual change and instruction-based conceptual change is not in actuality so large because conceptual development during the middle elementary school years and after is directly or indirectly influenced by systematic science instruction. Even when such science education does not function well, some scientific concepts that students learned in incomplete ways may work as something like a placeholder in the students' knowledge system and contribute to restructuring it eventually. Thus conceptual change during and after the elementary school years may often be a mixture of spontaneous and instruction-based conceptual changes.

☐ Conceptual Change in the Domain of Naive Biology

Returning to the domain of biology, we discuss conceptual change in naive biology. Compared with lay adults' intuitive biology, young children's naive biology has five weaknesses: (a) limited factual knowledge, (b) limited applicability of biological reasoning to classes of biological phenomena (focusing on eating, being vigorous and lively, and growing, almost neglecting, say, reproduction and etiological aspects), (c) a lack of inferences based on complex, hierarchically organized biological categories, (d) a lack of mechanical causality, and (e) a lack of some conceptual devices, such as "evolution" or "photosynthesis." During the early elementary school years, children gradually overcome weaknesses (a) and (b) through enrichment and (c) and (d) through spontaneous conceptual change. Specifically, the use of inferences based on complex, hierarchically organized biological categories and of mechanical causality requires fundamental restructuring of biological knowledge, whereas the accumulation of more and more factual knowledge and more coherent application of biological reasoning can be achieved by enrichment only.

In contrast, the acquisition of basic conceptual devices of scientific biology, such as photosynthesis or the Darwinian idea of evolution, requires instruction-based conceptual change, because children almost never acquire them without instruction, and incorporating them meaningfully into the existing body of knowledge can usually be achieved only with its restructuring. For example, one who does not know the phenomenon of photosynthesis cannot understand the basic difference between animals and plants (i.e., plants can produce nutriment themselves) and thus may construct a wrong integrative theory for both animals and plants, accepting the false mapping of water for plants to food for animals. The Darwinian idea of evolution must also be difficult for children to grasp. Because naive biology assumes living things, but not nonliving things, to be able to adjust themselves to their ecological niche or ways of life, children are ready to accept any biological entity's gradual adaptive changes over generations (Evans, 2001) and thus to form a version of the Lamarckian idea of evolution (Marton, 1989). The Darwinian idea of evolution has been fully accepted, even among biologists, since only the 19th century. We assume that, unlike spontaneous conceptual change in naive theories, conceptual change through the understanding of conceptual devices is very hard to bring about, even with educational intervention, and thus occurs only among a limited portion of older children or adolescents, as described above in the case of the Darwinian idea of evolution.

In what follows, we primarily consider spontaneous conceptual change. We first sketch qualitative changes in the salient mode of inference and those in preferred causality with increasing age; that is, changes from similarity-based to category-based inference on the one hand, and those from vitalistic to mechanical causality on the other. Next, we show that the pre- and postchange modes of inference and causalities coexist even in adults, although the pre-change mode of inference and causality are no longer salient in adults' biology. It can sometimes be used as a fallback in everyday lives.

Developmental Shift From Similarity-Based to Category-Based Inference

In Chapter 3 we characterized young children's biology as human-centered or personifying in nature. Our experimental demonstrations used prediction/explanation questions requiring children to construct their answers. However, we cannot use this method to examine developmental changes in modes of inference from preschoolers to adults, because in this method the change in ways of inference would be confounded with children's increased general verbal abilities with age. Thus, instead of the person analogy task, we, like in Carey (1985), have adopted the task of inductive projection from humans, or the attribution of human properties. This method relies less on children's verbal ability. We considered it as admittable, because personification involves both the so-called person analogy and inductive projection from humans to other nonhuman entities, and the latter can be regarded as a special case of the person analogy (Inagaki & Hatano, in press).

Suppose children are asked the following attribution question, "Does X have a property Y?", where Y is a property that they know people have and that they do not know whether X has. If children have personifying biology, they will make the following inference: First, they will judge whether X is similar to humans, as for the target property. If they judge it as dissimilar, they will answer "No" to the above question. If they perceive some similarity between humans and the target entity X, they will tend to answer "Yes" in proportion to its judged similarity, unless they have additional knowledge that it is impossible for X to have the property Y. We call such a mode of inference "similarity-based attribution," which is the same as Carey's (1985) "comparison-to-people model." The attributional profile of this mode of inference is a gradually decreasing pattern, as shown by the solid line in Figure 7.1, when varied objects are arranged on a continuum according to their phylogenetic affinity to a person. Thus similarity-based attribution inevitably generates both under-

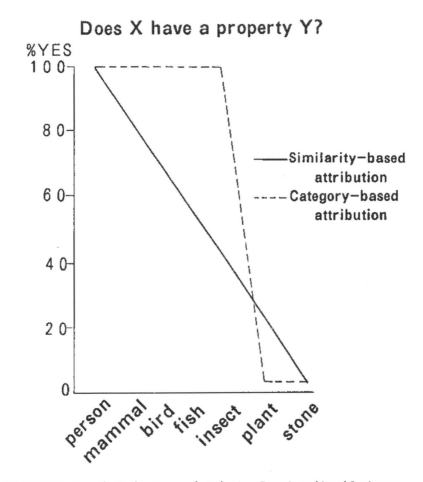

FIGURE 7.1. Hypothetical patterns of attribution. From Inagaki and Sugiyama (1988).

and overattribution errors, for the objects. By underattribution errors we mean that children fail to attribute a specific (human) property to those objects having it, and by overattribution errors, we mean erroneous attribution of the property to those not having it.

Another apparently contrasting type of inference is a deductive attribution arrived at by relying on such higher order biological categories as mammals, vertebrates, and so on (e.g., "The grasshopper is an invertebrate and the invertebrates have no bones, so the grasshopper must have no bones"). We call it category-based attribution. This attribution generates correct responses as long as the target object is allocated to the proper category and the attributional boundary is correct. Its attributional profile is a flat pattern with a sharp break as shown in the dotted line in Figure 7.1, although the location of the sharp break on the continuum may vary from uniquely human to restricted-animal to all-living-thing properties.

Carey (1985) claimed that 4-year-olds attribute animal properties based on the "comparison-to-people model," whereas 10-year-olds rely little on it. To put it differently, we can expect that younger children use similarity-based inference, while older children rely on category-based attribution. How does this shift from the similarity-based to the category-based take place? More specifically, is the shift abrupt or gradual? We assume that pure similarity-based attribution progresses toward pure category-based attribution by being more and more strongly constrained by categorical knowledge, as children come to realize its usefulness through various experiences, including formal schooling. Even young children check the plausibility of similarity-based inference with factual knowledge (Inagaki & Hatano, 1987) and, though not often, with inference based on biological functions. Therefore, we can identify an "intermediate" way of attribution, which might be called a constrained similarity-based attribution, that is, inferences primarily based on similarity but constrained by categorical knowledge. The attributional profile of this intermediate way can be a variety of mixed patterns between a flat pattern with a sharp break and a gradually decreasing pattern.

However, we assume that a pattern with a decreasing part on the person/animal side and a flat part on the plant/nonliving thing side would occur most often, because children use object-specific knowledge (Inagaki & Hatano, 1987) or categorical knowledge to reject the "Yes" response obtained by projecting human properties to nonhuman entities. It is not likely that children possess object-specific knowledge that enables them to answer "Yes" when they do not project human properties to the object according to its similarity to people. This likely intermediate pattern would thus reduce overattribution errors to plants and nonliving things more than underattribution errors to those animals that are apparently dissimilar to humans.

We examined whether the above developmental shift from similarity-based to category-based attribution would occur through an analysis of both group data (Inagaki & Sugiyama, 1988, Experiment 1) and of individual data (Experiment 2). For the attribution of unobservable anatomical/physiological properties, we predicted, as Carey (1985) found, that there would be developmental changes from similarity-based to category-based attribution between ages 4 and 10.

In contrast, for mental properties, which were not taught explicitly in school biology, we predicted that there would be a delayed shift, and thus even adults might sometimes make similarity-based attributions. This is because the attribution of mental properties requires more inference than does the attribution of anatomical/physiological properties. For example, when a child is asked, "Does a grasshopper have bones?", he or she can find an answer by making an inference based on knowledge about higher order category membership and category-attribute associations. The child can reason, "It is an insect, so it can't possibly have bones." However, for the question of "Does a grasshopper feel happy?", he or she must further consider that a brain is required to feel happy, along with whether a grasshopper has a brain. As C. Johnson and Wellman (1982) reported, it is fairly difficult for children to grasp associations between a brain and mental properties, especially mental properties such as having feelings and sensations.

We also predicted that intermediate patterns of attribution, that is, the constrained similarity-based attribution, would be found in between the two contrasting patterns of attribution, between younger children and adults for anatomical/physiological properties, and among older children and adults for mental properties. This prediction implies that adults would be able to reduce overattribution errors. For example, they would exclude the possibility that trees feel pain, even when they perceive them to be somewhat similar to people, because they know that plants do not have a central nervous system enabling them to have feelings.

In the first experiment, 20 participants each from five age groups were involved: 4-year-olds (M=4;9), 5-year-olds (M = 5;9), second-graders (M = 8;1), fourth-graders (M = 10;2), and college students. Eight phylogenetically different objects were used as targets: a person, rabbit, pigeon, fish, grasshopper, tulip, tree, and stone. The objects are listed here in the order of perceived similarity to people, as established in another sample, but were presented in a random fashion in the experiment.

The participants were individually asked 10 property questions for each of the eight objects in the format, "Does X have a property Y?" The 10 properties were grouped into three types: (a) unobservable anatomical/physiological properties: having a heart, having bones, breathing, and growth; (b) unobservable mental properties: the abilities to think, feel happy, and feel pain; (c) observable properties: having eyes, the ability to move, and speaking to a person. Questions about the observable properties were included to confirm that there were no developmental differences in attributional accuracy about these properties. In fact, it turned out that the participants in all age groups had almost equally high percentages of correct knowledge about these observable properties of the target objects. All the property questions were asked about an object before the inquiry proceeded to another object.

For each of the seven unobservable property questions, we computed proportions of "Yes" response to the eight target objects, phylogenetically ordered from a person to a stone, in each age group. As already shown in Figure 7.1, the category-based attribution should be a pattern consisting of a big gap (decline) and two flat parts before and after it, and the similarity-based attribution, a pattern showing gradual decrease from a person to a stone. Thus we examined whether there existed a big gap (an arbitrary criterion of a difference of 40% or more between two consecutive objects) somewhere on the continuum, and whether the two parts before and after the gap were flat (i.e., all the successive differences were less than 10%). Then we classified the attributional patterns, for each property by each age group, into three types, category-based, similarity-based, and intermediate (e.g., the pattern having a big gap but only one flat part).

Results supported all three of our predictions. For the anatomical/physiological properties, there was a progression from 4-year-olds' predominant reliance on similarity-based attribution to adults' predominant reliance on category-based attribution. The intermediate pattern of attribution was found between similarity-based and category-based attribution, mostly among 5-year-olds, second-, and fourth-graders. One example is shown in Figure 7.2. Thus the shift seemed to occur primarily during the elementary school years. For mental properties, participants in all age groups mostly made similarity-based attribution. An illustrative example is shown in Figure 7.3.

For the above findings from the analyses of group data, there exists an alternative interpretation, which is that this apparent similarity-based pattern for a group of participants may have been generated by their disagreement in attributional boundaries. More specifically, the above shift in patterns for anatomical/physiological properties may have been due to greater variability among younger children in the category extensions or in category-attribute associations than among adults, and adults' "similarity-based" patterns for mental properties may have only represented category-based attribution with different category-attribute associations. To exclude this alternative interpretation, we conducted Experiment 2 that examined whether the similarity-based pattern would be found within individuals as well.

Another group of 5-year-olds and of college students participated in this experiment. Target objects were five members each belonging to the same higher order categories (i.e., mammals, birds, fish, insects, and plants) but differing in appearance (e.g., size), as well as a person and a stone.

Each participant was individually asked to attribute two anatomical/physiological properties (having bones and the heart) and two mental properties (feeling pain and feeling happy) to each of the above 27 objects. The question formats were the same as those of Experiment 1 described above: "Does X have a property Y?" In other words, property

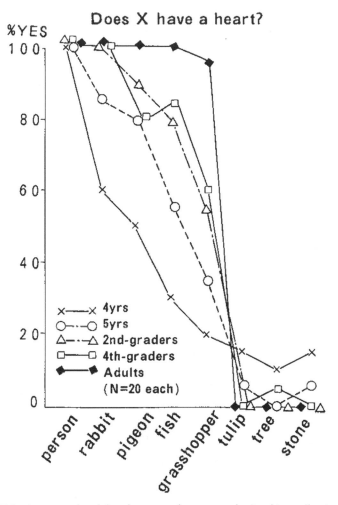

FIGURE 7.2. An example of developmental patterns obtained in attribution of the anatomical physiological properties. From Inagaki and Sugiyama (1988).

questions referred to the name of the target object, but did not refer to the name of the category. All the property questions were asked about an object before the inquiry proceeded to another object.

After all the property questions, the participant was required to classify into five categories all 25 of the above-described objects, excluding the person and the stone. This classification task was added in order to confirm that participants had relied on similarity-based attribution for judgment of these properties even though they were able to classify most of the objects correctly. Thus twenty 5-year-olds and twenty college students who classified most of the objects correctly were used in the analyses.

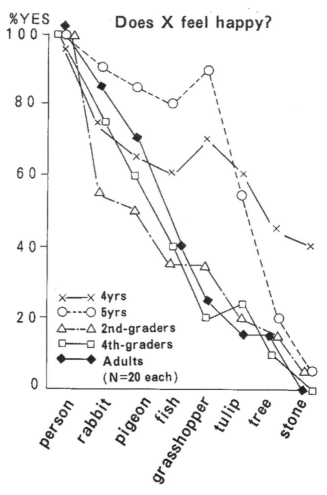

FIGURE 7.3. An example of developmental patterns obtained in attribution of the mental properties. From Inagaki and Sugiyama (1988).

   We classified the responses of each participant for each property into one of three patterns, that is, category-based, similarity-based, and others (classified as neither similarity-based nor category-based). If a participant makes category-based attributions, he or she should always answer "Yes" or always answer "No" to the question of whether each of the five objects belonging to the same category has a target property. Thus, the data pattern will consist of two flat parts with a sharp break. On the other hand, if a participant makes similarity-based attributions, he or she should give "Yes" responses to some members and "No" responses to others belonging to the same category when the category is located near the boundary of "Yes" responses and "No" responses; as a result, the ratio of "Yes" responses to each category should decrease as the categories become phylogenetically farther from people.

Results of Experiment 2 confirmed our interpretation of the result obtained by analyses of group data in Experiment 1, as shown in Table 7.1. For anatomical/physiological properties, 73% of the preschoolers' patterns fit the definition of similarity-based attribution. In contrast, 90% of the adults' patterns were category-based attributions. The developmental difference in frequency of the two patterns was highly significant.

For mental properties, about half of the young children's patterns reflected similarity-based attributions, versus only 13% reflecting category-based attributions. More than 50% of adults' patterns were also similarity-based attributions; about 40% were category-based. The difference between young children and adults in ratio of similarity-based to category-based patterns was marginally significant.

The results described above clearly indicate that there exist qualitative changes in the salient mode of inference, that is, from preschoolers' use of inference based on similarity to people to older children's and adults' reliance on higher order category-based inference, and that these changes proceed gradually from preschool years to middle childhood to adult ages.

We hastily add that we are not claiming that young children can never make inferences based on higher order biological categories. They can do so if they are urged to with some help, at least when they possess the pieces of knowledge about the higher order category membership of the target and relevant category-property relationships. However, they seldom possess such pieces of knowledge and are unlikely to rely on category-based inference spontaneously.

To paraphrase this shift, preschool children have a graded concept of living things organized in terms of their similarity to humans, but as they grow older, they come to possess a concept of living things that is divided into hierarchically organized categories, where humans are probably seen

TABLE 7.1. Percentages of each attributional pattern in each age group

Age group	Anatomical/physiological properties			Mental properties		
	S-based	C-based	Others	S-based	C-based	Others
5-year-olds	73	18	10	48	13	40
Adults	10	90	0	53	43	5

Note. S-based means similarity-based attribution; C-based means category-based attribution. $N = 20 \times 2$ in each age group.

just as animals. K. Johnson, Mervis, and Boster (1992) obtained relevant findings for 7-year-olds, and even 10-year-olds, in their experiment, using a triad task, which required the participants to find two similar things from among, say, human/nonhuman primate/nonprimate triads. Whereas the 7- and 10-year-olds tended to treat humans as isolates by showing reluctance to acknowledge similarities between humans and nonhumans, the adults did not show such a tendency; the adults responded by basing their judgments on membership within or outside the primate category.

Interestingly, this change in the salient mode of inference is accompanied with, if not induced by, change in metacognitive beliefs and values about particular modes of inference. Hatano and Inagaki (1991) examined whether the shift from similarity-based to category-based inferences would be induced, at least in part, by a metacognitive belief about the usefulness of higher order categories, namely, the belief that category-based inference is more dependable than similarity-based inference. Children of second-, fourth-, and sixth-grade were required to evaluate, in a questionnaire format, a given set of reasons that were allegedly offered by same-age children in a dialogue with a teacher. That is, they were asked to judge the plausibility of three different types of reasons, each of which was preceded by a "Yes/No" judgment to such a question as, "Does an eel have bones?" or "Does a tiger have a kidney(s)?" Two of the three reasons represented similarity-based inference and category-based inference, respectively. The former referred to the target's surface similarity to people, such as, "I think a tiger has a kidney, because it is generally like a human," and the latter referred to higher order categories like "mammals," such as, "I think a tiger has a kidney, because both a human and a tiger are mammals." The other reason, clearly not category-based nor similarity-based, was a distractor, for example, "I think a tiger does not have a kidney, because it is not as intelligent as a human." The same children were also given a similar attribution task as the one used in Inagaki and Sugiyama (1988).

It was found that as children grew older, the number of respondents who judged the category-based reason to be plausible and the similarity-based one to be implausible significantly increased, whereas the number of respondents who evaluated the similarity-based reason as plausible and the category-based one as implausible decreased, suggesting that children came to acquire a metacognitive belief about the usefulness of higher order categories. Moreover, even among the second-graders, those children who consistently favored category-based reasons tended to show an attributional pattern closer to the pure category-based attribution than was shown by those who favored similarity-based reasons.

Hatano and Inagaki further examined, by using indirect, "projective"-type questions, whether older students differentiated more clearly a fictitious child who gave a category-based reason from a child who gave a similarity-based reason in the rating of his or her academic talent. Another group of second-, fourth-, and sixth-graders were given a questionnaire. It described two hypothetical pairs of children of the same grade as the students, who, in dialogue with their teacher, gave a judgment of whether rabbits and ants had a pancreas (or tigers and grasshoppers had bones) and the reason for it. The reason given by one of each pair was in fact similarity-based, and the other, category-based (these labels were not given). The participating students were asked to rate how good academically the fictitious child who had given the reason would be, and how likable the child would be as a friend, in a four-point scale.

Results were as follows: The fictitious child who had allegedly given a category-based reason was rated significantly higher in academic talent than the allegedly similarity-based child in all grades. However, the older the participants, the bigger was the magnitude of the difference. That is, the older students were much more negative than the younger ones in the rating of the fictitious child who had given the similarity-based reasons. Since the likability rating for this fictitious child did not differ significantly, it is not likely that these participants always gave favorable ratings for the category-based child. These results strongly suggest that children become reluctant to use similarity to people as an inferential cue for biological attributions as they grow older. It is likely that conceptual change in modes of biological inference is enhanced by social sanctions; for instance, children may stop relying on similarity to people in order to avoid being regarded as less talented.

Progression From Vitalistic to Mechanical Causality

We examine how another essential element of young children's naive biology, namely vitalistic causality, changes as they grow older. In Chapter 5, we have seen that young children's naive biology is vitalistic in nature; they tend to apply vitalistic causality to internal bodily phenomena. They consider that internal bodily phenomena are caused by activity of an internal organ having agency, and the organ's activity often involves transmission or exchange of "vital force." Since the vital force is an unspecified substance as illustrated in children's words, "vital power," "source of energy," "something good for health," and so on, vitalistic causality presumes unspecified mechanisms. Vital power seems to be a global conceptual entity that serves as a causal device in children's initial biology. It is expected that, as children learn more and more about biological phenomena including scientific words and their implications, through learning school biology, watching TV programs, or reading books, they come to acquire knowledge that enables them to specify mechanisms. In other words, the global conceptual entity of vital power is specified into a set of particular mechanisms. With this learning of specific mechanisms, children come to recognize mechanical causality (presupposing a specified mechanism) to be more reliable than vitalistic causality, and this induces the shift to mechanical causality.

To confirm this expectation, Inagaki and Hatano (1993, Experiment 2) examined whether young children's reliance on vitalistic causality would progress to the use of mechanical causality as they grow older. Not only 6-year-olds but also 8-year-olds and college students participated in this study. They were asked to choose one from among three possible causal explanations for each of six bodily phenomena, such as blood circulation and respiration. The three explanations represented intentional, vitalistic, and mechanical causality, respectively. Although several of the example questions and three alternative explanations were already shown in Chapter 5, we present here another example, blood circulation: "Why does the blood flow to different parts of our bodies? (a) Because we move our body, hoping the blood will flow in it [intentional causality]; (b) Because our heart works hard to send out life and energy with blood [vitalistic]; (c) Because the heart sends the blood by working as a pump [mechanical]."

As shown in Figure 7.4, the 6-year-old children chose vitalistic explanations as most plausible most often (54%) and chose intentional explanations second most often (25%). In contrast, the 8-year-olds chose mechanical causal explanations most often (62%) and opted for some

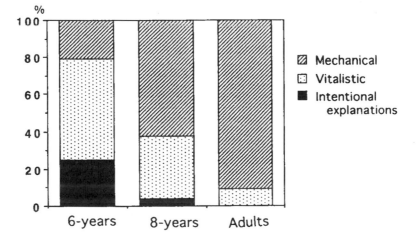

FIGURE 7.4. Percentages of choices for different types of casual explanations.

vitalistic ones (34%) as well, but seldom chose intentional explanations. The adults predominantly preferred mechanical explanations to explanations of the other two types.

Results of individual data analyses also confirmed this developmental change in preferred causality. Out of the twenty 6-year-olds, only one chose four or more intentional explanations for the six items (we call them intentional responders), whereas nine chose four or more vitalistic explanations (vitalistic responders). Among 8-year-olds, there was only one vitalistic responder; there were 10 mechanical responders who made four or more mechanical choices; 6 out of 9 "Others" respondents were children who chose vitalistic and mechanical explanations equally (three each), and 2 were children who made three vitalistic choices and two mechanical choices. Among adults, there were 19 mechanical responders and one vitalistic responder. This pattern of findings also suggests that there exists change in preferred causality from vitalistic to mechanical, with increasing age.

Developmental change in preferred causality for biological phenomena is not confined to Japanese children and adults. Morris, Taplin, and Gelman (2000), carrying out a careful replication of Inagaki and Hatano's (1993) Experiment 2, confirmed this tendency among English-speaking children and adults in Australia. When asked to choose one from among three causal explanations for each of the six bodily phenomena, Australian 5-year-old kindergartners showed a clear preference for vitalistic explanations over mechanical ones, whereas college students and, to a lesser extent, 10-year-old children chose the mechanical explanation most often. Results from the individual data analyses confirmed the results of the group analysis, indicating that 30% of the 5-year-olds were vitalistic responders, while 48% of the 10-year-olds and 80% of the adults were mechanical responders.

Again, we would like to emphasize that the observed shift is for preferred causality, and it is premature to conclude that young children cannot rely on mechanical causality in explaining bodily processes. However, they are unlikely to be attracted by mechanical explanations because they do not have well-understood examples of specific mechanisms for bodily processes.

When the above findings on the shift in preferred causalities are combined with those on the shift in the salient mode of inference, we can conclude convincingly that there occurs conceptual change in children's naive biology, from 5-years-old or so through middle childhood and adulthood; from young children's personifying and vitalistic biology to older children's and adults' biology based on category-based inference and mechanical causality.

Pre-Change System Still Exists in Adults' Intuitive Biology

Is older children's and adults' intuitive biology no longer personifying at all? Is the similarity-based inference completely replaced by the category-based inference in older children and adults? Does their intuitive biology no longer rely on vitalistic causality? Answers to these questions are not affirmative. The fact that there exists a shift from similarity-based to category-based inferences does not mean that older children and adults never rely on similarity to people in their inferences. Likewise, as discussed in Chapter 5, the fact that there is a developmental shift from reliance on vitalistic causality to that on mechanical causality does not denote that adults never take vitalistic views for biological understanding. We first describe the similarity-based inference in adults.

Adults' Reliance on Similarity-Based Inference

Remember that a substantial number of adults as well as older children still relied on similarity to people in attributing mental properties to various animals. As impressively indicated in Table 7.1, even adults showed the similarity-based pattern at a substantial rate (more than 50% of the time) in attributing mental properties to animate entities. This suggests that even adults sometimes rely on similarity-based inference.

This tendency is not limited to attribution of mental or psychological properties. In another experiment using reaction times (Morita, Inagaki, & Hatano, 1988), we found that college students relied on similarity-based attribution to some extent not only for mental properties but also anatomical/physiological ones in a situation where quick responding was required. In this experiment, 4 pairs of animals belonging to the same category but differing in judged similarity to humans (e.g., a tiger vs. a fur seal; a tortoise vs. a snake; a penguin vs. a swallow; a mantis vs. a grasshopper) were used as targets, and 4 additional objects (e.g., a rose, a stone, etc.), as fillers. These 4 pairs were selected from 16 animals by another group of students who were required to rate them on a 9-point scale in terms of similarity to people. The former of each pair was perceived by these raters as more similar to people than the latter. First, 31 college students were told the correct higher order category that each object belongs to, and then they were required to give Yes/No responses as quickly as possible to 7 property questions for each of the 12 objects (i.e., the 4 pairs of animals and 4 fillers). The property questions consisted of two unobservable anatomical/physiological properties (i.e., has bones and breathes), two mental properties (i.e., feels pain and feels sad), two observable animal properties (i.e., has a mouth and has eyes) and one human property (i.e., speaks language). Answers to these questions were to be all "Yes" for humans. There were 84 property questions altogether.

It was found that these students made more "Yes" responses to the more human-like members of the animals (e.g., a tortoise in the above example) in attributing unobservable properties. In addition, when their responses were identical within pairs, "Yes" responses were quicker for the more similar members than for the less similar ones, whereas "No" responses were slower for the more similar members than for the less similar ones (see Figure 7.5). The interaction effect was significant. This suggests that even college students use the similarity-to-humans as a cue when relying on category-based inference is nearly impossible because of the time pressure.

It is not feasible to explain the above results in terms of prototypicality, for example, that the more typical member of the pair was more readily assigned target properties shared by most members of the category. This is because the member of the pair that is more similar to humans is not always more prototypical within the category; for example, a penguin is more similar to humans, but less prototypical within the category of birds than a swallow. Moreover, some of the target properties (e.g., feeling sad) are typical of humans, and are in fact not attributed to other animals frequently.

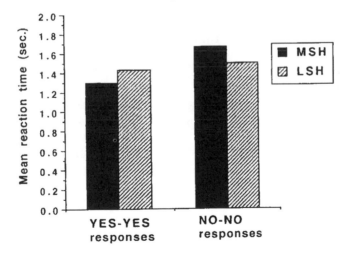

FIGURE 7.5. Mean reaction times for "Yes" and "No" responses to the members more similar to humans (MSH) and the less similar to humans (LSH) when a participant's responses were identical within pairs of animals.

Thus, we can summarize that the college students relied on similarity to people in attributing mental as well as unobservable biological properties under time pressure. This means that the developmental shift from similarity-based to category-based inference is only a part of the whole story; the similarity-based mode of inference is retained and may be used even by adults as a fallback strategy.

Adults' Use of Vitalistic Causality

Inagaki and Hatano (1993) and Morris et al. (2000) revealed that older children and college students preferred more strongly mechanical causality to the vitalistic one. However, this does not necessarily mean that adults never rely on vitalistic causality in any situation. Instead, we claim, vitalistic causality is never completely superseded by mechanical causality with increasing age; rather, it may continue to work as a basis of understanding some biological phenomena and to be used in situations where people are not required to give precise and detailed answers based on scientific biology (Hatano & Inagaki, 1996, 1997). In fact, a few college students in Experiment 2 of Inagaki and Hatano (1993) seemed to use vitalistic causality as an informal or fallback mode of explanation. One student who consistently chose vitalistic explanations answered at the interview after the experiment, "We usually choose those including 'oxygen' or 'the heart works like a pump' because we have learned in school to do so. However, I chose others because they were most convincing and comprehensible to me."

Miller and Bartsch (1997), conducting a modified replication of Inagaki and Hatano's (1993) Experiment 2, found that American college students were vitalists, contrary to Inagaki and Hatano (1993); that is, these students preferred to apply vitalistic explanations for bodily phenomena as often as the 6- and 8-year-olds did. Although we cannot reject a possibility that this result was an artifact produced by methodological problems in their study, as Morris et al. (2000) pointed out (instead of requiring participants to choose one from among three alternatives, they asked the participants to make a choice between intentional and vitalistic explanations, and between vitalistic and mechanical explanations) it is possible that these adults indeed preferred vitalistic explanations for bodily phenomena, because the students may have been interviewed in a situation in which answers based on scientific biology were not highly valued. It is plausible that even adults still consider vitalistic explanations reasonable for bodily phenomena and offer such explanations when they are not obliged to give an answer based on scientific biology.

We should note the fact that not only young children but also a substantial ratio of lay adults hold the idea of resistance to illness as one case of vitalism in everyday life; they believe in folk preventive medicine that advocates the importance of one's resistance to illness and that offers various specific recommendations for improving resistance. When asked what factor was considered the most important as a cause for getting a cold, about 70% of Japanese college students offered physical factors as contributing to illness susceptibility, that is, irregular daily routines or the lack of self-control of health, fatigue, deterioration of physical strength, sudden change of temperature, and so on. For example, "Bodily resistance to illness is lost due to shortage of sleep and/or fatigue," "Insufficient sleep or staying out in cold weather increases bodily susceptibility to illness," or "The body cannot adjust to sudden changes of temperature" (see Inagaki & Hatano, 1999a).

We can generalize the above results as follows: Although the pre- and post-change knowledge systems are qualitatively different, there are some continuities between them (Hatano, 1994). The occurrence of conceptual change does not mean that components of the pre-change system are replaced by the post-change system and disappear completely. We claim that old components retain as less salient fallback models or strategies in the new system. This is consistent with recent research findings indicating that multiple models (Yates et al., 1988) or multiple strategies (e.g., Siegler & Jenkins, 1989) coexist within the same individual. This is also in line with the claim offered by Perner (1991) as to the development of theories of mind or the claim by Subbotsky (1997) as to phenomenalistic causal reasoning. An important implication of these claims is that the post-change knowledge system of educated adults may not be as drastically different from young children's pre-change knowledge system as it appears.

Another Conceptual Change?

The qualitative changes that we have discussed so far occur in later childhood, that is, after 5 years of age. Considering that a great majority of investigators now believe that even preschool children possess a form of naive biology, only those changes before 5 years of age can be relevant to the issue of conceptual change that has been the target of debate, namely, whether naive biology emerges from intuitive psychology through conceptual change. Does another conceptual change take place earlier? Since in Chapter 8 we will discuss in detail the issue of whether young children interpret biological phenomena within the framework of intuitive psychology, we concentrate here on the issue of whether naive biology emerges from naive psychology through conceptual change.

It is true that there are some qualitative changes in children's predictions and explanations for biological phenomena approximately between ages 3 and 5. As we reviewed in the preceding chapters, many studies have shown that 5-year-old children can clearly differentiate human biological properties and phenomena from psychological ones in terms of modifiability and controllability. They also understand illness causality biologically. Around age 5, children can distinguish living entities including animals and plants from nonliving things and begin to recognize commonalities between animals and plants. Some studies have shown that 5-year-olds can choose biological explanations presented from a number of alternative causal explanations for biological phenomena, and at times even offer biological explanations themselves.

In contrast, (a) 3- and 4-year-olds' predictions for biological phenomena are not highly consistent and are easily influenced by contexts or by types of questions. (b) They sometimes rely on psychological causal devices as often as on biological ones for biological phenomena, whereas they seldom apply biological causality to social-psychological phenomena. However, (c) when biological and psychological causal devices are explicitly contrasted, they tend to choose the biological ones for biological phenomena.

We propose two possible interpretations for the observed change during these years. It may be that, although children as young as 3 possess naive biology as well as psychology, psychological knowledge is more readily retrieved generally and thus sometimes interferes with the retrieval of its biological counterpart (as suggested above (b)). It probably takes a few years before young children clearly recognize that it is not naive psychology but biology that can explain those bodily processes and phenomena that are needed for us to be active and lively but are beyond our intentional control. It could thus be called a kind of conceptual change, somewhat similar to a relevance shift (Keil, 1999). This interpretation is harmonious with Carey's (1985) original position, though it differs from hers in attributing a form of naive biology to young children (based on (c) above). An alternative interpretation is that the observed change is just trivial, because it is a product of the fact that 3-year-olds' naive biology is still being established. For many theories, there is some delay between acquisition and firm establishment, and such theories are unlikely to be used promptly until they are well established. Naive psychology as an established neighbor theory may sometimes penetrate into biological reasoning, but only until the establishment of naive biology.

Although more studies are needed, we prefer the second interpretation, because even 3-year-olds respond differently to biological and psychological phenomena unless they respond in a random fashion. In addition, they tend to choose biological causal devices for biological phenomena when these devices are given explicitly. In other words, we assume that the observed change in biological reasoning between ages 3 and 5 is not a matter of conceptual change but of a gradual construction of naive biology.

☐ How Does Conceptual Change Occur?

In this final section, we discuss the issue of how conceptual change occurs in general, using primarily the case of naive biology as an example, because conceptual changes in core domains of thought are considered to be similar to each other in their mechanisms and conditions, though different in content. Although the issue of how conceptual change occurs and the specification of its mechanisms is "one of the fundamental problems of cognitive psychology today" (Vosniadou, 1994, p. 3), the available data are limited. This is partly because recent developmentalists have focused on the specification of the initial form of a naive theory and, to a much lesser extent, on the description of the state after conceptual change, without analyzing the process of change itself (e.g., Carey, 1985; Wellman, 1990). Relying on not only findings obtained in conceptual development but also some evidence from the history of science and science education, we thus propose possible mechanisms of conceptual change and conditions for its occurrence. To put it differently, we consider primarily mechanisms and conditions of spontaneous conceptual change, but take into account findings from studies on instruction-based conceptual change or scientists' activities, when they are relevant.

The critical difference between spontaneous and instruction-based conceptual changes seems to be the extent to which a cognizer consciously recognizes inconguity in his or her existing knowledge system and to which he or she intentionally attempts to solve them. Whereas spontaneous conceptual change seems to proceed slowly but steadily without the cognizer's explicit recognition of incongruity, the instruction-based conceptual change usually takes place only when students explicitly recognize the inadequacy of their conceptual knowledge by a teacher's instructional attempts to induce such recognition in them.

It is clear that in every case increased knowledge is required for conceptual change, and that the pre-change system serves as a cognitive constraint on conceptual change. In other words, conceptual change is a cognitive attempt to resume coherence of the knowledge system that has been disturbed by new pieces of information, through complex interactions of constituent elements of the current knowledge system.

Let us propose two contrasting mechanisms, one local and bottom-up, the other goal directed and top-down. If the system includes all candidate concepts, conceptions, and conceptualizations, each of which has its own subjective truth value (i.e., how strongly it is believed to be true), conceptual change can be described as radical changes in the truth-value of a range of connected pieces of knowledge (or beliefs, these two expressions being used interchangeably). We can thus assume that one type of mechanism for conceptual change is the spreading of truth-value alteration. When new inputs change the truth value of some pieces of knowledge, the changes bring about changes in the truth-value of other connected pieces, which may induce further changes in their neighbors. In the long run, there can be a drastic change in almost all pieces through continued spreading and recurring effects as well as further inputs to facilitate the truth-value alteration. This type of conceptual change is a bottom-up process and does not require the cognizer's conscious grasp of incongruity among beliefs and intentional attempt to reduce it. The relationships among beliefs are divided into dyadic relations with one another, each of which is characterized only in terms of whether two beliefs are roughly consonant, dissonant, or neither (one belief's being true implies the other belief's being true, false, or nothing). Here the change is gradual, takes time, and is based on a large amount of input.

The other type of conceptual change, which might be called deliberate belief revision, sometimes occurs. A representative subtype of this is similar to the process of comprehension monitoring (Markman, 1981) or repair (e.g., Ackerman, 1984; Glenberg & Epstein, 1985) in the sense that existing beliefs are consciously and deliberately rewritten (and new beliefs are introduced) in the process, in order to remove recognized inconsistencies (e.g., disconfirmed predictions based on the current set of beliefs) and make the knowledge system coherent again. In another subtype, deliberate belief revision is induced by what we call "discoordination" (Hatano, 1998), that is, the recognition that the current set of beliefs is not well connected or not powerful enough to be the basis for understanding the world. In both cases, removal of incongruity is not achieved as the accumulation of small local changes, as in the case of spreading of the truth-value alteration. It is a top-down, goal-directed process.

Instruction-based conceptual change usually takes the form of deliberate belief revision. In contrast, spontaneous conceptual change usually proceeds less consciously and less deliberately, although it is not always bottom-up. It is often initiated when a new piece of information induces unexpected incongruity. Suppose that children have a conception of birds consisting of a set of beliefs, such as "birds are flying animals," "birds are bigger than bugs," "birds lay eggs," "birds have wings," and so on. If they learn that a penguin is a bird but does not fly, it is dissonant with the first belief; or when they learn that a bat flies but isn't a bird, the target belief may become less trustworthy. As a result of these local, minor truth-value alterations and their recurring effects, children's conception of birds may change, as the flying-animals belief, being dissociated from other beliefs about birds, becomes less and less trustworthy. Alternatively, however, such incongruous pieces of information may induce a deliberate attempt to revise the conception. Of course, we human beings can ignore or tolerate incongruity to some extent, but let us suppose children are sensitive and open to the incongruous information. They may thus be tempted to modify their conception of birds, for instance, into something like, "birds are animals that have a basic body structure convenient for flying, but cannot necessarily fly."

Similarly, children who have found that similarity to people does not always lead to valid attributions, or that their peers often use and highly evaluate category-based inference, may weaken a little their belief in similarity-based inference. Alternatively, they may decide to compare similarity-based and category-based inferences systematically. Those who are afraid that vitalistic explanations are not welcome by adults (including the science teacher) and those who know some mechanical concepts and terms may shift to offering mechanical explanations either via spreading of truth-value alteration or via deliberate belief revision. We believe that spontaneous conceptual change involves a combination of the two mechanisms.

Conditions for Inducing Conceptual Change

What conditions are likely to induce conceptual change? It should be pointed out that, although accumulated knowledge is a necessary condition for conceptual change (e.g., Carey, 1985), it is not a sufficient condition. We propose three additional conditions, two cognitive requisites that seem necessary and the sociocultural context that is facilitative. Since spontaneous conceptual change occurs without systematic intervention, these conditions are usually met, but theoretically it is significant to conceptualize them explicitly.

First, some metacognitive abilities that enable one to assess and monitor incongruity within the existing knowledge system are needed for conceptual change (especially deliberate belief revision) to occur, because it is an incongruity-reducing process. In most cases, as children grow older, their knowledge accumulates, and at the same time their metacognitive knowledge and skills also develop. In other words, the increase of knowledge and the development of metacognitive knowledge and skills proceed hand-in-hand in normal cognitive development. Thus, the necessity of metacognitive knowledge and skills for conceptual change is often overlooked.

However, we can offer solid evidence for the importance of metacognitive ability for conceptual change by examining knowledge that individuals with the Williams syndrome have acquired. Individuals with Williams syndrome tend to talk in great detail with only superficial understanding, on the one hand, and lack analytic and metacognitive knowledge and skills, on the other. S. Johnson and Carey (1998) compared individuals with Williams syndrome, whose average verbal mental age was 11 years, with two groups of normally developing children whose average mental ages were 10 years and 6 years, respectively, in terms of the acquisition of general knowledge of animals (e.g., the size of their animal lexicon) and folkbiological concepts that were supposed to be normally acquired through conceptual change between ages 6 and 12 years (e.g., concepts of being alive or dead). They found that, although the participants with Williams syndrome performed at the level of the normal children of age 10 on the tasks concerning general knowledge of animals, their performance on the folkbiological knowledge tasks was at the level of normal 6-year-olds.

Although a number of alternative interpretations could be offered, we consider this finding as strongly suggesting the role of metacognitive skills in the acquisition of knowledge through conceptual change. In the course of normal development, we assume, children use metacognitive skills more or less unconsciously, and as a result, the process of belief revision may proceed slowly and gradually because a piece of new information induces local incongruity. This may be one of the reasons why conceptual change occurring in development takes place gradually over years, as is well illustrated in the developmental shifts in a domain of biology in the previous section.

Some conceptual change observed among scientists may occur more quickly than conceptual change occurring in the course of childhood conceptual development. Scientists can carefully monitor coherence among pieces of knowledge constituting a theory and be sensitive to and respond to a small amount of disconfirmation or discoordination in their knowledge system, thanks to their advanced metacognitive abilities. A good example is the "thought experiment," including limiting case analyses, as represented by Galileo's famous thought experiment showing that heavier objects do not fall faster than lighter ones (Nersessian, 1992). Some science instruction aims at bringing about conceptual change in less time by making students aware of the incongruity in their knowledge through the presentation of contradictory evidence.

The second condition for conceptual change is that an alternative concept, conception, or conceptualization (or the set of its constituent pieces) is available at least potentially in the existing knowledge structure. As indicated above, conceptual change via a spreading of the truth-value alteration is possible only when the candidate pieces of conceptual knowledge are included in the system. The deliberate belief revision is possible only when a cognizer can think of an alternative belief. If people do not think of any alternative theory, model, or interpretation, they may stick to the old conceptual device even when predictions from it are not supported.

An alternative concept, conception, or conceptualization may be prepared gradually and slowly in development of the target naive theory; alternatively, it can be brought in from outside the target theory by using some "borrowing" heuristics. Examples of the former case include the following.

1. Pieces of information needed to construct an alternative idea are accumulated slowly because they are not attended initially (e.g., on a balance beam, young children pay attention to the number of weights but ignore their distance from the center).
2. An idea stays implicit, in other words, it is "implemented" but not represented (e.g., being able to solve a concrete problem but unable to describe how to solve it).
3. An idea is available only in a particular context and has yet to be generalized (e.g., from biological understanding of illness as caused by germs only when there are obvious routes of contagion, such as coughing, to a generalized illness causality in terms of the germ theory).

Analogies and conceptual placeholders are two major "borrowing" heuristics. Conceptual change may often be triggered by an analogy that suggests an alternative view. Using analogies, people map their knowledge about the source to the present new case (target) so that they can make a coherent interpretation of the set of observations for the target, or even build a tentative theory.

Analogies are sometimes applied spontaneously, and other times presented by teachers and other adults. Photosynthesis is one of the difficult notions in understanding biology, because it is against the intuitive grasp of the commonality among all living things that naive biology indicates. That plants can produce their own nutriment is usually beyond children's imagination. However, Yuzawa (1988) reported that a "production factory" analogy—processing materials with proper means like baking bread from flour using heat—helped junior high students understand photosynthesis. Dunbar (1995) also reported that scientists in real-world laboratories often rely on analogy to generate new ideas when faced with inconsistent experimental findings.

Another possibility for deriving an alternative concept, conceptions, and conceptualizations is to assume a conceptual placeholder that does not include much substantive information initially. Solomon and Johnson (2000) reported findings suggesting that conceptual change occurs when children are exposed to a scientific concept that can serve as a conceptual peg in a sociocultural context. Here, children of 5–6 years were first made aware of the inadequacy of their understanding of biological inheritance by a conversation with a teacher, and then they were given a rudimentary notion of genes and opportunities to use this notion. This intervention, though lasting only about 20 minutes, led the children to make adult-like judgments on inheritance to some extent. This strategy is often adopted in science education. However, considering that young children in highly technological societies are often presented with a scientific concept that would serve as a conceptual peg through conversation with adults, watching TV programs, reading a book with adults, and so on in everyday life, spontaneous conceptual change also could occur in a similar way in everyday life, though it would take a longer time than the instruction-based one.

Third, sociocultural contexts in which children are exposed to various, sometimes incongruous, pieces of information may make conceptual change more likely to occur. As already mentioned, children's learning that others possess different beliefs from their own may reduce the truth-value of relevant beliefs and also induce attempts to revise the beliefs. This is because, though human beings have not only confirmation biases but also tendencies to ignore incongruous information (Festinger, 1957), they cannot do so when they engage in interaction with others for an extended period of time. One of such contexts enhancing conceptual change is social interactions including group discussion. Social interactions can be sources for generating recognized inconsistencies or discoordinations in individuals' existing knowledge systems, because different perspectives are presented in the interactions, and they can also be sources for providing possible solutions. In this sense, discussion can contribute to the occurrence of conceptual change. Indeed, it has been reported that social interaction can be a powerful mechanism for inducing conceptual change among scientists (Dunbar, 1995).

However, a number of studies have revealed that even among less sophisticated thinkers, discursive interactions may induce conceptual change. For example, Hatano and Inagaki (1997) provided data to support this claim; many school-aged children (10 years of age) changed their ways of reasoning about a monkey's physical characteristics through whole-class discussion—from reasoning based on the animal's similarity to humans to reasoning based on a more sophisticated (Lamarckian) conception of evolution and specific biological taxonomy. Willams and Tolmie (2000) also reported that socially generated cognitive conflict (or inconsistencies) is effective for acquiring a more advanced conception of inheritance in their intervention study using children aged 8–12. Their dialogue analyses indicated that the effects of group discussion could be attributed to resolution of conceptual conflict within the groups holding different conceptions.

Toward an Integrative and Moderate Model of Conceptual Change

Let us make a brief comparison with other notions of conceptual change proposed so far. In what point does our notion of conceptual change differ from others? We take the position that conceptual change, as a profound change in a child's underlying conceptual structures, can take place during childhood, and at the same time we assert that the pre- and post-change knowledge systems have some continuity. In naive biology, for example, the pre- and post-change modes of inference or causalities coexist even among adults, though the former system becomes less salient and is used as a fallback.

How is our notion related to a newly proposed idea that children and adults differ only in shifting the relevance of already present explanatory systems (Keil, 1998, 1999)? This relevance shift notion of "conceptual change" denotes that children and adults differ not in underlying conceptual structures but in the relevance of these structures; children often possess several theories available to them early on, but they differ remarkably from adults in realizing where these theories are most relevant. It should be noted that according to this conceptualization, conceptual change is no longer clearly distinguished from enrichment. We agree with this notion of continuities in conceptual structures among young children, older children, and adults. Even preschool children possess naive theories of core domains, such as biology and psychology, and if they are urged to do so, they may be able to reason using biological categories and relying on mechanical causality in primitive ways. However, this does not mean that all developmental differences are just quantitative, a matter of how salient a variety of competing ideas are and how adaptively they can be applied to problem situations.

In addition, we cannot ignore possibilities that instruction-based conceptual change or instructionally influenced spontaneous conceptual change can take place, especially in later cognitive development. It can produce new conceptual tools through which older children and lay adults can see the world differently than young children do. We should pay more attention to the bridge or interaction between conceptual development and instruction, as claimed and researched by Vosniadou and Ioannides (1998).

Finally, our notion of conceptual change has emphasized the sociocultural factors involved. We fully agree that an increased amount of knowledge is a necessary condition for conceptual change (e.g., Carey, 1985; Smith et al., 1985; Wiser, 1988) and that the pre-change system provides as cognitive or internal constraints in conceptual change. However, the roles of other people and tools as sociocultural or interactive constraints are also very important in conceptual change. We believe that most leading investigators studying conceptual change have been too cognitive and too individualistic. The issue of motivation inducing conceptual change has also been neglected, with a few notable exceptions (e.g., Pintrich, Marx, & Boyle, 1993).

8
CHAPTER

Toward a Better Understanding of Conceptual Development

Our experimental findings, as well as those of other investigators, have demonstrated that Piaget (1929), in spite of his great insight, was not completely right. Although young children are animistic and personifying, they possess naive knowledge needed to differentiate the living from the nonliving and the bodily from the mental. They reason about human biological (life-sustaining) behaviors in terms of vitalistic causality, whereas they reason about social-psychological behaviors in terms of intentional causality.

The findings also have shown that Carey's (1985) original formulation needs substantial revision: Although, as she aptly pointed out, young children know little about the physiological mechanisms involved in bodily processes and fail to apply mechanical causality to biological phenomena, they nonetheless possess a form of biology based on vitalistic causality separate from psychology. Young children do not differentiate the body and the mind as clearly as modern Western scientists do, especially for illness causality, but this does not mean that they do not differentiate between biology and psychology in terms of target phenomena and modes of causality. In fact, her current position (Carey, 1995, 1999) seems much more congruent with ours.

Like Piaget and Carey, we are convinced that young children's naive biology is human centered, but, unlike Piaget and Carey, we emphasize positive features of personification in biological understanding. We think

181

that if, as Keil (1992) suggested, humans possess knowledge acquisition devices specialized for biological phenomena, the devices partly exist in the fact that humans, too, have a body that needs food and/or water. This prepares humans, even young children, to analogically understand other living things as having a body that takes in food/water.

☐ What Young Children Know About Biological Phenomena

We summarize briefly the entire argument we have reviewed in the preceding chapters. Let us start with what young children's knowledge system for biological phenomena has and what it does not. The experimental findings gathered so far generally indicate that children as young as 5 years of age possess three essential components of biology, that is, the living/nonliving and the mind/body distinctions, a mode of inference enabling one to produce consistent and reasonable predictions for animals and plants (personification), and a nonintentional causal explanatory framework for biological phenomena (vitalism). These components correspond, respectively, to the three features that Wellman (1990) lists in characterizing framework theories: ontological distinctions, coherence, and a causal-explanatory framework.

However, the experimental findings also reveal that young children's naive biological knowledge has several limitations. Young children's biological knowledge is limited in quantity, and they apply biological reasoning to a limited set of biological phenomena (focusing on eating, being vigorous and lively, and growing, but almost neglecting reproducing and etiological aspects). They lack inferences based on complex, hierarchically organized biological categories and they lack an appreciation of mechanical causality for physiological-biochemical processes. Moreover, they have yet to learn various conceptual devices in scientific or school biology (e.g., "evolution," "photosynthesis").

The use of inferences based on hierarchically organized biological categories and that of mechanical causality requires conceptual change (i.e., fundamental restructuring or qualitative change in knowledge), whereas the accumulation of factual knowledge and coherent application of biological reasoning can be achieved by accretion or enrichment. Whether the acquisition of basic conceptual devices in scientific or school biology is accompanied by conceptual change as theory change is not beyond dispute, but incorporating these devices meaningfully into the child's existing body of knowledge can usually be achieved only with its partial restructuring.

☐ Conclusions About Four Target Issues in the Naive Biology Debate

In this section we present our conclusions on four theoretical issues that have been debated among researchers on naive biology (Hatano & Inagaki, 1994b, 1996): (a) whether young children are animistic, and if so, why; (b) the age by which most children have acquired naive biology; (c) whether naive biology emerges from psychology; and (d) whether the development of naive biology involves conceptual change.

About Animism

Both Piaget's and Carey's studies on children's biological understanding concerned animism. With regard to the interpretation about childhood animism, we present a third alternative to Piaget (beyond R. Gelman and Carey).

Piaget (1929) asserted that young children are animistic (or, as we have termed it, personifying) and took this animistic tendency as a sign of intellectual immaturity, reflecting the fact that young children have not yet acquired basic differentiations of entities, such as the animate/inanimate distinction. Although there were many replication studies conducted within the Piagetian framework in earlier years, studies of young children's biological understanding or naive biology since the 1980s, as we have seen in Chapters 2 and 3, shed new light on childhood animism. These recent studies have shown that young children are able not only to distinguish between animals and non-animals but also to differentiate living things, including animals and plants, from nonliving things.

R. Gelman et al. (1983) claimed that, based on their data, children are seldom animistic unless they respond in play mode. According to them, Piaget induced play-mode responses by asking a series of peculiar questions, for example, referring to the consciousness of clouds. This play-mode explanation offers an interesting alternative to Piaget's explanation of the animistic responses that he and his followers (e.g., Laurendeau & Pinard, 1962) observed. However, this alternative provides only a partial answer to the issue of animism, because young children, even when they are intellectually serious, also make animistic or personifying remarks fairly often, though not as often as Piaget claimed.

We, like Carey (1985), have claimed in this book that, though young children are able to classify entities into ontological categories, they apply their knowledge about human beings to other living things or even to inanimate objects, in order to infer an entity's unknown attributes or reactions. This is probably because they do not have rich categorical knowledge and thus have to rely on analogies in inference. Since they are intimately familiar with humans while necessarily ignorant of most other entities, at least when growing up in highly technological societies, they can most profitably use their knowledge about humans as a source analog for making analogies.

However, we differ from Carey in the following respect: Whereas Carey (1985) stresses the false or distorted interpretations of biological phenomena in terms of human psychology, we emphasize that the animistic, or personifying, tendencies of young children are products of their active mind and have a basically adaptive nature. Young children's personification or person analogy, which can be a basis for biological as well as psychological reasoning, can lead them to accurate predictions for living things functionally similar to humans. It can also provide justifications for a variety of experiences, sometimes even with phylogenetically less similar objects like trees or flowers. Thus personification allows young children to accumulate biological knowledge promptly and with understanding.

Of course, young children may carry the person analogy beyond its proper limits and produce false inferences, as revealed in typical examples of animistic reasoning. However, they can also generate appropriate "educated guesses" by such analogies, relying on their only familiar source analog of a person (Holyoak & Thagard, 1995). Thus animistic errors and/or overattribution of human characteristics to nonhuman objects should be regarded as negative by-products unluckily generated by this basically sensible process of reasoning. Because their attempts at personification are guided by a few constraints for inferences, such as checking the plausibility of the inference against what is known about the target, they do not produce so many overpersonifying errors, except for assigning mental states to nonhumans (Inagaki & Hatano, 1991).

Personification plays an especially important role in young children's understanding of plants as biological entities, as those taking energy from outside and using its surplus for growth. Mapping the relation between humans and food to that between plants and water is intuitively appealing, especially because young children do not know that plants can produce the needed nutriment themselves (through photosynthesis). They surely overpersonify plants sometimes, but personification serves as the basis for acquiring the integrated category of living things, including both animals and plants.

In short, we emphasize the adaptiveness of inferences based on the knowledge about humans. Personification reveals young children's adaptive mind as well as their limited biological knowledge. The finding that young children use their enriched knowledge acquired through raising animals as source in analogy (Inagaki, 1990a, 2001a) also supports, though indirectly, the interpretation of animism or personification as an attempt by the active and constructive human mind to make educated guesses often based on poor biological knowledge.

How can we account for animistic thinking among indigenous adults? According to Atran (1998), in cultures throughout the world it is common to classify all entities into four ontological categories and to arrange animals and plants hierarchically and more or less accurately, because such taxonomies are products of the human mind's natural classification scheme. Indigenous people generally possess rich knowledge about major animals and plants in their ecological niche. Therefore, their animistic and personifying remarks, except about poorly understood nonnatural entities like God (Barrett & Keil, 1996), cannot be attributed to a paucity of biological knowledge. Those remarks seem instead to be products of cultural beliefs acquired through, among other things, discourse about a specific class of entities. Mead's (1932) early observation that children in the Manus tribes were less animistic than adults lends support to this conjecture. Aptly assigning some human properties (e.g., consciousness) to nonhuman animals, plants, or even nonliving things was considered as a sign of mature thought in those tribes. It should also be noted that animistic or personifying explanations, widespread among indigenous folks, are more about the metaphysical or imaginative universe than about the world of everyday, ordinary things (Atran, 1990). Even in contemporary Japanese culture, outside of science lessons, it is not considered a silly idea that large, old inanimate entities (e.g., giant rocks, mountains) have consciousness. These explanations cannot be a sign of intellectual immaturity, because these forms of reasoning emerge no earlier than biological reasoning developmentally (Rosengren, Subbotsky, & Harris, 2000).

Another possible interpretation for adults' animistic remarks is that adult participants also can respond in a play or fantasy mode or metaphorically. According to Dennis (1953), who asked more than 150 college students living in New York City whether a variety of objects (e.g., the sun, a lighted match, the ocean, an electric clock, etc.) were alive, about half of the students stated that one or more of these objects were alive, and the lighted match, the sun, and the ocean elicited animistic responses from one third of the students. These students' typical remarks were as follows: For the lighted match: "Living, because it has flames which indicate life." For the sun: "Living because it gives forth energy. Gives us power, warmth, light, and energy. Makes things—living things—thrive and exist." As readers will notice, these animistic answers are apparently equivalent to those given by young children in Piaget's interview (see Chapter 1), except that some of the adults' answers reflect their large vocabularies. Similar results were found among more than 700 students from colleges and high schools in Beirut, Lebanon (Dennis, 1957). However, it is highly unlikely that these adults believed that the sun is alive in the same sense as a dog or a tulip is; they were simply tempted to metaphorically extend the meaning of "alive."

On Whether Young Children Possess a Form of Biology

Many recent studies on naive biology were stimulated by Carey (1985), who made three provocative assertions, namely, that children younger than 10 years of age or so do not possess naive biology separated from psychology, that young children thus interpret biological phenomena in terms of psychology, and that naive biology emerges from psychology through conceptual change in a strong sense. These assertions were somewhat counterintuitive for conceptual development researchers who believed in early competence and domain specificity of thought. However, unlike Piaget, Carey did not attribute young children's allegedly psychological, distorted interpretation of biological phenomena to their intellectual immaturity in general; she claimed that young children could not understand biology because they were totally ignorant of the physiological mechanisms involved.

Whether young children possess a form of biology is partly a definitional issue. On the one hand, because children (and many lay adults, too) clearly lack scientific biology, we may claim that they do not possess any form of biology by establishing the criterion for naive biology approximately that of scientific biology. On the other hand, because a majority of researchers, including Carey, admit that even young children possess a more powerful knowledge system for biological phenomena than a schema or script in the sense that the system allows them to offer explanations or construals, we may claim that they possess a form of biology if we set a different (but still appropriate) criterion for naive biology.

In our first paper on naive biology (Hatano & Inagaki, 1987), we asserted that, although it is true that young children lack knowledge in scientific biology and often rely on personification, they possess the biological knowledge needed to differentiate the bodily from the mental, and thus their frequent use of personification does not necessarily mean that they fail to possess biology separated from psychology. We also proposed that young children's reasoning about biological (life-sustaining) behaviors is based on vitalistic causality. Vitalistic causality is not psychological but biological in nature, and it is seldom applied to social-psychological behaviors, which are explained in terms of intentional causality.

We hope we have shown in the preceding chapters, more or less convincingly, that children as young as 5 years of age do possess a form of biology separate from psychology, at least in its essential distinctions and causal devices. We think, as Carey (1995) now seems to, that a not-too-ambitious but still reasonable criterion includes whether young children distinguish biological phenomena from psychological ones and whether they have causal devices that can be regarded as distinctively biological. We also think that separating bodily processes and properties from mental ones is the primary distinction, and such intermediate forms of causality between mechanical and intentional as vitalism and (life-)teleology can be regarded as biological in the sense that they resonate with the biological world even if they are not unique to it.

The issue of the age at which naive biology is established is now a minor one, because the differences among researchers in the age of acquisition are not large enough to be interesting. On the one hand, even proponents of the early acquisition of naive biology cannot radically lower the age of acquisition. Whereas there is a consensus that even 3-year-olds have acquired naive physics and psychology, it is still debatable whether they appreciate a biological domain of thought including humans, non-human animals, *and* plants, whether they possess a uniquely biological mode of reasoning, and whether they apply it to a wide range of biological phenomena, such as nutrition, being taken ill, growth and death, and reproduction. On the other hand, even Carey (1999), a vocal representative of the late acquisition proponents, agreed in one of her recent publications that children have constructed an intuitive theory of biology by age 6 and that "some 4- and 5-year-olds have already made it" (p. 303). Thus agreement is more evident than disagreement: Children have acquired naive biology by ages 4, 5, or 6 years, at the least before the formal teaching of science. The exact age may vary from population to population and according to specific criteria by which children's biological knowledge is assessed.

There are several reasons to believe that humans construct a theory of biology quite early, even if they do not have it as a distinct theory from the beginning. The natural classification scheme of the human mind (Atran, 1998), which categorizes entities into humans, nonhuman animals, plants, and nonliving things, seems to serve as a basis for naive biology. Skeletal principles differentiating between animate and inanimate entities (R. Gelman, 1990) and abstract knowledge assuming different insides for natural kinds versus artifacts (Simons & Keil, 1995) also seem to contribute to its early construction, because they are taken for granted before a large amount of factual knowledge has been accumulated.

However, naive biology (or a causal explanatory framework unique for biological properties and processes) may be established later than psychology and physics for several reasons. Understanding bodily processes, an essential component of naive biology, may be delayed because it presupposes awareness of these processes, which may emerge around age 4 (Inagaki, 1997). Naive biology also presupposes the construction of an integrated category of living things that includes plants, which appear so different from animals.

A new, strong opponent to the early acquisition position is Au. Au and her associates, as they half-admitted (Au & Romo, 1999), set a strict criterion for attributing naive biology (and psychology) to children and adults, that is, requiring explanations in terms of "uniquely biological" causal mechanisms, not just reliance on causal devices that are neither psychological nor physical. Because vital power is unspecified substance, energy, or information, vitalistic causality seldom offers specific mechanisms that satisfy their criterion. Therefore, we agree with Au and Romo (1999) that, according to their criterion, children (and lay adults) who have not learned much about scientific biology do not have a form of biology. However, we doubt that setting such a strict criterion is productive for future research on naive biology or conceptual development.

On Whether Biology Emerges From Psychology

Let us move on to the debate concerning whether biology emerges from psychology. Are biological phenomena initially explained in terms of intentional causality (as Carey originally claimed), or are biological phenomena construed biologically from the beginning to the extent that they are construed at all (as Keil claims)? Our answer to this question is complicated, because there are intricate relationships between naive biology and its neighboring theories. Moreover, Carey (1995) later elaborated the question that she raised in her earlier book (1985). According to her, her earlier claim that naive biology emerges from naive psychology admits three interpretations: weak (animals' psychological phenomena are explained by naive psychology but their biological phenomena are either unexplained or explained by domain-general mechanisms), medium-strong (both naive biology and psychology emerge from an undifferentiated theory), and strong (all behaviors and properties of animals are initially explained by naive psychology). She has now accepted that "the strong version of the claim is wrong" (p. 283) but believes that the other options may be tenable.

We must doubt that either of the two remaining options can be a legitimate interpretation of her claim that naive biology emerges from naive psychology. The medium-strong interpretation indicates that both naive biology and psychology emerge from an undifferentiated theory, which is *neither* biology nor psychology. In the weak interpretation, animals' biological phenomena are not explained by naive psychology. Aside from that, our answer is partially consistent with these tenable interpretations.

On the one hand, we assert that children as young as 4 can distinguish bodily functions from mental ones; in other words, they never distort all biological observations so that they can be incorporated into the framework of intuitive psychology, nor are they totally ignorant of mediating processes between input and output. Moreover, treating humans and other animals as behavioral beings does not mean that what they do should always be explained in terms of intentional causality. Behaviors, especially in the case of nonhuman animals, might sometimes be explained biologically, in terms of the bodily state, for example, and biological explanations can induce important practical implications in the wild environment; some predators are not very dangerous when they are fully fed, we may beat some formidable nonhuman animals when they are suffering from disease, and so on. On the other hand, we assume that young children, and sometimes lay adults too, take the mind and the body to be not totally independent. In addition, because psychology is established earlier, we assume, it influences young children's explanation for or interpretation of biological phenomena.

However, there still remains an important disagreement between Carey and us. We assume that biological knowledge was critically important for millions of years for human beings as hunters-gathers, because they had to (a) identify proper varieties of animals and plants as food (based on their taxonomic knowledge), and (b) select, whenever possible, healthy individual animals or plants to take. Such knowledge was needed by almost everyone. We therefore claim that naive biology is one of the core domains of thought and is thus a privileged or innate domain. In contrast, Carey (1995, 1999) continues to believe that biology is a derived domain that must come from something else—most likely from psychology, because both have humans as the representative example.

We have three arguments against Carey on this issue. First, as we have seen in Chapter 6, the acquisition of naive biology is fairly early, easy, and uniform. If humans are not endowed with domain-specific principles and constraints for acquiring it, it would be unlikely that it is differentiated so early from physics and psychology. The acquisition of naive biology does not require any systematic instruction nor extensive experience, though it may be accelerated by formal or informal teaching.

Second, it is not surprising that biological knowledge does not seem to appear very early in development—no biology module is assumed among Leslie's (1994) three modules (one of which is about physical objects, and the remaining two, mental states) and no biology domain among Carey's (1999) three innate domains (physics, psychology, and number)—because infants seldom need biological knowledge, since they do not need to take care of their health nor try to find food themselves. We do not take it for granted that all privileged or innate domains emerge very early. A nonepistemic example is that if the judgment of facial and bodily attractiveness is for mate selection and propagation of one's genes, sensitivity to those cues is important, but only from puberty on and may thus appear fairly late (Thornhill & Gangestad, 1999).

Third, if naive biology emerges from psychology, then autistic children must reveal a delayed acquisition of naive biology because they have great difficulty in developing a theory of mind. However, available evidence (e.g., Baron-Cohen, 1991; Peterson & Siegal, 1997) shows that this is not true. Experiences enhancing or inhibiting the development of a theory of mind (e.g., having a sibling or another intensive communication partner within the family) do not seem to have similar influences on the acquisition of naive biology.

At the same time, however, we believe that in young children's mind, naive psychology seems to be more dominant than naive biology. In this sense, our position is not compatible with Keil (1992), who asserts, "As we look at younger and younger children, we do not see their judgments becoming more and more psychologically driven" (p. 132). A considerable number of studies reviewed in Chapter 4 showed that both biological and psychological causal devices are applied to biological phenomena, though biological causal devices are considered more important for biological phenomena than psychological devices when these are in conflict. In contrast, only psychological devices are induced by psychological phenomena.

Recall Wellman et al.'s (1997) study. It clearly showed that even 3-year-olds understand the psychology/physics contrast for human movements and actions, but the data regarding biology were not conclusive in that the 3-year-olds gave as many psychological explanations as biological ones for the stories about biologically caused human actions. Inagaki's (1997) results also strongly suggest that the biology/psychology differentiation may take longer to develop than 2 or 3 years after birth. In that study, although preschool children could distinguish biological phenomena from psychological ones in their causal reasoning, their reasoning about biological phenomena was sometimes influenced by social or psychological variables, especially when these variables were salient or when the biological variables were not explicitly indicated. In Inagaki and Hatano's study (1993, Experiment 3 and 3a), although most of the kindergarten children applied vitalistic causal explanations to biological phenomena, about 20% of them used intentional causal explanations for them, whereas all the children applied only intentional explanations to social/psychological phenomena.

On Conceptual Change in Naive Biology

Does the development of naive biology undergo conceptual change? The answer to this question again varies depending on the definition of the key term, in this case how we define conceptual change (as against enrichment). Our claim is this. Conceptual change occurs in naive biology in the sense that its causal explanatory principle changes qualitatively and also the mode of biological reasoning for predicting and explaining a variety of behaviors shifts from one to another. We have proposed that young children's initial form of biology is vitalistic, that is, that their biology indicates that the target bodily phenomenon is caused by the working of a "vital force," which is nonobvious and can be conceptualized as unspecified substance, energy, or information. We have also proposed that young children often rely on similarity-based inference, though they can use category-based inference under some conditions (S. Gelman & Markman, 1986).

Vitalistic biology is partially displaced, if not completely superseded, by "mechanistic" biology as children learn more and more about physiological mechanisms, through which a specific bodily system enables a person, irrespective of his or her intention, to exchange specific substances with the environment or to carry them to and from bodily parts. Around the same age, children who have accumulated fairly rich knowledge about specific animals and plants and also their taxonomic relationships, tend to adopt primarily category-based inferences much more often than similarity-based inferences.

Another qualitative change in responding to biological phenomena seems to occur in earlier years (between ages 3 and 5). However, we attribute that change to the shift from incomplete to complete establishment of naive biology (rather than conceptual change similar to the relevance shift). In other words, although very young children's predictions and explanations for biological phenomena are sometimes influenced by naive psychology, that does not mean that naive biology emerges from psychology. Naive psychology as one of the established neighbor theories may sometimes penetrate into "biological" reasoning until the more consolidated establishment of naive biology. Naive physics may also do so, though less often, when the agent is a nonliving entity, as Au and Romo (1996, 1999) asserted.

To conclude, conceptual change does occur in the development of na-ive biology, but within the domain of biology. Biology does not emerge from psychology, as Carey (1985) originally claimed.

☐ Implications for Education and Health

What implications can we derive from the studies of naive biology for educational and health practices?

Educational Implications

The growing body of research on naive and intuitive biology has signifi-cant implications for education, especially for the teaching and learning of biology. This is because, as pointed out by Olson and Torrance (1996), any attempt of teaching is based on understanding of child's mind, and vice versa. Our understanding of how children's mind works and grows can direct, or even specify, the content and methods of teaching. Let us discuss very briefly educational implications of three major generaliza-tion from the review: (a) young children possess naive biology that often produces reasonable predictions and explanations; (b) children's biologi-cal knowledge, though it may have some shared core components, is in-stantiated differently in different cultures; and (c) children's naive biology serves as the basis for learning school biology and is transformed, or re-structured, by it.

The first generalization concerns learners' initial state of knowledge before instruction. Detailed descriptions of the initial state must be very helpful for designing an effective course of instruction, because instruc-tion aims at changing learners' knowledge from an initial state to a goal state (Glaser & Bassok, 1989). For instance, our understanding of what young children know sheds light on "how to ease their transition into formal school settings" (Bransford, Brown, & Cocking, 1999, p. 67). The view that even young children possess a form of biology implies that start-ing instruction of biology at kindergarten or lower elementary grades is possible and can be effective. This implication is clearly distinct from that of Carey (1985) and others, who assume that young children have no form of biology, because, according to the latter, we have to teach biology as a totally new discipline in school or postpone its teaching until the 4th grade or so. It should be pointed out that biology instruction for young children does not always mean systematic teaching of scientific biology. Rather, it is recommended for educators to "respect" but elaborate children's reasoning based on their naive biology. To illustrate, educators need to anticipate and acknowledge children's use of personification as one of biologically plausible reasoning, but at the same time help children notice the limitations of personification. For children who tend not to attribute some animal properties to an animal dissimilar to humans, for example, educators can bring to their attention the fact that the animal shares those properties with humans. Motoyoshi (1979) succeeded in producing such recognition among her daycare center children who insisted that a tortoise does not excrete, by encouraging them to carefully observe the tortoise, when it was put on a sheet of white paper.

The second generalization indicates that there can be diverse routes in the development of biological understanding. This generalization encourages educators to build a curriculum for biology instruction by taking students' cultural perspectives into account. In other words, it gives support to the idea of ethnographic translation of instructional materials and procedures (Serpell & Hatano, 1997), rejecting the idea of importing educational programs from other cultures as they are. Local cultural practices, such as raising a particular kind of animal among children at home or school, and various forms of contact with the natural world such as hunting and fishing, should be exploited. Young children often show great interest in the kinds of animals being raised by their friends as well as by themselves, and they can readily use knowledge about those animals as the source for analogical reasoning and understanding. Therefore, those kinds of animals might be used for teaching about bodily structures and processes.

The third generalization concerns meaningful learning of school biology and conceptual change. It suggests that educators activate students' naive or informal biological knowledge and relate it to formal biology instruction as much as possible. It implies that naive biology, which is personifying and vitalistic in nature, can provide students with a conceptual framework for learning school biology meaningfully. Remember Inagaki and Kasetani's (1994) study in Chapter 3, where giving hints to use knowledge about humans facilitated kindergartners' understanding of procedures for raising squirrels.

A recommendation of activating knowledge about humans is found in a teacher's guidebook titled the *Kyokuchi Method in Science Education*, prepared by a Japanese research and development group. In the unit on animals' bodily structures and their ways of living (Takahashi, 1980), school-aged children are given the following problem: "Which is a bigger eater, a starfish or a sea anemone?" By being given a hint such as, "Taking exercise makes *you* hungry, doesn't it?", students are likely to figure out the animal's characteristic successfully.

As described in Chapter 2, young children have difficulty recognizing commonalities between animals and plants, but giving a brief, vitalistic explanation for biological phenomena such as growth can facilitate their recognition. In other words, children seem to think that plant growth occurs by taking in vital power from water, because those who lack the understanding of photosynthesis in plants tend to map food for animals to water for plants. At an early stage of learning biology, the activation of the idea of vital force would help children recognize commonalities that animals and plants share. At a later stage, we speculate, the water-for-plant is food-for-animal analogy might help them wonder how plants can take in vital power from water alone and motivate them to explore another mechanism specific to plant growth. Photosynthesis, or the essential difference between animals and plants in terms of self-movement versus self-generation of nutriment, might be learned meaningfully in these contexts. Future studies regarding interactions between naive and school biology will, we hope, specify how naive biology should be elaborated by formal instruction toward "scientific" biology, as well as how it should be relied on to help students understand school biology better (Inagaki, 1990b). The better we understand the process of conceptual change, the more solid will be the foundation we build in designing biology instruction.

Implications for Health Practices

Naive biology is closely related to various aspects of medicine. We have shown that young children can distinguish bodily functions from mental ones; in other words, they never distort all biological observations so that they can be incorporated into the framework of intuitive psychology, nor are they totally ignorant of mediating processes between input and output. They can understand bodily phenomena or processes, including illness, in terms of vitalistic causality, although they do not know the specific physiological mechanisms involved. However, as also shown, young children, and lay adults too, believe that the mind and the body are not totally independent but interdependent to some degree, especially in their understanding of illness causality. They recognize that susceptibility to illness is important in determining whether a person becomes ill and that not only physical aspects but also social or psychological aspects of daily activities contribute to health and illness, although the former aspects are more important than the latter.

We can derive some implications from these findings for health practices and health education. We propose three of them. The first implication is that we should regard children who are taken ill as capable of understanding their illness and necessary treatments. Because children who are suffering from illnesses can understand their bodily phenomena and processes "biologically," parents or health practitioners can expect children's guided cooperation based on informed consent. Needless to say, practitioners should give explanations translated into vitalistic terms, rather than purely technical or scientific (mechanical) terms. Thoughtful explanations for the significance and necessity of medical treatments would remove unnecessary fear, frustration, and confusion from child patients and create favorable conditions for treatments. This recommendation can be applied even to preschool-aged children.

The second implication is that even young children can understand preventive medicine or health practices. They not only know that they may be taken ill through exposure to sick people or contagion, but also that whether they become ill depends on their susceptibility to illness. Moreover, they know that susceptibility to illness is determined by their daily activities. From the perspective of health practice and education, personal responsibility for health should be emphasized (e.g., eating a balanced diet, engaging in regular daily routines, avoiding stress in everyday life, and so on) by appealing to or triggering their notion of vital power and their understanding of mind–body interdependence. Such responsibility may include the avoidance of unnecessary and close contacts with sick people, although this is problematic, as will be discussed in the next paragraph. However, many other recommended activities are desirable, as far as children themselves trying to engage in them with some biological understanding.

It should be pointed out that this emphasis on personal responsibility for maintaining health or preventing disease should be offered by health educators with great care. This is the third implication. Emphasizing that we can reduce the risk of becoming ill through self-control is double-edged in that it may develop a prejudice against sick people and/or restrict opportunities for natural interactions with them. As we have seen in Chapter 4, children are at least prepared to accept that whether they become ill depends on their susceptibility to illness, which is determined by their daily activities. A corollary of this belief is that a sick person may be responsible for his or her illness to some extent. Although this corollary is problematic, the emphasis on self-control for good health may increase a sick person's guilt feelings, and/or result in blaming other sick persons for their failure in self-control (Wilkinson, 1988). A germ theory interpretation of diseases is guilt-free, because the causes of illness are attributed to exogenous factors. However, this interpretation may make children overly cautious about the risk of contagion (Kalish, 1998; Springer & Ruckel, 1992), which tends to violate the basic human rights of patients.

Considering the last two implications simultaneously, we must develop a balanced and sensitive program for health education. On the one hand, children need to be instructed about causal mechanisms of germ transmission, but in a way that clearly eliminates undue anxiety over having contact with a sick person. The program must also indicate that preventing contagion is not always possible, and thus patients should not be blamed. Fortunately, Au and Romo (1996) report that at least middle elementary school children can understand the causal mechanisms of AIDS transmission following appropriate biological instruction. On the other hand, we must emphasize the notion of self-care and personal responsibility for health, as the above second implication indicates. For effective health practices and education, we not only need to integrate the vitalistic causality of Oriental medicine and the germ theory of Western medicine, but also keep a balance between emphasizing children's initiatives for their own health and the protection of sick persons' human rights.

☐ On Notions of Domains and Naive Theories

As indicated at the beginning, the goal of this book is twofold: to present a monograph on young children's naive biology, and to elaborate our model of conceptual development. In the last two sections of this last chapter, we thus discuss theoretical implications of studies of naive biology for conceptual development in general. Because confusion over and difficulty with the current views of conceptual development are primarily due to imprecise or imbalanced characterization of the key constituent notions, as indicated in Chapter 1, we concentrate here on how the studies of naive biology help us reconceptualize the notions of domains and naive theories and of constraints for knowledge acquisition.

The notion of domains and that of naive theories are closely related: Domains correspond to sets of phenomena that are covered by respective naive theories; naive theories represent those domains' knowledge systems that enable children and lay adults to offer coherent and differentiated predictions (and sometimes plausible explanations) regarding relevant phenomena based on causal schemas. Therefore, we discuss theoretical implications that our review of studies on naive biology has for these two notions together in this section.

As for "domains" and "naive theories," there are two related, difficult problems for conceptual development investigators. The first problem is, assuming that our knowledge constructed in the course of development is divided into domains, what are bases for this division? More specifically, is the division of knowledge into domains a cultural product or is it determined primarily on cognitive bases?

The second, related problem is how in actuality do young children differentiate core domains of thought. Each core domain probably emerges as a framework for predicting and interpreting typical "behaviors" of representative objects that are covered by the domain; in the case of naive physics, such behaviors are motion of inanimate, solid objects, and in the case of naive psychology, the social activity of humans. But how do young children come to presume a few separate domains? It may be because human infants or toddlers possess a few distinct modes of causal reasoning, and each of them serves as the core of a core domain of thought; they incorporate into the domain only those objects that tend to reveal behaviors that can readily be explained by the particular mode of causal reasoning. Alternatively, entities may be first classified into several groups in terms of their perceptual similarities, and then the domain-general mechanism of causal reasoning (e.g., from covariation to causation proposed by Cheng, 1997), interacting with those entities, produces domain-specific causal devices. Still another possibility is that young children are socialized to choose the proper causal device for interpreting a given phenomenon through social learning.

Based on the discussion in earlier chapters, we offer the following four characterizations and specifications.

1. The division of domains is based on our intuition to some extent, but the cognitive boundary between neighboring domains or theories is not always clear; there can be some ambiguity in the assignment of a phenomena just based on cognitive intuition; the core domains of thought must be a joint product of cognition and culture.

Recent studies have demonstrated that individual competence varies considerably from domain to domain, no matter how the term "domain" is defined. Piaget's stage theory, which posited that an individual's competence depended on his or her logico-mathematical structures applicable across domains, has been challenged or even rejected by many current researchers (R. Gelman & Baillargeon, 1983; Laboratory of Comparative Human Cognition, 1983; Siegler, 1978; Wellman & Gelman, 1992). Many contemporary researchers believe that, because each domain is under a different set of constraints, the course and process of development vary from domain to domain; in other words, knowledge is acquired, in part, in a unique fashion in each domain.

However, as pointed out in Chapter 1, it is very hard to indicate how our entire knowledge is divided into domains. Considering the universality of folkbiology, a portion of knowledge is split into the domain of biology on a cognitive basis that is at least partially innate. At the same time, however, naive biology and naive psychology may partly overlap, because the mind and the body are not always distinguished as clearly as in modern Western science a la Descartes. Whereas humans everywhere have some effective means to cope with illnesses (Maffi, 1996), whether illness causality should be treated just in terms of biology (or its subdivision called medicine) or in terms of psychology or metaphysics as well varies from culture to culture. People in the East and West may attribute a given disease to different sets of factors. It will be interesting to examine in detail how people from different cultural backgrounds intuitively divide the total body of knowledge they possess.

2. *Young children's choice of the domain or theory to which a given phenomenon is assigned is somewhat unstable as well as inaccurate, in that it can be influenced by types of questions and contexts; however, they have some intuition about the appropriateness of causal schemas, that seems similar to lay adults'.*

As demonstrated by Wellman et al. (1997), 4-year-olds can give causal explanations differentially for human movements and actions that require biological, psychological, or physical reasoning. Although 4-year-olds' mapping is not always very accurate, they must have some intuition for what kinds of causal schemas are needed to predict and explain phenomena belonging to different domains/theories.

Young children believe that illness susceptibility is influenced not only by physical aspects of daily activities but also by moral behaviors (Inagaki, 1997). Their reasoning seems less compartmentalized than older children's and adults', in other words, more inclusive in identifying causes of illness. However, young children recognize biological factors as more important for illness when these factors are explicitly contrasted with moral factors. Also highly relevant here is the finding by Simons and Keil (1995) that young children possess pieces of "abstract" knowledge, which are partially valid, before acquiring pieces of detailed factual knowledge. This abstract knowledge about the insides of animals and artifacts may serve to induce different causal schemas for these entities belonging to different ontological categories. These results suggest that, though it is possible that a given phenomenon may sometimes induce knowledge belonging to neighboring domains in young children's reasoning, it is unlikely that lay adults and young children apply different kinds of explanatory schemas for the same phenomena consistently. In this sense, domain-specificity of thought holds across ages.

3. *Coherence of responses is especially high within a given subdomain, except for very young children; however, coherence of responses across subdomains of single domains or theories may not be high.*

Our attributing a theory to children presupposes their coherent responding (to differentiate the possession of a theory from a set of correct responses based on specific pieces of knowledge). A cautionary note is needed for the acquisition of naive theories, however. Children's knowledge may be more advanced in some subdomains than others that eventually belong to the same theory. Thus their responses are not highly coherent within a given total domain or theory. To put it differently, naive theories do not cover initially all phenomena they can, nor are their implications fully extended or exploited. We do believe that children's reasoning in its constituent subdomains is constrained by their naive theory of the domain, but this contraint may not be as strong as expected.

Possessing a naive theory implies some coherence both within and between subdomains, but how much coherence should be required is still a debatable question. Our preferred choice is to require only a modest extent of coherence in the use of causal devices across a few core subdomains, because otherwise, we believe, we fail to see commonalities in cognition between lay adults and young children. For example, we may be tempted to conclude that whereas lay adults have naive theories, young children do not. Good news for this rather lenient criterion is that children come to be able to, within a few years after fulfilling the lenient criterion, apply causal devices more coherently to "peripheral" subdomains as well and choose valid explanations from a number of alternative causal explanations or even offer plausible explanations themselves.

4. Naive theories develop under the influence of the corresponding scientific theories; scientific theories emerge from the corresponding naive theories through several phases of conceptual change.

A considerable number of conceptual development researchers treat naive theories and scientific theories as if they were constructed independently. The similarities between the naive theories and scientific theories, for instance in their cognitive content and processes of change, are often attributed to the fact that both are products of the natural schemes of the human mind, and the differences between them are different levels of the understanding of aspects of the world. Commonalities between naive theories and "scientific" theories that appeared many years ago in history are thus attributed to these theories' representing comparable stages of cognition. However, our notion of sociocultural constraints and our discussion on conceptual change imply that naive and scientific theories interact in several ways.

We should not forget that children's naive theories are constructed in part on the "scientific" theories held by leading members of their community, or on lay adults' version of scientific theories, as sociocultural constraints. Such lay scientific theories are a kind of shared beliefs and probably reflect, to some extent, scientific theories of some previous years. To put it differently, scientists' theories are distributed to the general public to form lay scientific theories, which are incorporated by children through socialization practices. In particular, conceptual changes or theory changes in later childhood, such as the shift from vitalistic to mechanistic biology, are partly due to the influence of scientific theories. They are not cognitive changes that occur spontaneously. Thus, the similarities between naive theories and scientific theories may be a result of children's cultural learning or conceptual development under sociocultural constraints.

It should also be noted that scientific theories are a collection of individual scientists' theories, which emerge from the corresponding naive theories through several phases of conceptual change, because scientists used to be young children. Moreover, because in the process of conceptual change the prior theory serves as acquired cognitive constraints, there must be some commonalities between naive theories and scientific theories due to this cognitive inheritance.

☐ On the Notion of Constraints

The notion of "constraints" for learning and development, which are supposed to play key roles in conceptual development and change, is not well articulated in the current views. There are two types of problems with this notion in conceptual development: conceptual and empirical. The empirical problem is that there have been very few studies that directly examined what constraints operate in what ways *in conceptual development.* Unlike constraints in word learning, about which we know quite a bit (see, for example, Markman, 1992; Tomasello, 1992), discussions on constraints in conceptual development must be speculative, because of the small number of relevant studies. An equally serious problem is conceptual in nature. More specifically, as alluded to in Chapters 1 and 6, (a) researchers often emphasize their favorite type of constraints while almost ignoring other types; (b) they disagree how best to conceptualize "innate constraints"; and (c) "sociocultural constraints," the workings of which characterize uniquely human development, have not been assigned their due roles. Therefore, based on our review of the studies on naive biology, we would make a brave attempt to suggest several characterizations of constraints in conceptual development and change in the core domains.

   1. Constraints direct a developing individual's attention to particular aspects of the world and lead them to particular ways of encoding; the constraints also restrict a set of hypotheses and interpretations for him or her to entertain.

   Constraints operating in the core domains should serve to, either internally or externally, control and direct attention or coding and to restrict the range of hypothesis space to be searched. A unique set of constraints in each core domain draws attention to relevant aspects of the target objects or phenomena so that even young children can readily distinguish those that should be interpreted within the domain from those that should not. In the case of naive biology, there seem to be a set of constraints, both cognitive and sociocultural, directing attention to those aspects of living things that serve to distinguish them from nonliving things. We now know that even infants can differentiate animals (including humans) that spontaneously move from those inanimate entities that do not move by themselves. Slightly older children pay attention to eating and its connection to bodily states and changes in humans.

Another set of constraints serves to eliminate in advance a large number of logically possible interpretations or hypotheses. Considering that even rats tend to attribute their bodily disturbance to novel food eaten (Garcia, 1981), it seems likely that human are endowed with similar specific constraints, such as trying to find the cause among a variety of foods for diarrhea whereas seeking a physical cause for a cut. Moreover, how people talk about illness causality limits the range of interpretations for given ailments. It is assumed that, because those spontaneous tendencies and guided biases in the seeking of an interpretation enable humans to search the hypothesis space highly selectively, they can reach, in most cases, a reasonable interpretation promptly and thus can accumulate pieces of knowledge constituting a core domain of thought.

It should be noted that these constrains are domain-specific learning mechanisms. Children acquire naive theories based on their experience with the target phenomena, but this acquisition process is enhanced by relevant constraints. The notion of constraints is introduced to solve learnability problems, in other words, to explain the early differentiated understandings of important aspects of the world; it is highly unlikely that domains can be differentiated so early just by domain-general learning mechanisms.

2. Prior knowledge of a domain surely serves as constraints, but its role may be limited in the early phase; it becomes more important in later development.

Once a form of naive theory becomes available, it serves as a set of constraints for further learning or for elaboration and revision processes. Therefore, nobody doubts the significance of prior knowledge as constraints in later conceptual development. However, in explaining infants' and young children's fascinating competence, we cannot rely heavily on prior knowledge.

It should be emphasized that, unlike the process of expertise, conceptual development progresses extremely fast at the initial phase, is led by good intuition based on a small database, and proceeds from abstract to concrete (Wellman, in press). Some constraints are indispensable for bootstrapping, in other words, when the initial theory of the domain is to be constructed. Innate or very early constraints and interactive sociocultural constraints seem to play a more critical role at this phase.

It should also be emphasized that much of prior knowledge has a sociocultural origin; it is constructed based on, though not transmitted through, experiences accumulated in earlier generations in the form of culture. Children may incorporate shared beliefs of the community (e.g., "one has to eat a lot in order to grow") that make sense to them, without directly observing the facts. Such indirect experiences are also represented in the form of domain-specific prior knowledge, which works as acquired cognitive constraints in further development.

3. There are domain-specific tendencies and biases that, if not innate, are acquired very early.

We believe that humans are endowed with a set of innate domain-specific constraints for the core domains of thought, but we believe that it is more accurate to describe them as "innate or acquired very early," because they do not operate at birth. In the case of biology, we can observe the operation of most constraints no earlier than several months olds. We assume that humans possess innate domain-specific constraints for acquiring naive biology, as we discussed in Chapter 6, because of empirical findings showing its early, easy, and uniform acquisition without systematic intervention or any other powerful experiential factors and because of evolutionary-psychological considerations on its importance for the survival of the human species.

We assume that innate or early cognitive constraints take the form of biases and preferences, because such constraints can effectively mitigate learnability problems and because it is hard to believe that specific pieces of knowledge can be genetically transmitted or neurally prewired. Moreover, since the process of evolution is very slow, possessing specific pieces of innate knowledge may be detrimental when ecological environments change.

4. Sociocultural constraints operate as general contexts that restrict children's access to resources based on which they construct naive theories; the constraints also enhance conceptual development in interactive ways.

We claim that sociocultural factors influence conceptual development from the beginning, because children need experiences in sociocultural contexts or socioculturally provided data to build naive theories. In this process, sociocultural contexts necessarily produce variations in conceptual development.

Conceptual development is also enhanced by such sociocultural constraints as other, more knowledgeable people and physical, symbolic, and social tools that are shared by members of a community or its subgroup. Sociocultural constraints enable children not only to be competent in problem solving and comprehension but also to acquire knowledge and skills readily.

As children begin to learn in a uniquely human way, in other words, as they acquire the ability to mentally represent other people's mental representations (Tomasello et al., 1993), they become able to share with other people the goals, methods, and concepts of activities. Raising an animal at home serves as a good example that shows how children learn foundational knowledge through participation in culturally organized activities (Inagaki, 1990a). The participating children tend to learn routinely used procedures promptly, because their observation and their choice of procedures are directed by joint attention with or by imitation of the more mature partners, and to acquire a sort of conceptual knowledge about the raised animals by being helped by guided comprehension activities. Those tools or artifacts that are used in the raising activities also serve to direct children's attention and narrow the range of procedures and interpretations they consider at the time of the activities.

5. *All three types of constraints work often in coordinated or compensatory ways.*

We would like to emphasize that, because the acquisition of naive theories has been and still is important for humans, there are multiple constraints that draw children's attention to particular aspects of the world and that restrict the range of hypotheses and interpretations to consider. In children's early interaction with the immediate environment, innate constraints and interactive sociocultural constraints operate either conjointly or complimentarily. For example, parents may rely on their children's innate tendency to pay attention to important aspects of the environment or try to control the input their children receive by joint attention.

It is also important to recognize that, as children acquire more and more pieces of information, prior knowledge tends to take the dominant role in their interaction, because it is more specified and adapted to their current ecological and cultural niche. In a sense, the current version of prior knowledge represents both innate constraints and interactive sociocultural constraints that operated in the past. Speaking generally, each of the three kinds of constraints has some limitations: Prior knowledge cannot work at the beginning, innate constraints are too skeletal though strong, and interactive sociocultural constraints are not guaranteed to operate though they can be specific. However, taken together, they nicely help developing individuals acquire naive theories promptly.

We would also like to emphasize that these constraints operate at multiple levels. Children's interaction with the immediate environment, in which innate and interactive constraints work, is controlled in a global fashion by larger sociocultural contexts that influence what are readily accessible to the children. Innate constraints are tendencies and biases that restrict the possible range of naive theories children can acquire, but they acquire a specific theory based on other constraints that operate within the limit of innate constraints and that futher narrow down the course of knowledge acquisition.

☐ Remaining Issues

Since Carey (1985), young children's naive biology has been an exciting topic for research in conceptual development. As more and more ambitious researchers have joined to study it, a richer database has been built and finer conceptualizations have been offered about this specific issue. In addition, through attempts to examine key constituent notions like the ones discussed in this chapter, a better understanding of fundamental issues in developmental studies on cognition, like the nature of domains, theories, and constraints, has been achieved. However, we are well aware that many hard problems remain in the study of naive biology in particular and conceptual development in general. Let us list several of them as the postscript to the present monograph.

What is urgently needed in the study of naive biology is (a) to integrate nativistic and cultural accounts of acquisition and change, (b) to better characterize the causality (or causalities) used in the initial form of biological reasoning, (c) to put in order such subdomains as bodily processes, illness causality, inheritance, and so on in terms of ease of understanding, and (d) to clarify the relationships between the amount of specific knowledge and modes of reasoning.

As for enhancing our understanding of conceptual development in general, using naive biology as the target case, intensive research is needed (a) to better conceptualize the nature of naive theories, in relation to mental models on one hand and early scientific theories on the other, (b) to specify how a variety of constraints operate in conceptual development and change, (c) to sketch the process of bootstrapping or how the construction of a new domain of thought is initiated, and (d) to understand later conceptual development in relation to education and schooling. Moreover, it is expected that, as our understanding of naive physics and naive psychology also progresses, it will be intriguing to examine commonalities and differences in development among major theories about aspects of the world understood by young children.

As we indicated at the beginning of this book, the target entities of naive biology, that is, human bodily processes as well as nonhuman animals and plants, are topics of apparent concern and importance to young children. Children are not only fairly knowledgable about these targets but also willing to talk about them. In this sense, studies of biological understanding provide investigators with advantageous opportunities to examine conceptual development and change in general.

REFERENCES

Ackerman, B. P. (1984). The effects of storage and processing complexity on comprehension repair in children and adults. *Journal of Experimental Child Psychology, 37*, 303–334.

Anzai, Y., & Simon, H. (1979). The theory of learning by doing. *Psychological Review, 86*, 124–140.

Atran, S. (1990). *Cognitive foundations of natural history: Towards an anthropology of science*. Cambridge, UK: Cambridge University Press.

Atran, S. (1998). Folkbiology and the anthropology of science: Cognitive universals and cultural particulars. *Behavioral and Brain Sciences, 21*, 547–609.

Au, T. K., & Romo, L. (1996). Building a coherent conception of HIV transmission: A new approach to AIDS education. In D. Medin (Ed.), *The psychology of learning and motivation* (Vol. 35, pp. 193–241). New York: Academic Press.

Au, T. K., & Romo, L. (1999). Mechanical causality in children's "folkbiology." In D. Medin & S. Atran (Eds.), *Folkbiology* (pp. 355–401). Cambridge, MA: MIT Press.

Au, T. K., Romo, L., & DeWitt, J. (1999). Considering children's folkbiology in health education. In M. Siegal & C. C. Peterson (Eds.), *Children's understanding of biology and health* (pp. 209–234). Cambridge, UK: Cambridge University Press.

Backscheider, A. G., Shatz, M., & Gelman, S. A. (1993). Preschoolers' ability to distinguish living kinds as a function of regrowth. *Child Development, 64*, 1242–1257.

Baron-Cohen, S. (1991). The theory of mind deficit in autism: How specific is it? *British Journal of Developmental Psychology, 9*, 301–314.

Barrett, J. L., & Keil, F. C. (1996). Anthropomorphism and God concepts: Conceptualizing a non-natural entity. *Cognitive Psychology, 35*, 219–247.

Bertenthal, B. I. (1993). Perception of biomechanical motions by infants. In C. Granrud (Ed.), *Visual perception and cognition in infancy* (pp. 175–214). Hillsdale, NJ: Erlbaum.

Bibace, R., & Walsh, M. E. (1981). Children's conceptions of illness. In R. Bibace & M. E. Walsh (Eds.), *Children's conceptions of health, illness, and bodily functions* (pp. 31–48). San Francisco: Jossey-Bass.

Boster, J. S. (1991). The information economy model applied to biological similarity judgment. In L. B. Resnick, J. M. Levine, & S. D. Teasley (Eds.), *Perspectives on socially shared cognition* (pp. 203–225). Washington, DC: American Psychological Association.

Bransford, J. D., Brown, A. L., & Cocking, R. R. (1999). *How people learn: Brain, mind, experience, and school*. Washington, DC: National Academy Press.

Bransford, J. D., & McCarrell, N. S. (1975) A sketch of a cognitive approach to comprehension: Some thoughts about understanding what it means to comprehend. In W. B. Weimar & D. S. Palermo (Eds.), *Cognition and the symbolic processes* (pp. 189–229). Hillsdale, NJ: Erlbaum.

Bullock, M. (1985). Animism in childhood thinking: A new look at an old question. *Developmental Psychology, 21*, 217–225.

Caramazza, A., & Shelton, J. R. (1998). Domain-specific knowledge systems in the brain: The animate-inanimate distinction. *Journal of Cognitive Neuroscience, 10*, 1–34.

Carey, S. (1985). *Conceptual change in childhood.* Cambridge, MA: MIT Press.

Carey, S. (1988). Conceptual differences between children and adults. *Mind and Language, 3*, 167–181.

Carey, S. (1991). Knowledge acquisition: Enrichment or conceptual change? In S. Carey & R. Gelman (Eds.), *The epigenesis of mind: Essays on biology and cognition* (pp. 257–291). Hillsdale, NJ: Erlbaum.

Carey, S. (1995). On the origin of causal understanding. In D. Sperber, D. Premack, & A. J. Premack (Eds.), *Causal cognition: A multidisciplinary debate* (pp. 268–302). Oxford, UK: Clarendon Press.

Carey, S. (1999). Sources of conceptual change. In E. Scholnick, K. Nelson, S. Gelman, & P. Miller (Eds.), *Conceptual development: Piaget's legacy* (pp. 293–326). Mahwah, NJ: Erlbaum.

Carey, S., & Spelke, E. (1994). Domain-specific knowledge and conceptual change. In L. A. Hirschfeld & S. A. Gelman (Eds.), *Mapping the mind: Domain specificity in cognition and culture* (pp. 169–200). New York: Cambridge University Press.

Cheng, P. W. (1997). From covariation to causation: A causal power theory. *Psychological Review, 104*, 367–405.

Chi, M. T. H. (1978). Knowledge structures and memory development. In R. S. Siegler (Ed.), *Children's thinking: What develops?* (pp. 73–96). Hillsdale, NJ: Erlbaum.

Chi, M. T. H., Glaser, R., & Rees, E. (1982). Expertise in problem solving. In R.J. Sternberg (Ed.), *Advances in the psychology of human intelligence* (Vol. 1, pp. 7–75). Hillsdale, NJ: Erlbaum.

Chi, M. T. H., Hutchinson, J. E., & Robin, A. F. (1989). How inferences about novel domain-related concepts can be constrained by structured knowledge. *Merrill-Palmer Quarterly, 35*, 27–62.

Clement, J. (1982). students' preconceptions in introductory mechanics. *American Journal of Physics, 50*, 66–71.

Coley, J. D. (1995). Emerging differentiation of folkbiology and folkpsychology: Attributions of biological and psychological properties to living things. *Child Development, 66*, 1856–1874.

Coley, J. D. (2000). On the importance of comparative research: The case of folkbiology. *Child Development, 71*, 82–90.

Coley, J. D., Medin, D. L., Proffitt, J. B., Lynch, E., & Atran, S. (1999). Inductive reasoning in folkbiological thought. In D. Medin & S. Atran (Eds.), *Folkbiology* (pp. 205–232). Cambridge, MA: MIT Press.

Contento, I. (1981). Children's thinking about food and eating: A Piagetian-based study. *Journal of Nutrition Education, 13*, 86–90.

Dennis, W. (1953). Animistic thinking among college and university students. *Scientific Monthly, 76*, 247–249.

Dennis, W. (1957). Animistic thinking among college and high school students in the Near East. *Journal of Educational Psychology, 48*, 193–198.

diSessa, A. A. (1983). Phenomenology and the evolution of intuition. In D. Gentner & A. L. Stevens (Eds.), *Mental models* (pp. 15–33). Hillsdale, NJ: Erlbaum.

Dunbar, K. (1995). How scientists really reason: Scientific reasoning in real-world laboratories. In R. J. Sternberg & J. E. Davidson (Eds.), *The nature of insight* (pp. 365–395). Cambridge, MA: MIT Press.

Eimas, P. D., & Quinn, P. C. (1994). Studies on the formation of perceptually based basic-level categories in young infants. *Child Development, 65*, 903–917.

Elman, J. L., Bates, E. A., Johnson, M. H., Karmiloff-Smith, A., Parisi, D., & Plunkett, K. (1996). *Rethinking innateness: A connectionist perspective on development.* Cambridge, MA: MIT Press.

Estes, D., Wellman, H. M., & Woolley, J. D. (1989). Children's understanding of mental phenomena. In H. Reese (Ed.), *Advances in child development and behavior* (pp. 41–87). New York: Academic Press.

Evans, E. M. (2001). Cognitive and contextual factors in the emergence of diverse belief systems: Creation versus evolution. *Cognitive Psychology, 42,* 217–266.

Festinger, L. (1957). *A theory of cognitive dissonance.* Evanston, IL: Row, Peterson.

Garcia, J. (1981). Tilting at the paper mills of academe. *American Psychologist, 36,* 149–158.

Gellert, E. (1962) Children's conceptions of the content and functions of the human body. *Genetic Psychology Monographs, 65,* 291–411.

Gelman, R. (1979) Preschool thought. *American Psychologist, 34,* 900-905.

Gelman, R. (1990). First principles organize attention to and learning about relevant data: Number and the animate-inanimate distinction as examples. *Cognitive Science, 14,* 79-106.

Gelman, R., & Baillargeon, R. (1983). A review of some Piagetian concepts. In J. H. Flavell & E. M. Markman (Eds.), *Handbook of child psychology, Vol. III. Cognitive development* (pp. 167–230). New York: Wiley.

Gelman, R., Spelke, E., & Meck, E. (1983). What preschoolers know about animate and inanimate objects. In D. Rogers and J. A. Sloboda (Eds.), *The acquisition of symbolic skills* (pp. 297–326). New York: Plenum.

Gelman, S. A. (1999). Essentialism. In R. A. Wilson & F. C. Keil (Eds.), *The MIT encyclopedia of the cognitive sciences* (pp. 282–284). Cambridge, MA: MIT Press.

Gelman, S.A., Coley, J. D., Rosengren, K. S., Hartman, E., & Pappas, A. (1998). Beyond labeling: The role of maternal input in the acquisition of richly structured categories. *Monographs of the Society for Research in Child Development, 63*(1, Serial No. 253).

Gelman, S. A., & Hirschfeld, L. A. (1999). How biological is essentialism? In D. Medin & S. Atran (Eds.), *Folkbiology* (pp.403–446). Cambridge, MA: MIT Press.

Gelman, S. A., & Kremer, K. E. (1991). Understanding natural cause: Children's explanations of how objects and their properties originate. *Child Development, 62,* 396–414.

Gelman, S. A., & Markman, E. M. (1986). Categories and induction in young children. *Cognition, 23,* 183–209.

Gelman, S. A. & Wellman, H. M. (1991) Insides and essences: Early understandings of the non-obvious. *Cognition, 38,* 213–244.

Gentner, D. (1983). Structure-mapping: A theoretical framework for analogy. *Cognitive Science, 7,* 155–170.

Gentner, D., & Markman, A. B. (1997). Structure-mapping in analogy and similarity. *American Psychologist, 52,* 45–56.

Glaser, R. (1984). Education and thinking: The role of knowledge. *American Psychologist, 39,* 93–104.

Glaser, R., & Bassok, M. (1989) Learning theory and the study of instruction. *Annual Review of Psychology, 40,* 631–666.

Glenberg, A. M., & Epstein, W. (1985). Calibration of comprehension. *Journal of Experimental Psychology: Learning, Memory, and Cognition, 11,* 702–718.

Golinkoff, R. M., Harding, C. G., Carlson, V., & Sexton, M. E. (1984). The infant's perception of causal events: The distinction between animate and inanimate objects. In L. P. Lipsitt & C. Rovee-Collier (Eds.), *Advances in infancy research* (Vol. 3, pp. 145–165). Norwood, NJ: Ablex.

Goodnow, J., Miller, P., & Kessel, F. (1995). *Cultural practices as contexts for human development.* San Francisco: Jossey-Bass.

Gopnick, A., & Meltzoff, A. N. (1997). *Words, thoughts, and theories.* Cambridge, MA: The MIT Press.

Gopnick, A., & Wellman, H. M. (1994). The theory theory. In L. A. Hirschfeld & S. A. Gelman (Eds.), *Mapping the mind: Domain specificity in cognition and culture* (pp. 257–293). New York: Cambridge University Press.

Goswami, U. (1996). Analogical reasoning and cognitive development. In H. Reese (Ed.), *Advances in child development and behavior* (Vol. 26, pp. 91–138). New York: Academic Press.

Greeno, J. G. (1983). Forms of understanding in mathematical problem solving. In S. G. Paris, G. M. Olson, & H.W. Stevenson (Eds.), *Learning and motivation in the classroom* (pp. 83-111). Hillsdale, NJ: Erlbaum.

Group El Sol (Ed.) (1987). Children's utterances from age 2 to 9 years. Tokyo: Shobunsha. [in Japanese]

Gutheil, G., Vera, A., & Keil, F. C. (1998). Do houseflies think? Patterns of induction and biological beliefs in development. *Cognition, 66*, 33–49.

Hart Jr., J., Berndt, R. S., & Caramazza, A. (1985). Category-specific naming deficit following cerebral infarction. *Nature, 316*, 439–440.

Hatano, G. (1994). Introduction. *Human Development, 37*, 189–197.

Hatano, G. (1998). Comprehension activity in individuals and groups. In M. Sabourin, F. Craik, & M. Robert (Eds.), *Advances in psychological sciences. Vol. 2: Biological and cognitive aspects* (pp. 399–418). Hove, UK: Psychology Press.

Hatano, G., & Inagaki, K. (1986). Two courses of expertise. In H. Stevenson, H. Azuma, & K. Hakuta (Eds.), *Child development and education in Japan* (pp. 262–272). New York: Freeman.

Hatano, G., & Inagaki, K. (1987). Everyday biology and school biology: How do they interact? *The Quarterly Newsletter of the Laboratory of Comparative Human Cognition, 9*, 120–128.

Hatano, G., & Inagaki, K. (1991). *Learning to trust higher-order categories in biology instruction.* Paper presented at the meeting of the American Educational Research Association, Chicago.

Hatano, G., & Inagaki, K. (1992). Desituating cognition through the construction of conceptual knowledge. In P. Light & G. Butterworth (Eds.), *Context and cognition: Ways of learning and knowing* (pp. 115–133). London: Harvester/Wheatsheaf.

Hatano, G., & Inagaki, K. (1994a). *Bodily organ's "intention" in vitalistic causal explanations.* Paper presented at the 36th annual meeting of Japanese Educational Psychology Association. [in Japanese]

Hatano, G., & Inagaki, K. (1994b). Young children's naive theory of biology. *Cognition, 50*, 171–188.

Hatano, G., & Inagaki, K. (1996). Cognitive and cultural factors in the acquisition of intuitive biology. In D. R. Olson & N. Torrance (Eds.), *Handbook of education and human development: New models of learning, teaching and schooling* (pp. 683–708). Oxford, UK: Blackwell.

Hatano, G., & Inagaki, K. (1997). Qualitative changes in intuitive biology. *European Journal of Psychology of Education, 12*, 111–130.

Hatano, G., & Inagaki, K. (1999). A developmental perspective on informal biology. In D. L. Medin & S. Atran (Eds.), *Folkbiology* (pp. 321–354). Cambridge, MA: MIT Press.

Hatano, G., & Inagaki, K. (2000). Domain-specific constraints of conceptual development. *International Journal of Behavioral Development, 24*, 267–275.

Hatano, G., Siegler, R. S., Richards, D. D., Inagaki, K., Stavy, R., & Wax, N. (1993). The development of biological knowledge: A multi-national study. *Cognitive Development, 8*, 47–62.

Hickling, A. K., & Gelman, S. A. (1995). How does your garden grow? Early conceptualization of seeds and their place in the plant growth cycle. *Child Development, 66*, 856–876.

Hickling, A. E., & Wellman, H. M. (2001). The emergence of children's causal explanations and theories: Evidence from everyday conversation. *Developmental Psychology, 37*, 668–683.

Hills, A. E., & Caramazza, A. (1991). Category-specific naming and comprehension impairment: A double dissociation. *Brain, 114*, 2081–2094.

Hirschfeld, L. A. (1995). Do children have a theory of race? *Cognition, 54,* 209–252.

Hirschfeld, L. A., & Gelman, S. A. (1994). Toward a topography of mind: An introduction to domain specificity. In L. A. Hirschfeld & S. A. Gelman (Eds.), *Mapping the mind: Domain specificity in cognition and culture* (pp. 3–35). New York: Cambridge University Press.

Holyoak, K. J., & Thagard, P. (1995). *Mental leaps: Analogy in creative thought.* Cambridge, MA: MIT Press.

Inagaki, K. (1989). Developmental shift in biological inference processes: From similarity-based to category-based attribution. *Human Development, 32,* 79–87.

Inagaki, K. (1990a). The effects of raising animals on children's biological knowledge. *British Journal of Developmental Psychology, 8,* 119–129.

Inagaki, K. (1990b) Young children's everyday biology as the basis for learning school biology. *The Bulletin of the Faculty of Education, Chiba University, 38* (part I), 177–184.

Inagaki, K. (1996). *Effects of raising goldfish on young children's grasp of common characteristics of animals.* Paper presented at 26th International Congress of Psychology, Montreal.

Inagaki, K. (1997). Emerging distinctions between naive biology and naive psychology. In H. M. Wellman & K. Inagaki (Eds.), *The emergence of core domains of thought: Children's reasoning about physical, psychological, and biological phenomena* (pp. 27–44). New Directions for Child Development, No. 75. San Francisco: Jossey-Bass.

Inagaki, K. (2000). *Young children's vitalistic explanations for eating and other related bodily phenomena.* Paper presented at 27th International Congress of Psychology, Stockholm.

Inagaki, K. (2001a). *Effects of raising mammals on young children's biological inference.* Paper presented at the SRCD meeting, Minneapolis.

Inagaki, K. (2001b). *Young children's distinction between living kinds and complex artifacts: How living and nonliving entities recover from trouble.* Paper presented at the SRCD meeting, Minneapolis.

Inagaki, K., & Hatano, G. (1987). Young children's spontaneous personification as analogy. *Child Development, 58,* 1013–1020.

Inagaki, K., & Hatano, G. (1990) *Development of explanations for bodily functions.* Paper presented at the 32nd annual convention of the Japanese Association of Educational Psychology, Osaka. [in Japanese]

Inagaki, K., & Hatano, G. (1991) Constrained person analogy in young children's biological inference. *Cognitive Development, 6,* 219–231.

Inagaki, K., & Hatano, G. (1993). Young children's understanding of the mind-body distinction. *Child Development, 64,* 1534–1549.

Inagaki, K., & Hatano, G. (1996). Young children's recognition of commonalities between animals and plants. *Child Development, 67,* 2823–2840.

Inagaki, K., & Hatano, G. (1999a). Children's understanding of mind-body relationships. In M. Siegal & C. C. Peterson (Eds.), *Children's understanding of biology and health* (pp. 23–44). Cambridge, UK: Cambridge University Press.

Inagaki, K., & Hatano, G. (1999b). *Roles of naive biology in young children's memory of facts about animals.* Paper presented at the 8th European Conference for Research on Learning and Instruction, Gothenburg, Sweden.

Inagaki, K., & Hatano, G. (in press). Conceptual and linguistic factors in inductive projection: How do young children recognize commonalities between animals and plants? In D. Genter & S. Goldin-Meadow (Eds.), *Language and thought in mind: Advances in the study of language and thought.* Cambridge, MA: MIT Press.

Inagaki, K., & Kasetani, M. (1994) *Effects of inducing person analogies on young children's understanding of procedures for raising animals.* Paper presented at the 12th meeting of the International Society for the Study of Behavioral Development, Amsterdam.

Inagaki, K., & Oshima, N. (2001). *Comprehension of a picture book about atopic disease among young children with and without the disease.* Paper presented at the meeting of the European Association for Research on Learning and Instruction, Fribourg.

Inagaki, K., & Sugiyama, K. (1988) Attributing human characteristics: Developmental changes in over- and underattribution. *Cognitive Development, 3,* 55–70.

Jaakkola, R. (under review). Are plants and animals the same kind of things? Children's projection of novel causal properties.

Johnson, C. N., & Wellman, H. M. (1982) Children's developing conceptions of the mind and brain. *Child Development, 53,* 222–234.

Johnson, K. E., Mervis, C. B., & Boster, J. S. (1992). Developmental changes within the structure of the mammal domain. *Developmental Psychology, 28,* 74–83.

Johnson, S. C., & Carey, S. (1998). Knowledge enrichment and conceptual change: Knowledge acquisition in people with Williams syndrome. *Cognitive Psychology, 37,* 156–200.

Kalish, C. (1996). Preschoolers' understanding of germs as invisible mechanisms. *Cognitive Development, 11,* 83–106.

Kalish, C. (1997). Preschoolers' understanding of mental and bodily reactions to contamination: What you don't know can hurt you, but cannot sadden you. *Developmental Psychology, 33,* 79–91.

Kalish, C. W. (1998). Young children's predictions of illness: Failure to recognize probabilistic causation. *Developmental Psychology, 34,* 1046–1058.

Kalish, C. (1999). What young children's understanding of contamination and contagion tells us about their concepts of illness. In M. Siegal & C. C. Peterson (Eds.), *Children's understanding of biology and health* (pp. 99–130). Cambridge, UK: Cambridge University Press.

Kawashima, R., Hatano, G., Oizumi, K., Sugiura, M., Fukuda, H., Itoh, K., Kato, T., Nakamura, A., Hatano, K., & Kojima, S. (2001). Different neural systems for recognizing plants, animals, and artifacts. *Brain Research Bulletin, 54,* 313–317.

Keil, F. (1981). Constraints on knowledge and cognitive development. *Psychological Review, 88,* 197–227.

Keil, F. C. (1983). On the emergence of semantic and conceptual distinctions. *Journal of Experimental Psychology: General, 112,* 357–385.

Keil, F. C. (1989). *Concepts, kinds, and cognitive development.* Cambridge, MA: MIT Press.

Keil, F. C. (1990). Constraints on constraints: Surveying the epigenetic landscape. *Cognitive Science, 14,* 135–168.

Keil, F. C. (1992). The origins of an autonomous biology. In M. R. Gunnar & M. Maratsos (Eds.), *Modularity and constraints in language and cognition. The Minnesota Symposia on Child Psychology* (Vol. 25, pp. 103–137). Hillsdale, NJ: Erlbaum.

Keil, F. C. (1994). The birth and nurturance of concepts by domain: The origins of concepts of living things. In L. A. Hirschfeld & S. A. Gelman (Eds.), *Mapping the mind: Domain specificity in cognition and culture* (pp. 234–254). New York: Cambridge University Press.

Keil, F. C. (1995). The growth of causal understandings of natural kinds. In D. Sperber, D. Premack, & A. J. Premack (Eds.), *Causal cognition: A multidisciplinary debate* (pp. 234–262). Oxford, UK: Clarendon Press.

Keil, F. C. (1998). Cognitive science and the origins of thought and knowledge. In W. Damon (Ed.), *Handbook of child psychology,* 5th ed., Vol. 1: R. M. Lerner (Ed.), *Theoretical models of human development* (pp. 341–413). New York: Wiley.

Keil, F. C. (1999). Conceptual change. In R. A. Wilson & F. C. Keil (Eds.), *The MIT encyclopedia of the cognitive sciences* (pp. 179–182). Cambridge, MA: MIT Press.

Keil, F. C., Levin, D. T., Richman, B. A., & Gutheil, G. (1999). Mechanism and explanation in the development of biological thought: The case of disease. In D. Medin & S. Atran (Eds.), *Folkbiology* (pp. 233–284). Cambridge, MA: MIT Press.

Keil, F. C., & Wilson, R. A. (2000). Explaining explanation. In F. C. Keil & R. A. Willson (Eds.), *Explanation and cognition* (pp. 1-18). Cambridge, MA: MIT Press.

Kelemen, D. (1999a). Function, goals and intention: Children's teleological reasoning about objects. *Trends in Cognitive Sciences, 3,* 461–468.

Kelemen, D. (1999b). The scope of teleological thinking in preschool children. *Cognition, 70*, 241–272.

Kelemen, D. (1999c). Why are rocks pointy? Children's preference for teleological explanations of the natural world. *Developmental Psychology, 35*, 1440–1452.

Kister, M. C., & Patterson, C. J. (1980). Children's conceptions of the causes of illness: Understanding of contagion and use of immanent justice. *Child Development, 51*, 839-846.

Koizumi, A., Miyahara, S., & Muramatu, H. (Eds.) (1990) *Ningen: Kokoro to Karada* (Human beings: Mind and body). Tokyo: Syogakkan. [in Japanese]

Kuhn, D. (1989) Children and adults as intuitive scientists. *Psychological Review, 96*, 674-689.

Laboratory of Comparative Human Cognition. (1983). Culture and cognitive development. *Handbook of child psychology*, 4th ed., Vol. 1: W. Kessen (Ed.), *History, theory, and method* (pp. 295–356). New York: Wiley.

Lakoff, G., & Johnson, M. (1980). *Metaphors we live by*. Chicago: University of Chicago Press.

Laurendeau, M., & Pinard, A. (1962) *Causal thinking in the child*. New York: International Universities Press.

Leslie, A. M. (1994). ToMM, ToBy, and agency: Core architecture and domain specificity. In L. A. Hirschfeld, & S. A. Gelman (Eds.), *Mapping the mind: Domain specificity in cognition and culture* (pp. 119–148). New York: Cambridge University Press.

Lockhart, K., Stegall, S., Roberts, K., & Yip, T. (1997). *Unlearned optimism: Children's beliefs about the stability of negative traits*. Paper presented at the meeting of Society for Research in Child Development, Washington, DC.

Looft, W. R., & Bartz, W. H. (1969) Animism revived. *Psychological Bulletin, 71*, 1–19.

López, A., Atran, S., Coley, J. D., Medin, D., & Smith, E. E. (1997). The tree of life: Universal and cultural features of folkbiological taxonomies and inductions. *Cognitive Psychology, 32*, 251–295.

Lutz, D., & Keil, F. (in press). Early understanding of the division of cognitive labor. *Child Development*.

MacWhinney, B., & Snow, C. (1985). The child language data exchange system. *Journal of Child Language, 12*, 271–296.

MacWhinney, B., & Snow, C. (1990). The child language data exchange system: An update. *Journal of Child Language, 17*, 457–472.

Maffi, L. (1996). "The Blisters": Smallpox and an early case of Mayan self-help. In S. K. Jain (Ed.), *Ethnobiology in human welfare* (pp. 112–119). New Delhi, India: Deep Publications.

Mandler, J. M., & McDonough, L. (1993). Concept formation in infancy. *Cognitive Development, 8*, 291–318.

Mandler, J. M., & McDonough, L. (1998). On developing a knowledge base in infancy. *Developmental Psychology, 34*, 1274–1288.

Markman, E. M. (1981). Comprehension monitoring. In W. P. Dickson (Ed.), *Children's oral communication skills* (pp. 61–84). New York: Academic Press.

Markman, E. M. (1992). Constraints on word learning: Speculations about their nature, origins, and domain specificity. In M. R. Gunnar & M. Maratsos (Eds.), *Modularity and constraints in language and cognition. The Minnesota symposia on child psychology* (Vol. 25, pp. 59–101). Hillsdale, NJ: Erbaum.

Marton, F. (1989). Towards a pedagogy of content. *Educational Psychologist, 24*, 1–23.

Massey, C. M., & Gelman, R. (1988). Preschooler's ability to decide whether a photographed unfamiliar object can move itself. *Developmental Psychology, 24*, 307-317.

Mayr, E. (1982). *The growth of biological thought*. Cambridge, MA: Harvard University Press.

McMenamy, J., & Wiser, M. (1997). *Germ and folk theories: Young children's understanding of the causes, transmission, and treatment of illness*. Paper presented at the meeting of the Society for Research in Child Development, Washington, DC.

Mead, M. (1932). An investigation of the thought of primitive children with special reference to animism. *Journal of the Royal Anthropological Institute, 62,* 173–190.

Medin, D., & Atran, S. (Eds.). (1999). *Folkbiology.* Cambridge, MA: MIT Press.

Miller, J. L., & Bartsch, K. (1997). Development of biological explanation: Are children vitalists? *Developmental Psychology, 33,* 156–164.

Morita, E., Inagaki, K., & Hatano, G. (1988). *The development of biological inferences : Analyses of RTs in children's attribution of human properties.* Paper presented at the 30th annual convention of the Japanese Association of Educational Psychology, Naruto. [in Japanese]

Morris, S. C., Taplin, J. E., & Gelman, S. A. (2000). Vitalism in naive biological thinking. *Developmental Psychology, 36,* 582–613.

Motoyoshi, M. (1979) Essays on education for day care children: Emphasizing daily life activities. Tokyo: Froebel-kan. [in Japanese]

Munakata, Y., McClelland, J. L., Johnson, M. H., & Siegler, R. S. (1997). Rethinking infant knowledge: Toward an adaptive process account of successes and failures in object permanence tasks. *Psychological Review, 104,* 686–713.

Murakawa, M. (1993). Understanding the mistery of how a baby born. *Broadcasting Education,* September, 42–46. [in Japanese]

Murayama, I. (1994). Roles of agency in causal understanding of natural phenomena. *Human Development, 37,* 198–206.

Nersessian, N. (1992). How do scientists think? Capturing the dynamics of conceptual change in science. In R. N. Giere (Ed.), *Minnesota studies in philosophy of science: Vol. 15. Cognitive models of science.* Minneapolis: University of Minnesota Press.

Nguyen, S. P., & Rosengren, K. S. (2000). *Magical and biological explanations for illness: A cross-cultural study of Vietnamese-American and European-American children's causal reasoning.* Paper presented at the meeting of International Society for the Study of Behavioral Development, Beijing, China.

Ohmori, S. (1985) *Chishikito gakumonno kouzou* [The structure of knowledge and science]. Tokyo: Nihon Hoso Shuppan Kyokai. [in Japanese]

Olguin, R. (1995). *The birth of children's first biological theory.* Paper presented at the meeting of Society for Research in Child Development, Indianapolis.

Olson, D. R., & Torrance, N. (1996). Introduction: Rethinking the role of psychology in education. In D. R. Olson & N. Torrance (Eds.), *The handbook of education and human development: New models of learning, teaching, and schooling* (pp. 1–6). Oxford, UK: Blackwell.

Perner, J. (1991). *Understanding the representational mind.* Cambridge, MA: MIT Press.

Peterson, C. C., & Siegal, M. (1997). Domain specificity and everyday biological, physical, and psychological thinking in normal, autistic, and deaf children. In H. M. Wellman and K. Inagaki (Eds.), *The emergence of core domains of thought: Children's reasoning about physical, psychological, and biological phenomena* (pp. 55–70). San Francisco: Jossey-Bass.

Piaget, J. (1929). *The child's conception of the world.* London: Routledge & Kegan Paul.

Pinker, S. (1997). *How the mind works.* New York: Norton.

Pintrich, P. R., Marx, R. W., & Boyle, R. A. (1993). Beyond cold conceptual change: The role of motivational beliefs and classroom contextual factors in the process of conceptual change. *Review of Educational Research, 63,* 167–199.

Poulin-Dubois, D., Lepage, A., & Ferland, D. (1996). Infants' concept of animacy. *Cognitive Development, 11,* 19–36.

Poulin-Dubois, D., & Shultz, T. R. (1990). Infant's concept of animacy: The distinction between social and nonsocial objects. *The Journal of Genetic Psychology, 151,* 77–90.

Quinn, P. C., & Eimas, P. D. (1998). Evidence for a global categorical representation for humans by young children. *Journal of Experimental Child Psychology, 69,* 151–174.

Resnick, L. B. (1987). Constructing knowledge in school. In L. S. Liben (Ed.), *Development and learning: Conflict or congruence?* (pp. 19–50). Hillsdale, NJ: Erlbaum.

Richards, D. D., & Siegler, R. S. (1984). The effects of task requirements on children's life judgments. *Child Development, 55,* 1687–1696.

Richards, D. D., & Siegler, R. S. (1986). Children's understandings of the attributes of life. *Journal of Experimental Child Psychology, 42,* 1–22.

Rochat, P. (1998). Self-perception and action in infancy. *Experimental Brain Research, 123,* 102–109.

Rochat, P., Morgan, R., & Carpenter, M. (1997). Young infants' sensitivity to movement information specifying social causality. *Cognitive Development, 12,* 441–465.

Rogoff, B. (1990). *Apprenticeship in thinking: Cognitive development in social context.* New York: Oxford University Press.

Rosengren, K. S., Gelman, S. A., Kalish, C. W., & McCormick, M. (1991). As time goes by: Children's early understanding of growth. *Child Development, 62,* 1302–1320.

Rosengren, K. S., Subbotsky, E., & Harris, P. (Eds.). (2000). *Imagining the impossible: Magical, scientific, and religious thinking in children.* New York: Cambridge University Press.

Ross, N., Medin, D., Coley, J., & Atran, S. (under review). Cultural and experiential differences in the development of folk biological induction.

Rozin, P. (1990). Development in the food domain. *Developmental Psychology, 26,* 555–562.

Rozin, P., Millman, L., & Nemeroff, C. (1986). Operation of the laws of sympathetic magic in disgust and other domains. *Journal of Personality and Social Psychology, 50,* 703–712.

Russell, J. (1992). The theory theory: So good they named it twice? *Cognitive Development, 7,* 485–519.

Schult, C. A., & Wellman, H. M. (1997). Explaining human movements and actions: Children's understanding of the limits of psychological explanation. *Cognition, 62,* 291–324.

Serpell, R., & Hatano, G. (1997). Education, schooling, and literacy. In J. W. Berry, P. R. Dasen, & T. S. Saraswathi (Eds.), *Handbook of cross-cultural psychology, Vol. 2: Basic processes and human development* (pp. 339–376). Boston, MA: Allyn and Bacon.

Shimizu, E. (1964). *Chigaubokuto torikaete* [Collection of young children's spontaneous remarks]. Tokyo: Doushinsha. [in Japanese]

Siegal, M. (1988). Children's knowledge of contagion and contamination as causes of illness. *Child Development, 59,* 1353–1359.

Siegal, M. (1997). *Knowing children: Experiments in conversation and cognition* (2nd ed.). Hove, UK: Psychology Press.

Siegler, R. S. (Ed.). (1978). *Children's thinking: What develops?* Hillsdale, NJ: Erlbaum.

Siegler, R. S., & Crowley, K. (1994). Constraints on learning in nonprivileged domains. *Cognitive Psychology, 27,* 194–226.

Siegler, R. S., & Jenkins, E. (1989). *How children discover new strategies.* Hillsdale, NJ: Erlbaum.

Sigelman, C., & Alfred-Liro, C. (1995). *Wear your coat: Age and ethnic differences in cold weather and germ theory of infectious disease.* Paper presented at the meeting of the Society for Research in Child Development, Indianapolis.

Simons, D. J., & Keil, F. C. (1995). An abstract to concrete shift in the development of biological thought: The *insides* story. *Cognition, 56,* 129–163.

Slaughter, V., Jaakkola, R., & Carey, S. (1999). Constructing a coherent theory: Children's biological understanding of life and death. In M. Siegal & C. C. Peterson (Eds.), *Children's understanding of biology and health* (pp. 71–96). Cambridge, UK: Cambridge University Press.

Slaughter, V. & Lyons, M. (in press). Learning about life and death in early childhood. *Cognitive Psychology.*

Smith, C., Carey, S., & Wiser, M. (1985). On differentiation: A case study of the development of the concepts of size, weight, and density. *Cognition, 21,* 177–237.

Solomon, G. E. A., & Cassimatis, N. L. (1999). On facts and conceptual systems: Young children's integration of their understandings of germs and contagion. *Developmental Psychology, 35*, 113–126.

Solomon, G. E. A., & Johnson, S. C. (2000). Conceptual change in the classroom: Teaching young children to understand biological inheritance. *British Journal of Developmental Psychology, 18*, 81–96.

Solomon, G. E. A., Johnson, S. C., Zaitchik, D., & Carey, S. (1996). Like father, like son: Young children's understanding of how and why offspring resemble their parents. *Child Development, 67*, 151–171.

Spelke, E. S. (1994). Initial knowledge: Six suggestions. *Cognition, 50*, 431–445.

Spelke, E. S., Phillips, A., & Woodword, A. L. (1995). Infants' knowledge of object motion and human action. in D. Sperber, D. Premack, & A. J. Premack (Eds.), *Causal cognition: A multidisciplinary debate* (pp. 44–78). Oxford, UK: Clarendon Press.

Springer, K. (1992). Children's awareness of the biological implications of kinship. *Child Development, 63*, 950–959.

Springer, K. (1995). How a naive theory is acquired through inference. *Child Development, 66*, 547–558.

Springer, K. (1996). Young children's understanding of a biological basis for parent-off-spring relations. *Child Development, 67*, 2841–2856.

Springer, K., & Keil, F. C. (1989). On the development of biologically specific beliefs: The case of inheritance. *Child Development, 60*, 637–648.

Springer, K., & Keil, F. C. (1991). Early differentiation of causal mechanisms appropriate to biological and nonbiological kinds. *Child Development, 62*, 767–781.

Springer, K., & Ruckel, J. (1992). Early beliefs about the causes of illness: Evidence against immanent justice. *Cognitive Development, 7*, 429–443.

Stavy, R., & Wax, N. (1989). Children's conceptions of plants as living things. *Human Development, 32*, 88–94.

Subbotsky, E. (1997). Explanations of unusual events: Phenomenalistic causal judgments in children and adults. *British Journal of Developmental Psychology, 15*, 13–36.

Super, C., & Harkness, S. (1986). The developmental niche: A conceptualization at the interface of child and culture. *International Journal of Behavioral Development, 9*, 545–569.

Takahashi, K. (1980). *Shinpan, rika wakaru oshiekata 1nen* [Teaching methods for helping 1st-graders understand science: New version]. Tokyo: Kokudo-sha. [in Japanese]

Taplin, J. E., Finney, D. A., & Gelman, S. A. (1998). *Theory-based constructs underlying children's causal understanding of illness*. Paper presented at the International Society for the Study of Behavioral Development, Berne.

Thornhill, R., & Gangestad, S. W. (1999). Facial attractiveness. *Trends in Cognitive Sciences, 3*, 452–460.

Toda, M. (2000). Emotion and social interaction: A theoretical overview. In G. Hatano, N. Okada, & M. Tanabe (Eds.), *Affective minds* (pp. 3–12). Amsterdam: Elsevier.

Tomasello, M. (1992). *First verbs: A case study in early grammatical development*. Cambridge, UK: Cambridge University Press.

Tomasello, M., Kruger, A. C., & Ratner, H. H. (1993). Cultural learning. *Behavioral and Brain Sciences, 16*, 459–552.

Vosniadou, S. (1989). Analogical reasoning as a mechanism in knowledge acquisition: A developmental perspective. In S. Vosniadou & A. Ortony (Eds.), *Similarity and analogical reasoning* (pp. 413–437). Cambridge, UK: Cambridge University Press.

Vosniadou, S. (1994). Introduction. *Learning and Instruction, 4*, 3–6.

Vosniadou, S., & Brewer, W. F. (1992). Mental models of the earth: A study of conceptual change in childhood. *Cognitive Psychology, 24*, 535–585.

Vosniadou, S., & Ioannides, C. (1998). From conceptual development to science education: A psychological point of view. *International Journal of Science Education, 20,* 1213–1230.

Vygotsky, L. S. (1978). *Mind in society.* Cambridge, MA: Harvard University Press.

Walker, S. J. (1999). Culture, domain specificity and conceptual change: Natural kind and artifact concepts. *British Journal of Developmental Psychology, 17,* 203–219.

Warrington, E. K., & McCarthy, R. (1983). Category specific access dysphasia. *Brain, 106,* 859–878.

Warrington, E. K., & Shallice, T. (1984). Category specific semantic impairments. *Brain, 107,* 829–854.

Wellman, H. M. (1990). *The child's theory of mind.* Cambridge, MA: MIT Press.

Wellman, H. M. (in press). Enablement and constraint. In U. M. Staudinger, & U. Lindenberger (Eds.), *Understanding human development.* Dordrecht, the Netherlands: Kluwer.

Wellman, H. M., & Gelman, S. A. (1992). Cognitive development: Foundational theories of core domains. *Annual Review of Psychology, 43,* 337–375.

Wellman, H. M., & Gelman, S. A. (1998). Knowledge acquisition in foundational domains. In W. Damon (Ed.), *Handbook of child psychology,* 5th ed., Vol. 2: D. Kuhn & R. Siegler (Eds.), *Cognition, perception and language* (pp. 523–573). New York: Wiley.

Wellman, H. M., Hickling, A. K., & Schult, C. A. (1997). Young children's psychological, physical and biological explanations. In H. M. Wellman & K. Inagaki (Eds.), *The emergence of core domains of thought: Children's reasoning about physical, psychological, and biological phenomena* (pp. 7–25). San Francisco: Jossey-Bass.

Wellman, H. M., & Inagaki, K. (Eds.) (1997). *The emergence of core domains of thought: Children's reasoning about physical, psychological, and biological phenomena.* San Francisco: Jossey-Bass.

Wilkinson, S. R. (1988). *The child's world of illness: The development of health and illness behavior.* Cambridge, UK: Cambridge University Press.

Williams, J. M., & Tolmie, A. (2000). Conceptual change in biology: Group interaction and the understanding of inheritance. *British Journal of Developmental Psychology, 18,* 625–649.

Wiser, M. (1988). The differentiation of heat and temperature: History of science and novice-expert shift. In S. Strauss (Ed.), *Ontogeny, phylogeny, and historical development* (pp. 28–48). Norwood, NJ: Ablex.

Wiser, M., & Carey, S. (1983). When heat and temperature were one. In D. Gentner & Stevens, A. L. (Eds.), *Mental models* (pp. 267–297). Hillsdale, NJ: Erlbaum.

Wolff, P., Medin, D. L., & Pankratz, C. (Eds.). (1999). Evolution and devolution of folkbiological knowledge. *Cognition, 73,* 177–204.

Yates, J., Bassman, M., Dunne, M., Jertson, D., Sly, K., & Wendelboe, B. (1988). Are conceptions of motion based on a naive theory or on prototypes? *Cognition, 29,* 251–275.

Yuzawa, M. (1988). Understanding the meaning of the situation of a problem and a reasoning schema. *Japanese Journal of Educational Psychology, 36,* 297–306. [in Japanese with an English summary]

AUTHOR INDEX

Ackerman, B. P., 174
Alfred-Liro, C., 86
Anzai, Y., 142
Atran, S., 4, 5, 9, 107, 121, 130, 134, 147, 185, 187
Au, T. K., 87, 100, 102, 107, 108, 109, 188, 191, 196

Backscheider, A. G., 25
Baillargeon, R., 197
Baron-Cohen, S., 190
Barrett, J. L., 185
Bartsch, K., 77, 106, 125, 170
Bartz, W. H., 7
Bassok, M., 192
Berndt, R. S., 137
Bertenthal, B. I., 132
Bibace, R., 68, 82
Boster, J. S., 134, 164
Boyle, R. A., 180
Bransford, J. D., 14, 192
Brewer, W. F., 109, 154
Brown, A. L., 192
Bullock, M., 38

Caramazza, A., 136, 137
Carey, S., 4, 5, 6, 7, 8, 9, 12, 15, 20, 21, 27, 40, 41, 46, 48, 49, 66, 68, 69, 70, 78, 82, 96, 97, 100, 104, 105, 108, 122, 127, 138, 152, 153, 156, 158, 172, 173, 175, 176, 180, 181, 183, 184, 186, 187, 188, 189, 192, 204
Carlson, V., 38
Carpenter, M., 132
Cassimatis, N. L., 86, 109
Cheng, P. W., 197
Chi, M. T. H., 11, 12, 14, 139
Clement, J., 154

Cocking, R. R., 192
Coley, J. D., 5, 70, 135, 143, 147
Contento, I., 96
Crowley, K., 8

Dennis, W., 185
DeWitt, J., 87, 107
diSessa, A. A., 15
Dunbar, K., 177, 178

Eimas, P. D., 46
Elman, J. L., 129
Epstein, W., 174
Estes, D., 97
Evans, E. M., 155

Ferland, D., 132
Festinger, L., 178
Finney, D. A., 86

Gangestad, S. W., 190
Garcia, J., 201
Gellert, E., 96
Gelman, R., 2, 7, 11, 36, 38, 46, 48, 96, 183, 187, 197
Gelman, S. A., 2, 12, 13, 22, 25, 26, 37, 78, 86, 106, 107, 121, 127, 143, 191, 197
Gentner, D., 44, 47
Glaser, R., 11, 139, 192
Glenberg, A. M., 174
Golinkoff, R. M., 38
Goodnow, J., 140
Gopnick, A., 12, 153
Goswami, U., 44
Greeno, J. G., 96
Group El Sol, 19
Gutheil, G., 27, 28, 47, 69, 88, 132

217

SUBJECT INDEX